Dear America

Dear America

Letters of Hope, Habitat, Defiance, and Democracy

Edited by

SIMMONS BUNTIN,

ELIZABETH DODD,

and

DEREK SHEFFIELD

TRINITY UNIVERSITY PRESS
Terrain.org / Terrain Publishing

Published by Trinity University Press
San Antonio, Texas 78212

Image credits: pages i–iii: istock/Jonathan Barbour; page 5: part 1 (Calls to Action), istock/ Mihajlo Maricic; page 41: part 2 (Extractions, Extinctions, and Depletions), iStock/Monika Podlaska; page 59: part 3 (Geographies of Exclusion), istock/Lemanieh; page 105: part 4 (Climate Change and Science Denial), istock/Don Mennig; page 133: part 5 (Memories (Imaginings) and Other Americas), istock/Josie Desmarais; page 181: part 6 (Ambient Violences and Misogynies), istock/Roschetzkylstockphoto; page 225: part 7 (The Power of Panic / The Power of Art), istock/Mathieu LE MAUFF; page 271: part 8 (Images from the Front), istock/blackdovfx; page 293: part 9 (The Power of Satire), istock/Page Light Studios; page 313: part 10 (Geographies of Inclusion and Renewal), istock/June Jacobsen; page 363: part 11 (Togethering), istock/Rawpixel

Cover design by ALSO
Book design by BookMatters, Berkeley
Cover art: iStock/agaliza

Printed in Canada

ISBN 978-1-59534-912-5 paper
ISBN 978-1-59534-913-2 ebook

CIP data on file at the Library of Congress

24 23 22 21 20 | 5 4 3 2 1

...in Order to form a more perfect Union, establish Justice,
insure domestic Tranquility, provide for the common defence,
promote the general Welfare, and secure the Blessings of Liberty...

PREAMBLE TO THE U.S. CONSTITUTION

Action is the antidote to despair.

JOAN BAEZ

Contents

Geographies of Exclusion

Climate Change and Science Denial

Memories (Imaginings) and Other Americas

Ambient Violences and Misogynies

The Power of Panic / The Power of Art

Images from the Front

The Power of Satire

Geographies of Inclusion and Renewal

Togethering

Introduction

Dear Reader,

When Alison Hawthorne Deming sent me her letter to America a week after the 2016 U.S. presidential election, I had just hung up the phone with my daughter, a college sophomore, biologist-in-training, and young woman who had just voted in her first presidential election—and now found herself devastated. It was the fourth or fifth time we'd talked since the election, and as her father I felt that I was in the position of talking her down from a ledge. A ledge on which we both teetered.

Alison's letter arrived just in time. A response to the shaken American landscape so vividly illuminated by Donald Trump's win, it was written—she told me in offering the letter for publication in *Terrain.org*—to encourage herself and others as we reeled with the disruption in our sense of national well-being.

I forwarded it to my daughter—and we stepped back from the ledge. But as we all know, the mountain is crumbling, and so we remain on that ledge, politically and perhaps literally.

After scheduling the piece for publication the very next day, I knew that Alison's wasn't the only voice that needed a venue. Likewise I knew that Alison's response wasn't the only wisdom we'd need as the administration turned over and America hurtled into the dark unknown. So coeditors Elizabeth Dodd, Derek Sheffield, and I invited other writers, artists, designers, politicians, and thinkers to offer their own letters. And they did, in numbers and with sustained energy that surprised us all.

Since publishing Alison's letter on November 17, 2016, we have added more than 160 additional responses in what one reader has called "the evolution of moral panic in America," a congress of the personal and the political, with a prominent focus on place and environmental and social justice.

In the book you now hold, we've combined some of these original letters with new contributions. They offer diverse and powerful responses to a shifting American and global landscape, running from shock through grief, truth-telling, and resolve. They acknowledge, too, that what for many is a suddenly changed America has, for many others, never been a country of equity or justice.

When I talk with my daughter today, and as we continue to lament a president, his administration, and representatives who disregard the Constitution, let alone common decency, we turn back to Alison's letter and her charge: "Think of the great spirit of inventiveness the Earth calls forth after each major disturbance it suffers. Be artful, inventive, and just, my friends, but do not be silent."

The voices in this essential anthology are anything but silent. Indeed, they are voices of hope, habitat, defiance, and, most importantly, democracy. Lend your ears, and then your own voice.

Patriotically yours,
Simmons Buntin

Calls to Action

Letter to America

ALISON HAWTHORNE DEMING

Dear America,

The heat is just beginning to wane here in Arizona in the November ending the hottest five years on record. I've had to adjust my inner thermostat too, living here in terrain associated in many of the world's religions with spiritual testing. The election results threaten to undermine every cause that I as an educator, poet, and essayist have worked for in the past fifty years: women's rights, civil rights, environmental justice, science literacy, civil discourse, and empathy—and underlying all, the informed and reflective thinking required for democracy to thrive.

Only 25 percent of the American electorate voted for Donald Trump. That means 75 percent of Americans did not vote for deportation of Mexicans, banning of Muslims, denigrating and denying science, wasting this glorious planet for the sake of personal and corporate gain, hate speech, racist and misogynist words and deeds, or autocratic decision-making. The reasons that only 25 percent of Americans voted for Hillary Clinton will become more clear with analysis, though some elements of this outcome I suspect will remain opaque.

The reasons that the remaining 50 percent of Americans did not vote for any candidate include despair, cynicism, principle, and challenges to the right to vote. I will not castigate nonvoters. I will praise them for not voting for a dangerous, ill-informed, disrespectful, undignified, greedy, and hate-filled bully. The fact that 75 percent of Americans did not vote for this candidate makes clear that Trump values are not American values. This vote says that whatever the reasons might have been for not voting, we need you now to avow your majority position in being publicly vigilant, articulate, respectful of difference, and caring toward the most vulnerable among our people and creatures with whom we share the planet.

We have seen language used to manipulate people, distort reality, deny facts, and betray our American ideals of liberty and justice. We need now to believe in the power of language to help us connect across our differences, express empathy, form new alliances, fuel our better natures, and live more fully the values we espouse. Surely surprising acts of resistance will rise from the spirit of resilience and solidarity energized by this dangerous turn in American leadership. Maybe all the women who attend the Million Woman March in Washington should wear the hijab in solidarity with those who feel the very real vulnerability arising from the threatening rhetoric of the campaign.

I think of this remembering the symbolic power of an action taken just days after the terrorist attacks in Paris in November 2015 when public protests were banned. Ten thousand pairs of shoes were lined up in the Place de la République—shoes from Pope Francis, shoes from the Dalai Lama, shoes of the living, and shoes of the dead. They stood in for the two hundred thousand people anticipated to gather on Paris streets ahead of the Paris climate summit.

Sure, take to streets, sign petitions, move to a red state and run for the school board, donate to organizations that work on the local level or promote human rights. Think of the great spirit of inventiveness the Earth calls forth after each major disturbance it suffers.

Be artful, inventive, and just, my friends, but do not be silent.

Yours,
Alison Hawthorne Deming

This Land Is (Still) Our Land

ANA MARIA SPAGNA

Dear America,

Even before her recent, too-damned-early death from cancer, I couldn't listen to Sharon Jones's version of "This Land Is Your Land" without weeping.

Tonight, I'm listening over and over.

True, I am a sucker for her voice on any song. Add horns and a funky bass line from the Dap-Kings, and I'll surely swoon. But this song, this song, this is the song I sang sitting cross-legged on the carpet at Jefferson Elementary School and around beach campfires at San Clemente with my parents' friends—this was the 1970s after all—and from the too-hot way back of the station wagon on family road trips from California to Saint Louis when we stopped at every national park. The song needles into me and betrays one of my deepest secrets: I am fiercely patriotic.

The road trips did it to me, yes. The land itself—your land, my land—stretching out: mountains and prairies and deserts and oceans. Natural beauty moved me always, but my allegiance could easily have affixed to the earth in general or more specifically to the nonhuman world. ("I'd sooner kill a man than a hawk," Robinson Jeffers famously once wrote, and at times his philosophy has perverse appeal.) But it didn't. Because of what I read.

In high school I took a combination American history and literature class that started with one question: What is truth? A question that shook my very Catholic heart. How could there be more than one? You mean, people could debate such things? From there, we were off to the Federalist Papers, *The Scarlet Letter*, Emerson and Thoreau—the usual suspects—but also Frederick Douglass, Willa Cather, *The Jungle* and *The*

Grapes of Wrath and *I Know Why the Caged Bird Sings*. America wasn't just land, it turned out, it was ideas, and we always seemed to be trying to make the ideas work better. That year I discovered Simon and Garfunkel's "America" and played it over and over. So we're all searching for America. So we're all empty and aching; at least we were in it together.

Despite the many flaws of our leaders. Our babysitter screeched into the driveway to holler that Nixon had "erased the goddamned tapes." A college professor announced in class that Reagan had sold arms to Iran to fund Nicaraguan rebels. (We figured, at first, he'd truly lost his liberal mind.) Clinton lied about Monica. Bush lied about WMDs. *Power, Corruption, and Lies* wasn't just an album title. There were always good reasons to stay vigilant. But not to give up.

When, two decades later, I went looking for stories to write, I met heroes and sheroes of the civil rights movement who told stories of their efforts and the real oppression they faced—arrests, beatings, lost jobs—with a shrug: It was no big deal. It was the right thing to do. Later Pauline Esteves, a Timbisha Shoshone elder in Death Valley, described to me how she'd been forcibly displaced as a child, had her adobe house hosed away as an adult, and still lived to be the lead negotiator when her tribe reclaimed its homeland from the U.S. government. For me to give into nonchalance draped in bitterness—to choose, say, not to vote—would betray these people and so many others.

The morning after the election I went running. Snow had crept low on the mountains, weak early winter sun shone on the river, still-yellow cottonwood leaves littered the gravel road, waiting to be churned to bits under tires. Neighbors passed in their super-sized American trucks, and I could hardly wave. Even though I always wave, every single morning, I didn't want to wave.

I waved anyway.

Sharon Jones and I come from wildly different worlds, the far ends of that ribbon of a highway, you might say. A black woman born in South Carolina, she moved north, with hopes of making it as a singer, but was told she was too black, too short, too fat to ever make it in show business. She worked as a corrections officer at Rikers prison before getting her break, with her own band, her own label, when she was forty. Me, I'm a white lesbian, a woods-dwelling former trail crew laborer originally from Riverside, California.

Until this week, when I finally looked it up online, I never knew why Sharon Jones names Riverside in "This Land Is Your Land" (because it's the hometown of Dap-King bassist Gabe Roth). A suburb in the vast crowded space between the Pacific and the Mojave, Riverside is the kind of place that many people disparage (I've done it myself), a regular sun-soaked suburb, neither shiny nor shoddy, crisscrossed by freeways, lined with palm trees, inhabited by workers waiting outside Home Depot for a day job and old women pushing handcarts to the food bank, kids on play-grounds, moms in traffic, my family, my friends. My land. Your land. Every time Sharon Jones belts out "from Riverside, California," I'm moved the way, surely, some voters feel when a candidate speaks to them directly.

But that's not all. It's not the shout-out, not the voice, not even nostalgia that gets to me most; it's the lyrics themselves, especially in the final two verses with Woody Guthrie's words tweaked only slightly.

In the third verse Sharon sings: *As I was walking, now they tried to stop me / They put up a sign that said private property / Well, on the back side, you know, it said nothin' / So it must be: That side was made for you and me.* (Hear that, Ammon Bundy?)

And in the fourth verse, even more rarely sung or heard: *One bright sunny morning in the shadow of the steeple / Down by the welfare office, I saw my people / As they stood hungry, I stood wondering: If this land is made for you and me.*

Not a proclamation but a question, and a good one.

I only saw her live once, shaking and stomping and shimmering across the high stage. The word "dancing" does not begin to describe this. She was not far from death then, and carried deep weariness tucked in a tight sequined dress. But that didn't stop her. She'd been told before she could never make it, but she made it anyway. She made it all the way until this week.

What we have in this country—in our country—is tenuous, every last bit of it. The land is threatened; nonhuman species are threatened. Ditto for our ideas. And then there are people, all of us, especially the vulnerable. Am I worried? I am. But I'm not giving up. I'm holding fast to this one word: *patriotic.* My word. Your word. I refuse to cede it even if I don't know yet how to protect all it stands for. For now, all I know how to do is to get up in the morning and go running by the river and wave at my neighbors.

Then come home and turn Sharon up loud. Again and again.

Yours,
Ana Maria Spagna

From the End of the Road

ERIN COUGHLIN HOLLOWELL

Dear America,

Dear Prairie Dog Town, Dear Corn Palace, Dear Largest Potato in the World,

Dear worn-out sneakers,

Dear Little Gem Diner windows covered with condensation from a hundred conversations and three stale pots of coffee at 2 a.m.,

Dear giant wood roaches that press their bodies onto the hot pavement after dark in a parking lot behind a community theater in Macon, Georgia,

Dear red apples in the hands of three children getting on the subway at 135th Street Station,

Dear statue of the Virgin Mary in a rusted out bathtub in the front yard,

Dear empty coffee mug on the desk of a woman still working in her cubicle at 3 a.m.,

Dear grocery carts, Dear pecans, Dear rhythmic tick of sprinklers on golf-courses,

Dear old roan mare carrying a teenage girl who wants to go to college and become a doctor,

Dear glacier missing the snow but insisting on blue shine even under persistent gray clouds,

Dear canvas jacket on the man nurturing the bougainvillea vine along the top of his unattached garage, his wife in the kitchen singing over dinner,

Dear bougainvillea with its blossoms like the memory of a first dance,

Dear origami cranes folded by a dancer visiting an arctic village after another suicide,

Dear old communist in his favorite threadbare grey cardigan opening up his bookstore with its shelves full of writing by Shakespeare and Milton and other long dead white guys,

Dear plastic bags on the feet of the woman sitting behind the Quick Stop on the turnpike,

Dear half-built house with an ocean view whose yard is subsiding into the sea,

Dear huckleberry milkshake sitting on a picnic table in Paradise, Montana,

Dear young man with the new snow machine that he bought with his summer salmon fishing wages,

Dear Trump signs in the yard of a big house where a tired man unloads a lawnmower out of his 1982 dented, once-red Chevy pick-up,

Dear jewel-green moss growing on the side of a fence in front of a mobile home on a back-road in Oregon, Dear goat cheese for sale, Dear thrown-away folding chair,

Dear caskets, Dear malls, Dear AK-15s,

Dear mason jar of water on the porch next to the woman who just hoed twenty rows of beans,

Dear eagles on their nest above the front-end loader scraping the ground beneath their cottonwood tree,

Dear sound of pebbles being tumbled in surf,

Dear key-card being slipped back into the pocket as the elevator goes up fifty-eight flights,

Dear charred chili pepper, Dear Piggly Wiggly Grocery Store, Dear snow shovel,

Dear library book drop,

Dear brown bear sleeping in her den, cubs two months from being born,

Dear sunrise, relentless and shifting,

> When will we open our eyes to our fellow travelers? When will we see?

Sincerely,
one small person at the end of the road

Americas

SETH ABRAMSON

Dear Americas,

At last count, there were nearly 319 million of you.

Despite what pollsters, pundits, and other self-interested data aggregators tell us—and what certain politicians would have us believe—a country is not a series of shifting tectonic plates roughly corresponding to discrete age, class, gender, racial, ethnic, and religious demographics. These lines are real and all too often consequential, but we also cross them innumerable times each day to live with hope and determination in America. And indeed we have to, even when—as it often does—it hurts us. And I firmly believe that all 319 million of us are hurting in our varying degrees and idiosyncratic ways.

So, no, I do not believe that we awoke on November 9 in a fundamentally different country than the one we inhabited on the morning of November 8.

That said, I do believe in something even more improbable than the notion that America's chief sociocultural differentiator is its myriad, hardened voting blocs: I believe that the nation has a spirit.

I don't say that our spirit is readily discernible, or necessarily exceptional, merely that we have one, that it changes over time, and that its composition affects and operations touch each of us to different degrees and none of us not at all. That this recent election opened such a gaping wound in the body politic is evidence enough for me that some indefinable thing, preelection, was shared by all of us, however uncomfortably.

When the presidential campaign began, I wrote in a Scandinavian academic journal that the spirit of America (or mood, to avoid any inadvertent religious connotations) was one of angry optimism.

Not merely anger, but angry optimism.

That's not a paradox.

I think that was America in 2016.

The nation's approval of the job Congress is doing is less than its approval of head lice. (Look it up.) We are turning away from our media institutions in droves, more convinced than ever before—not without reason—that they do more to misinform than inform. We are embittered by ceaseless wars abroad, by economic stagnation for the working- and lower-middle classes at home, by a sense that racial and ethnic divisions are deepening. Social media enforce envy and self-hatred, the swirl of new technologies generates new forms of misapprehension and self-doubt, and the ready connectivities of our time dredge up our latent fear of imminent self-annihilation—sometimes expressed as an open embrace of same.

So ours is an angry spirit.

But what I admire most about America is also, to our great shame, something that has often caused others around the world and many within our own borders enormous pain: our foolhardiness. We do not shirk from the seemingly impossible task—our national experiment in democracy being itself a seemingly impossible task—nor even entertain the possibility of impossibility. Instead, we push forward, often haltingly, sometimes vaingloriously, sometimes recklessly, but always with a sort of optimism that I cannot help but admire because I too often feel little of it myself.

Anger and optimism: America in 2016, I think.

But what we did not have, in 2016, was a political outlet for our optimism, as one presidential candidate offered only a steady, polltested incrementalism that has not for the last half-century significantly bettered the lives of tens of millions of our countrymen, while the other offered only the chaotic churn of ignorance, hatred, fear, bluster, hypocrisy, hyperconservative know- /do-nothingism, and a "post-truth" national discourse. These options were by no means coequally bad, or even in the vicinity of coequal. While the former was (not unreasonably) deemed deeply dispiriting by many, the latter should have been instantly received as intolerable by all. And yet we can clearly see, and many clearly did see in advance of the general election, that neither option gave the nation much cause for optimism. And the nation is addicted to its optimism—indeed, so much so that it has often convinced itself that folly, hubris, and brutality are in fact iterations of optimism, even when all of history and much of the rest of the world clamors otherwise.

So America—swathed as ever in optimism but also, as before, layers of self-denial, self-declared exceptionalism, and an almost casual brutalism—expressed in anger what it could not in any credible belief in its own near-term future.

It opted for darkness over DC, hatred over gridlock, empty rhetoric over partisanship. This wasn't, I don't think, born of a widespread preference for any of these false choices, merely the same refusal to any longer be responsible or socialized (in any measure responsible, or to any degree socialized) that we sometimes see in individual humans consequent to years and years and years of suffering severe physical abuse.

In this case, it is the spirit of America that has been abused. And it has been abused for decades. By talk radio, by redlining, by redistricting, by a hundred thousand pundits, by the bare fact that no one is a human to anyone else on the internet. And now our American polity has manifested its rejection of this systemic abuse in the person of a dastardly and dangerous overlord.

On November 8, about 46 percent of America voted to blow up both itself and the other 54 percent of America.

It was an irrational and foolhardy decision, though one whose internal metrics probably differed slightly for each of the sixty-odd million voters who helped make it happen.

Now we must regain our love and retain our optimism.

It is not wrong that we should go in wariness of conventional politics, and corporate media, and the dispirited masses massing in common areas online. Gerrymandering and campaign-finance corruption ruined consequential political activism, just as the twenty-four-hour news cycle and a dearth of investigative journalism did in mass media, and both social media and late postmodernism did in the internet.

The 46 percent who couldn't see it on November 8 will see it soon enough: Donald Trump is the answer to no question ever asked by America. He is the very worst of what we are or have ever been.

So I do not ask here that we merely pick up the pieces of a national fabric torn asunder. I hope, instead, that we will search for some different ones. I hope for new avenues for political activism, new methods of mass communication, and a new commitment to methods of problem-solving that lift, consequentially, all boats. I hope for a national spirit of studied audacity, informed naïveté, and humble idealism.

We've got nearly 319 million Americas to realize, America. It's a tall order. Impossible, even. Many a devious politician tells us that all is zero-sum, that what you get today was ripped away from your neighbor yesterday and vice versa, or else that all that is new is torn straight from an already tattered Constitution. So: policies, principles, and problem-solving praxes that benefit and honor all? Impossible.

And yet.

Perhaps—one more time—the impossible is possible every bit as much as the present is intolerable?

Having hit rock bottom on November 8—as a matter of our collective well-being if not our domestic policy, the latter of which will surely get darker still in the years to come—is there anywhere to kick but toward the surface of the water? The sky? Light?

So, I hope. I hope for America. And I'll continue to fight for the American experiment. Because nothing else but hope will do or ever has done for anyone, and America has always been far more about the fight than the finish.

And we are not finished.

Best,
Seth Abramson

Of Truth, Post-Truth, Alternative Facts, and Lies

You and I have a problem, dear America.

You have been telling me lies for all the sixty-odd years I have been alive, telling me sweet tales of exceptionalism and opportunity, whispering that no, no, it can't happen here.

And I, in turn, have been lying to myself for all those years, attempting to convince myself that your stories are true.

I no longer trust you, America, just as it seems you don't trust me—for otherwise, why would you tell me those sweet stories in the first place? As a result, we find ourselves at what a fine talker—the title character of Herman Melville's great American novel *The Confidence Man*, say—might call an epistemological crossroads.

Put another way, as many these days are saying, we're in a "post-truth era." But because "post-truth" is itself a post-truthful word, of a piece with its recent predecessors "truthy" and "truthiness," let us call our time what it is: the Age of Lies.

If it is indeed this Age of Lies, then the old rules no longer apply. And if the old rules don't apply, we need a few new ones, or at least a few rules of thumb, to help us navigate all the post-truths that are being thrown at us. Here are a few that I've found to be of use, and I offer them to my fellow Americans, if not to you, my mendacious America.

1.   Take it as a matter of faith, if it's not too oddly self-contradictory, that you should believe nothing. If the last election taught us anything, it is not to believe polls, for instance. If anyone comes to you and says

that six out of ten Americans opposes a woman's right to choose or supports some form of gun control, ask politely, "Are you sure you've counted them all?" Extrapolations, chi-squares, and all the rest seem to be all in keeping with the Age of Lies: the extrapolators are thinking wishfully, the poll respondents are lying through their teeth.

However, all that said, let's run a few numbers of our own. Let us say that half of all eligible American voters actually showed up. Of those, somewhat more voted for the blue candidate than for the red one. Let's simplify to say that half voted for each. So: one in four eligible American voters cast their lot for Donald Trump.

But of them, how many voted for him because they were enthusiastically *for* him, as opposed to enthusiastically *against* her? By an informal poll of friends and family—and I grew up in the South, where peckerwoods grow on trees—about one out of three. So let's say that one in ten of our fellow Americans is really inclined to fascism, or authoritarianism, or whatever you wish to call it. Which is probably the same as it's ever been: There is no difference in kind, only in the quality and volume of the noise they've been making.

Do you believe my numbers? If so, I love you. But you should not believe them, of course: You should scorn them, doubt them, disbelieve them until you've checked them for yourself.

2.   As a corollary: Interrogate any reputed facts that come your way, and relentlessly. Spend a portion of each day asking, Which came first, the chicken or the egg? I don't know, but I do know this: In 1960 humans consumed 6 billion chickens. There were about 2.5 billion humans then, so about 2.5 chickens per human. Today the number is 50 billion chickens eaten by 7 billion humans, or about seven chickens per human. And since the 1930s chickens have doubled in weight—which means chemicals are involved, and girth.

Interrogate your facts. Interrogate your sources as Detective Sergeant Joe Friday would interrogate a hippie. All right, it's an ancient reference, but I like it. We can update: As Bigfoot Bjornsen from Thomas Pynchon's *Inherent Vice* would interrogate a hippie.

3.   When evaluating the statements of others who mean for you to take them as facts, look for the passive voice. When someone says "mistakes were made," set your antennae on the most sensitive tuning. Anyone

who thinks he can lie to you will, passively and actively. This includes whole branches of industry, commerce, and government.

4.   No matter what your political, economic, religious, or cultural beliefs, practice symmetrical skepticism. Assume goodwill, but also assume that everything people tell you, whether your political opponents or those you count among your political friends and allies, is wrong until you have looked it up for yourself.

Suspect even what I've told you. Well—no. Would I lie to you? Never...

In the days of yore, when I got started in journalism, grizzled newspaper editors used to intone, "If your mother says she loves you, get it from two independent sources." That's precisely the attitude I mean for us all to take. It smacks of cynicism, but then, so does this whole era.

Symmetrical skepticism. It's essential. It's indispensable. On the matter of missing things and making mistakes, I try to remember, whenever I write, something that John McPhee once said: "Are you going to get it wrong? Of course! You were an English major." But getting it wrong doesn't mean it has to stay wrong. A serious writer, activist, thinker is going to sit there and bleed out the forehead until he or she understands the data and science at hand. Science takes time. So does education. And so does cultivating the exquisite sense of symmetrical skepticism that is too often missing from the world.

5.   If you're excited by a piece of news or a press release or some such discovery, wait a few days before you commit yourself to it. Mistakes are made (he said, passively). Corrections are issued—and sometimes reissued.

6.   In a democracy, everyone is entitled to an opinion. And given that our Supreme Court has ruled that a corporation counts as a person, that person is entitled to an opinion, too, it would seem.

But that does not mean that everyone's opinion is as worthy as everyone else's. Knowledge is not evenly distributed, universal, or unspecialized. The reality is that to have weight, opinions have to be matched by data, and by expertise—which is why we consult with the experts when we need to know something.

Yet we live in a time when expertise is devalued and experts are suspect. We live in a time when the ruling source of information is, and I quote, "the free encyclopedia that anyone can edit." The problem is, anyone can, and anyone does. The ruling premise is that everyone's opinion is as good as everyone else's, that the wisdom of the crowd is by definition, through sheer strength of numbers, superior to the wisdom of an individual. If enough people believe that Al Gore claimed to have invented the internet—he did not, by the way—well, then, Al Gore claimed to have invented the internet, regardless of whether he actually did or not.

So stay away from Wikipedia. Stay away from the blogs. The world is full of opinion but distressingly light on truth. Read the papers. Read a book.

All right, then: What qualifies one source to claim superiority over another? There are friendly librarians all around you who can help answer that question. All you have to do is ask. Make a friend of your friendly local reference librarian. Librarians live and breathe to help guide you toward the truth. Indeed, if there is any category of citizen that is essential to democracy, it is the librarian.

And journalists, too—but practice symmetrical skepticism there, too, for just about anyone who wants the title can claim it. At a minimum, look for a source that checks facts, that edits, that runs both letters to the editor and corrections. Look for journalists who have experience in print as well as online publications, allowing all the while that the grizzled veteran can get it wrong, too.

7.   On that note, be prepared to be wrong. Facts, as Ronald Reagan once observed, are stupid things. He did say that, didn't he? Why, yes, he did. But then he corrected himself immediately afterward. He was quoting John Adams, who once said, "Facts are stubborn things," and he made a little slip, which he immediately corrected. Reagan said, "Facts are stupid things—stubborn things, should I say," but few writers have bothered to note his correction.

Make mistakes. Then own up to them. Facts are stupid things, but they can entrap the most careful of us. And we are never so certain of ourselves as when we're wrong.

8.   Take some joy in this whole business of doubting. As the poet Ed Sanders says in his indispensable notes on life, what he calls the

"multi-decade research project," you have to sing meaning into the facts you have gathered.

You have to dig, to sift, to question, to research, to cross-examine, to interrogate—and then make sense of it all. It's not for the faint-hearted, but it's essential work.

Finally,

9. The Buddhist philosopher Thich Nhat Hanh suggests that you tape a little note to your telephone that asks, "Are You Sure?" I keep that question affixed to every computer I own. It doesn't keep me from being wrong, but it has spared me a bit of embarrassment from time to time.

Today's fact is tomorrow's fable; almost everything we know is wrong—and if we had any sense, we'd proceed with extra caution for that very reason. Are you sure about that yellow cake uranium from Niger? Are you sure there's no downside to drilling for shale oil? Are you sure there's no such thing as global warming? Are you sure what you're saying is true?

We have some gazing to do into each other's eyes, America. I won't stop believing in you, but I won't stop doubting you, either. Now stop lying to me, and let's get to work.

I don't know how to write
a letter to America,

MARTHA SILANO

but if I did I'd say that half of us, in November 2016,
were playing Taps, would mention someone threw
a bottle at a woman in a hijab: *Wherever you're from—*
go back.

Would want it to say, about landscape painting,
too many of them position the natives in the distance,
paddling tiny canoes.

Would want to share about a story I heard on NPR,
a woman carrying on about light bulbs. Said her husband
had to work in a factory that makes them. Otherwise,
he'd have no job.

Would have to include the man who was aching
to delimb, to buck, who'd voted for the man who said
he'd give him back his freedom to fell.

My letter would get very primeval with its protest space,
its activism arch. My instinct would be to include
a bake sale with resistance cake, you-can't-
be-kicked-out pie. Bread that would have to be torn.

My instinct would be to remove the donuts
in the shapes of *rapists* and *thugs*, replace them
with mercy muffins, refugee rugelach.

If I were to write it, I know I would fail.
I know I'd say something like *one lung doesn't*

make an empire-toppling wind,
which what does that even mean.

I know I'd be tempted to say something about faith,
how you can't leave out a single cell
or you'll never leave the tarmac,
how the cabin door won't close,
which doesn't matter who you voted for.

My letter, if I wrote one? Would have to include
those miners in Cumberland, Kentucky, using
their bodies to block a train carrying millions of dollars
of coal, keeping it from going forward
till they're paid what they're owed.

In my letter, if I wrote a letter, I'd have to share
that the last time I protested was 2001,
the night before we invaded Iraq.

Darkness has nothing on the searing light,
I'd written in a draft. I, who haven't been behind
on rent or mortgage, on a utility bill,
since grad school. *Grad school.*

What do I know about darkness, about light?

An American Song

EVER JONES

> Our past is bleak. Our future dim. But I am not reasonable.
> A reasonable man adjusts to his environment. An unreasonable man
> does not. All progress, therefore, depends on the unreasonable man.
> TONI MORRISON

Dear America,

I need a bedtime story, the stars are too far tonight; the night makes my window a mirror. There I am: brown eyes, buzzed hair, cinched tie above cinched breasts—a story between spaces.

You too, America, grown from the spaces between the story you tell and the lived one. Freedom for you and you, but not you. Liberty, for you, but never for you. Susan Griffin wrote: "The stories we tell ourselves, particularly the silent or barely audible ones, are very powerful. They become invisible enclosures."

Hush little baby, don't say a word...

I hear the sweet alto of Grandma Libby's reassuring voice, the grandma I loved best, who denied her mother's brown skin for a privileged life in Columbus, Ohio. Forty years ago her whispering song, but I can nearly feel the lavender cloth of sleep. That lift when the mind slips into a space away from the body. How space seems to become the story.

I want to write this letter like an exhalation; no beginning or end if it is still alive. (The rub between *still* and *alive*.)

I think that once I was whole. I don't believe this is your story.

A relative in central Ohio asked on Facebook, "What's so different from Obama that everyone is so upset now?" I said transpeople's suicides, I said Muslim registry, I said stop and frisk, I said law and order, I said encrypted email, I said my Mexican student's colleague telling her to go home, I said a wall, I said that Anastacia Reneé wrote a poem for her black son: "hide your babies, hide your babies, hide your babies."

I said none of this to her.

Mama's gonna buy you a mockingbird...

And if that bird doesn't sing, then she'll buy you a ring, then she'll buy you a looking glass, a billy goat, a cart and bull, a dog named Rover, and a horse and cart. This is an American song—your song.

Privilege is an insulation. "Rooms with no air," Griffin adds.

Charles Eisenstein suggests that "we as a society are entering a space between stories, in which everything that had seemed so real, true, right, and permanent comes into doubt." This is true for white people who weren't awake before Trump's election. My friends of color simply feel the intensity of the burn.

In the bedtime story, the baby is told to hush. Your little American babies. What will we do in this space between the story we knew last week and the one before us? There's a countdown to Trump's inauguration that I believe empowers his imagination. Let's turn it off. Do not hush. *You'll still be the sweetest little baby in town.*

Ever Jones

November, Third Trimester

JENNIFER CASE

Dear America,

I am tired. On the day of the election, I was thirty-six weeks pregnant. Now I am even farther along. I cannot climb a flight of stairs without losing my breath, and when I stand or sit for more than an hour, my feet swell against the seams of my shoes.

I am not sleeping well. I wake from random contractions: a rock-hard belly and a deep ache in my back. Soon I will birth this child, whether I want to or not, and the truth is, in the wake of the election, I'd rather not.

America: I worry for my children. I worry the culture they live in is too concerned with short-term comfort to face climate change. I worry my children's environmental memories will not be of camping trips or pumpkins or walks beneath the moon but of increasing catastrophes and wars over resources.

I worry for my daughter, and what messages she will receive from others about her body. I worry she will stop at a gas station at night, like I did one month before this election, and that men in the lone car next to her will catcall. I worry that she, like me, will leave with only three gallons in her tank.

I worry for my son. That he will be born into a time in which racist and homophobic comments fly like spittle from others' mouths, and that such comments will incite further violence. I worry this violence is the only news he will hear. I worry that hatred and intolerance, to him, will seem "normal."

I worry for myself. In a week or two, I will go into labor. I will be stripped down and monitored, in a city, a state, a country that has declared a predatory man can be president. I will rely on the hands of others to hold me and catch my child. I'm not sure I'll feel safe.

I know we are all scared and angry—including those who voted for Trump. A conservative colleague of mine with three children feels attacked by anti-Trump protesters; she has said feminists want mothers to hate their sons. A white, working-class relative of mine, struggling to pay the mortgage on her house, believes the government has done nothing to help her. She criticizes Obamacare and illegal immigrants, and she has applied for a permit to carry a concealed gun. Though I will never support Trump or his statements, I know the anger of these voters stems from fears and injustices that also need to be addressed.

America: I know that overcoming all these fears will take time and work.

Please show me that you, too, are willing to do that work.

Please show me that this is a world worthy of children.

Awaiting your reply,
Jennifer Case

It's Time to Teach My Daughter How

SUZANNE FRISCHKORN

It's time to teach my daughter how to shoot an arrow
How to use a knife
How to hit the center of a target
       It's bloody work, but she should know
It's time to teach her how to win a debate
While applying lipstick without a mirror
And how to hold her keys between her fingers in a parking lot
       It's time for her to hit the weight room
Join the cross-country team
Cast a spell, literally and figuratively
And it's time for her to develop telekinesis and clairvoyance
It's time she knows to never leave her drink unattended
Never drink on an empty stomach
Never drink before her period
And maybe what I mean to say is—never drink alcohol period
It's time to learn that one day she might switch
Grocery stores because a guy on staff there gives her the creeps
And even if it's less convenient to travel across town
       It's always best to trust her intuition
It's time to teach her that when a grown man stares at her
New breasts, she is not the one who should feel ashamed
America, she's her mother's daughter
       She's got this

My Mother's Vote

FENTON JOHNSON

Dear America,

It's October 2012, and I'm spending the autumn caregiving my inety-six-year-old mother in the family home in rural Kentucky when she says, "So, Fenton, who are you voting for, for president?" Politics and religion being forbidden topics south of the Ohio, the moment sets itself apart from the norm. I say, "I don't know, Mother," though I do, but I understand, in the way of southern manners, that the subtext of her question is, "Ask me who I'm voting for." And so I ask and she responds, "I think I'll vote for this Obama guy."

"You *will*?" I'm shocked out of manners, which takes quite a shock, since my mother understood early that manners were the only gifts she could afford to give her children and so she drilled them in deep—my mother, born in 1916 into the Jim Crow South; my mother, who like most women of my childhood adopted the formulation "nigra" as a genteel linguistic compromise between the impermissible Yankee "Negro" and the men's unspeakable N-word.

And then I shut my mouth. I want desperately to know the forces that brought her to this decision, but the moment seems too fragile, I'm afraid something I say will change her mind and so I leave the moment alone.

Across the next several weeks I seize every opportunity to say that if she wants to vote, I'll figure out a way to make that happen. But she puts me off and dodges the question and puts me off, until it's Election Day. I have a full day of errands, so over breakfast I say, "Now's your last chance, because if I'm taking you to the polls you have to let me know that so I can get back here in time," since Kentucky closes its polls at an absurdly early 6 p.m. "No," she says firmly. "I'm too old to vote." "Okay, well, whatever," I say, and go about my errands, and return around 5:30 to find my mother struggling to push open the door with her walker. "Where are you going?" I ask. "I've got to get down there to vote," she says. The polling place is a mile distant. "All right!" I say. "Let's get you in the car!"

I get to the polling place at 5:50 and screech to a halt in front of the door and get my mother into her walker. She turns out to be registered in Senator Mitch McConnell's wet dream of a polling place. There's a step to negotiate—a hazard and a barrier for the disabled. But I get her over that and inside, only to find that the booths are at the far end of a high school gym, fifty yards and more away, and are flimsy aluminum stands that provide no purchase or support. The polling volunteers all know my mother and offer a table and chair for her to vote, but there are no chairs with arms, only folding metal chairs that are more hazardous for an elderly person than the booths. I have no choice but to accompany her to the booth so that she can lean on my arm, though this feels a bit like sitting in on someone's confession.

The ballot is set in a typeface that would require a twenty-year-old to use a magnifying glass, and the voting booth provides the weakest of reading lights. So I take the ballot and read aloud the names, slowly and without inflection, and when I say "Barack Obama" she says, "I'm voting for him." I read the rest of the names, but at the end she says, "Obama." So I show her the box and she makes an X.

And I'm near to tears at witnessing this demonstration how despite all evidence to the contrary and the magnitude of the powers arrayed against it, change, positive change, affirmative change can happen: my mother, ninety-six years old, voting for an African American, take *that*, Senator McConnell! But instead of weeping I point out that she can't just make an X; it's a computer form and she has to black in the whole box (QED, a living demonstration of why Al Gore lost Florida in 2000). So, leaning heavily on my arm, she blacks in the box, and I leave her standing in her walker as I cross the additional hundred feet to the machine where I turn in her ballot.

■ ■ ■

Some years back I pointed out to a dear friend that much could be inferred from the fact that the United States chose as its national symbol the bald eagle, a bird that uses its size and power to steal food from smaller, more skilled animals who track and kill the prey. "A bully and a thief," I wrote. "An opportunist," she fired back. You will not be surprised to learn she voted for Donald Trump.

My lefty/liberal friends moan that they don't see how any intelligent person could vote for Donald Trump. In response I offer the suggestion with which philosopher William James opens his magisterial essay on pacifism, "The Moral Equivalent of War." "Pacifists ought to enter more deeply into the aesthetical and ethical point of view of their opponents. Do that first in any controversy . . . *then move the point*, and your opponent will follow."

Every Trump voter of my acquaintance was a college graduate who disliked the man intensely but (a) felt ignored by the Washington–New York–Boston–Silicon Valley elite the Obama presidency so carefully cultivated; (b) fell victim to the Republican Party's thirty-year smear campaign, Trump's lies, and Clinton's inability to redefine the tone of their encounter; and (c) was insulted by Clinton's repeated insistence that anyone who'd vote for Trump was racist and "deplorable." College biology taught them—inaccurately, as it turns out—that "survival of the fittest" is Nature's only measuring rod, and they believe that, in a world that capitalism is constantly telling them is dangerous—fear sells even better than sex—we need a president who is as nasty and manipulative and bullying as "they" are. That there is no readily identifiable "they" only increases my friends' fears. That biology now teaches that successful evolution requires cooperation and collaboration as much as competition is a message science is not doing nearly enough to disseminate.

The challenge is great—maybe insurmountable. Any critique of the 2016 election must begin with the reminder that Hillary Clinton comfortably won the popular vote and in a real sense achieved, in fact, a historic victory. But the slave owners of 1789 demanded and got a system that awarded them disproportionate power. With the concentration of the liberal vote in a few states, we are likely to see more elections like 2000 and 2016, with ever-increasing popular vote victories combined with ever-larger Electoral College losses.

Perhaps we are witnessing the disintegration of the American Empire, which if that could be accomplished peacefully might be for the best. But if the empire is to remain united, our work begins, not with the presidential election of 2020, but with the school board and state representative and county sheriff elections of 2017 and 2018.

Over and over I hear the question: How do we respond? Let me re-phrase the question: Where were you on Election Day? I went down to the local Democratic headquarters and made a few calls. Nice try, but it was wholly inadequate to the cause.

Watch and wait. Keep your wits about you. Stay calm. The great mistake of the Clinton campaign was engaging Donald Trump on his playing field of insult and ugliness. We can't win on that field. Let the thieves fall out, as they will, while we gather our strength and organize.

Recognize that while social media has its uses, Facebook and Twitter do not a successful campaign make. Why did my mother change her mind about going to the polls? Because on Election Day a volunteer called to ask her if she'd voted. Campaigns are won by shaking hands, knocking on doors, giving money, coming together, face time. As Obama and Trump taught us in different ways, there's no substitute for enthusiasm. Can I yell and scream and wave signs for social justice? You bet I can. Where might the left accomplish that? Once we had labor unions and union halls and first-rate regional media, newspapers, and locally owned television. Now we have . . . churches.

Get off your lazy weekend ass and join a liberal church or your local Democratic Party or your local environmental organization or *something*, some place where you come together with other like-minded people working for social justice. Turn off your dumb-down devices, pull out your earbuds, and connect, only connect. Come together to revere each other and the planet. For every homophobic, misogynistic megachurch, there are three struggling left-wing congregations or temples dedicated to loving-kindness and fellowship, where talk of God, if it happens, is undertaken in the most gender-neutral, user-friendly way, and whose leaders are, within the bounds of their tax-free status, eager to promote candidates who share your views.

Attend a Quaker meetinghouse and learn about nonviolent resistance. Define and honor your limits of action and then stretch them just a little bit in doing what you can. Prepare to put your body where your heart is. Action is the best way to stir yourself from the dumps. Don't underestimate the power of love. Get out there and do something subversive.

Carry this truth close to your heart: the closer the victory, the stronger the resistance. Unless, of course, we give up.

Okay, so roll your eyes. Don't join a liberal church. Don't head down to Democratic headquarters or your lefty nonprofit of choice. Instead, spend your Sundays at home on Facebook, send lots of tweets, and lose elections. Take your pick.

The struggle is unending, as it should be. Think of Frederick Douglass, born a slave, who endured the Civil War and the Thirteenth Amendment that ended slavery, then witnessed the corrupt election of 1876 and the end of Reconstruction and the rise of Jim Crow segregation. He died in 1895, with victory seemingly farther away than ever. But somewhere in his dying moments, I like to think he imagined Barack Obama, and my mother's vote.

Un abrazo fuerte and a spring-budding bough,
Fenton Johnson

The Windigo

ROBIN WALL KIMMERER

Dear Readers—America, Colonists, Allies, and Ancestors-yet-to-be,

We've seen that face before, the drape of frost-stiffened hair, the white-rimmed eyes peering out from behind the tanned hide of a humanlike mask, the flitting gaze that settles only when it finds something of true interest—in a mirror. Cruel eyes, a false face and demeanor of ravening hunger despite the unconscionable hoarding of excess while others go without. The spittle quickly licked away from the sly "fox in the henhouse" smirk that sends chills down your spine, a mouth that howls lies pretending it's an anthem.

Americans keep acting surprised by the daily assaults on American values once thought unassailable. I can't speak for all Native people, but we've smelled that carrion breath before. We know who this is, the one whose hunger is never slaked—the more he consumes, the hungrier he grows. We've met him on our shores, at the Thanksgiving table, at the treaty table, at the Greasy Grass, on the riverbank at Standing Rock, and in the courts. His mask does not fool us, and having so little left to lose and all that is precious to protect I call him the name of the monster that my ancestors spoke of around the winter campfire, the embodied nightmare of greed, the Windigo.

We know him. Perhaps this is why he has taken special efforts to poke Indigenous peoples in the eye, because we see him. He has proven himself an equal-opportunity offender to people black and brown. But with the spite of bullies everywhere, he has sharpened his stick with special vindictiveness for Native people from the first days of his administration, by reversing the glimpse of justice we held for one shining moment at Standing Rock, to dishonoring the Code Talkers, to undermining treaty obligations and threatening termination for our people, to casting Pocahontas's name as a slur that manages to taint every stereotype across a range of Indigenous identities, to denying protection for Gwich'an livelihoods, to sending drill rigs to penetrate sacred land.

He is the obscene of the Anthropocene, the colon of colonization, the grinder of salt into the original wound of this country, but lest I spend any more words on cathartic name-calling, let me say that Windigo is the name for that which cares more for itself than for anything else. It shrieks with unmet want—consumed with consumption, it lays waste to humankind and our more-than-human kin.

Windigo tales arose in a commons-based society where sharing was a survival value and greed made one a danger to the whole. But in a profit-based society, the indulgent self-interest that our people once held as monstrous is now celebrated as success. Americans are called on to admire what our people viewed as unforgivable.

The particular weapon of the Windigo-in-Chief is the executive pen, used against what has always been the most precious, the most contested wealth of Turtle Island—the land. With the stroke of that pen, he has declared that "oil is life" and that protecting the audacious belief that "water is life" can earn you a jail sentence. The same pen gutted the only national monument designed by Native people to safeguard a sacred cultural landscape, the Bears Ears. In opening those protected lands for uranium mining, he triumphantly claimed that he was returning public land to the people.

From his origins as a real estate developer to his incarnation as Windigo-in-Chief, he has regarded "public lands"—our forests, grasslands, rivers, national parks, wildlife reserves—all as a warehouse of potential commodities to be sold to the highest bidder.

Let us remember that what the United States calls "public lands" (and, if the truth be told, all of what the United States calls private property as well) are in fact ancestral lands; they are the ancestral homelands of 562 different Indigenous peoples. A time-lapse map of North America would show the original lands of sovereign peoples diminishing in the onslaught of colonization and the conversion from tribal lands to public lands, some through treaty-making, some through treaty-breaking, some through illegal sale, and some through what were termed "just wars," by executive action and "encroachment."

Not only was the land taken and her people replaced, but colonization is also the intentional erasure of the original worldview, substituting the definitions and meanings of the colonizer. That time-lapse map of land taking would also show the replacement of the Indigenous idea of land as a commonly held gift with the notion of private property, while the battle between land as sacred home and land as capital stained the ground red. Of course our ideas were dangerous to the idea of Manifest Destiny; resisting the lie that the highest use of our public land is extraction, they stood in the way of converting a living, inspirited land into parcels of natural resources.

Native people have a different term for public lands: we call them home. We call them our sustainer, our library, our pharmacy, our sacred places. Indigenous identity and language are inseparable from land. Land is the residence of our more-than-human relatives, the dust of our ancestors, the holder of seeds, the makers of rain; our teacher. Land is not capital to which we have property rights; rather it is the place for which we have moral responsibility in reciprocity for its gift of life. Here is the question we must at last confront: Is land merely a source of belongings, or is it the source of our most profound sense of belonging? We can choose.

Our ancestors had a remedy for Windigo sickness and the contagion it spreads. Those who endangered life with their greed were banished from the circle of what they would destroy. They were cast out from the firelight and the bubbling stewpot, from care and community. You colonists also have that power of banishment. Will you use it?

It's not enough to banish the Windigo himself—you must also heal the contagion he has spread. You, right now, can choose to set aside the mind-set of the colonizer and become native to place, you can choose to belong.

Colonists, you've been here long enough to watch the prairies disappear, to witness the genocide of redwoods, to see waters poisoned by the sickness of Windigo thinking. The Windigo has no moral compass; his needle swings wildly toward the magnetism of whatever profit beckons. Surely, however, the land has taught you differently, too—that in a time of great polarity and division, the common ground we crave is in fact beneath our feet. The very land on which we stand is our foundation and can be a source of shared identity and common cause. What could be more common and shared than the land that gives us all life? Rivers don't ask for party affiliation before giving you a drink, and berries don't withhold their gifts from anyone.

The moral compass guiding right relationship with land still remains strong in pockets of traditional Indigenous peoples. The sharp stick of the bully in the White House only hardens our resolve. The needle still points faithfully north, to what we call in my language Giiwedinong, the "going home star." When we acknowledge the truth that all public land is in fact ancestral land, we must acknowledge that by dint of history and time and the biogeochemistry that unites us all, your dust and your grandchildren will mingle here. They will know what you do here, they will reap the consequences of whether you choose to banish Windigo thinking. You could follow the "going home star" and make a home here grounded in justice for land and people.

Colonists become ancestors too. The question is, What kind of ancestor do you want to be?

Sincerely,
Robin Wall Kimmerer

Extractions,
Extinctions,
and Depletions

Notes to America

TAYLOR BRORBY

I.
Dear America, coal colored my childhood. Black, luminous lignite coal, exhumed from dusty Dakota prairie, put bread and milk on the table.

II.
Dear America, I remember burning coal. Before the first snowfall, Dad and I hopped in our silver Dodge pickup, the bench seat covered in a coarse blanket, and rumbled down the country road to fill the truck bed with coal. When we got home, I helped unload the black lumps, my hands struggling to hold the jagged not-quite-rock, not-quite-dust that would heat our home.

III.
Dear America, life on the northern Great Plains is defined by extractive economies. Coal. Water diversions. Oil. Grazing on public lands. My father's two brothers, as well as my grandfather, spent their entire careers in coal. My father worked at a coal-fired power plant in his last working years. Coal is in my blood.

IV.
Dear America, this summer, on a road trip west to hike to the source of the Missouri River, my friend John and I stayed at my uncle's house. He works in coal near Gillette, Wyoming; his house rattles when the three mines across the highway blast dynamite to get at lignite. One time, his grandson's rifle fell from the wall and hit his head.

V.
Dear America, over breakfast, while updating my aunt about my life, I told her how John and I saw mile-long coal trains leave Wyoming. "Everything leaves Wyoming full, and then comes back empty," she said.

VI.

Dear America, greatness is found in the breadth of the mixed-grass prairie. The world tends to be amazed at verticality—particularly the height of mountains. Instead, I relish the vastness of the prairie. In childhood, I heard pheasants thrum in the marshy land beyond the wheat field behind our house. I hurled crank baits into the Square Butte Creek, praying to God I'd catch a northern pike. Today I still smell the coffee-scented ponderosa pine in southwest North Dakota, climb buttes off little-traveled roadways, and catch toads in the baked mud on the banks of the Missouri and Yellowstone Rivers.

VII.

Dear America, I do not say this lightly: I intend to end the fossil fuel industry. North Dakota, home to the second largest oil play, roars with flares. Theodore Roosevelt National Park is ringed by fire. The Missouri River now contains radioactive material—these are not convenient facts for our great narrative.

VIII.

Dear America, a new narrative unfolds along the sage-scented banks of the Cannonball River in North Dakota. The Sacred Stone Spirit Camps of the Standing Rock Sioux Nation block construction of the Dakota Access Pipeline. Brown bodies, riddled with rubber bullets, soaked with water, face black-armored police in the black night. Another profit, another erasure of culture.

IX.

Dear America, my father is a lifelong union worker.

X.

Dear America, wealth is in our topsoil, in our waterways. It is in helping our neighbor build her new roof, and walking an elderly man across the street. Jobs can be created and can disappear—wealth, once lost, is gone forever. If the American Spirit is to thrive in the twenty-first century, it must come from our relationship to place and to one another. Without a place, we have nowhere to root ourselves, no safe anchor to weather the storm. Without each other, we walk our paths alone.

XI.

Dear America, a farmer in Iowa got arrested protesting the construction of a pipeline on her own land. *On her own land.*

XII.

Dear America, late at night, when I close my eyes, I go back in my mind to the breakfast table and think of my aunt. I think of how to keep Wyoming full, how to protect the pallid sturgèon I love. I think of the sage grouse in North Dakota doing the sagebrush step, and I remember that maybe the way forward is more like a dance—a gentle push here and pull there, striving to move together to make something beautiful of the place and people of our lives.

Refinery

GEORGIA PEARLE

Texas City

In my passenger seat she crosses
her legs, pulls down the sun visor.

Near midnight, and the Perseids
send slow artillery across our sky.

We've got a full tank, driving past
the derricks and pumpjacks;

the sucker rods bob in the fields
like bored horses. *My uncle died*

in that refinery, she says.
Chemical spill. No body left

to bury. Cousins got a settlement.
She flicks on the visor light

and keeps her gaze to its mirror,
lit, her own eyes on her own lips,

which she daubs a cimarron red,
her center fingertip bright and greased.

After the Election

AMANDA HAWKINS

Of course darkness.
Of course a milky white shroud.
Of course no high

and beautiful breach.
Instead, a curved black.

A body's foul
breath on the wind,
our sense of direction
obviously off.

The only sound
the slosh of waves,
the burst of air from the spout,

the muffled fog,

and the periodic pound of fists
against the kayaks' hard plastic.
Because our guide had made it clear:

his job was not to help us
get close to the whales.
His job was to keep the whales

a safe distance.

I Had Heard

BRIAN LAIDLAW

of the Don:

colossal, old.

surrounded.

burned, broken.

not at all conventional.

free of limbs.

very large, crooked and rugged.

zigzagging stiffly outward, seemingly lawless.

unexpectedly dissolving.

dense, bossy.

may be recognized while yet far off.

upheaved against.

the king   *not*   of behavior and port.

eighty or ninety.

the monarch of   the dying out of the species.

Note: This poem comes from an erasure of John Muir's *My First Summer in the Sierra*. The source text has a character—Muir's boss on the sheep-driving trail—nicknamed "The Don," who is a wealthy and incompetent shepherd.

Latte Capitalism

DEBORAH THOMPSON

Dear America,

Twelve white paper coffee cups sit on tables around me, each blazoned with a green iconic mermaid. Each cup has a corrugated cardboard sleeve with an additional mermaid. These brown-skinned mermaids, protecting their white-skinned sisters, stare at the clear mermaids—currently four of them in the shop—staring back from polypropylene cups. I see the mermaids steaming, each to each.

Most environmental writing looks at green and living things, teaching me to see and love the natural world around me. Lately, though, I've been thinking that I also need to learn to see the *unnatural* world around me, the one my cultural environment is set up both to naturalize and to render invisible. So today I'm doing my environmental writing in Starbucks.

The upright mermaids on cups all look down on the encircled mermaids stamped on brown paper bags, like the one currently serving as a plate for my morning muffin. The pastry looks freshly baked, but when I pointed to the one in the display case, the barista took out a cellophane duplicate, removed the muffin from the plastic bag, and put it in a brown paper bag, giving me an extra mermaid to send down the magic hole at the cream-and-sugar station.

In the time I've written the above paragraph, there's been a whole turnover of mermaids. So many fantastical females, commingling invisibly below that magic hole, along with green straws and stir sticks and the occasional plastic fork or spoon. We can't see this orgy of mermaids, of course. These trash chutes render all trash invisible.

That's a sure sign of repression at work. In his model of the psyche, Freud famously theorized the unconscious as the site where repressed thoughts, traumatic memories, and unacceptable impulses—our messy psychological undesirables—get buried. Such repressions make civilization possible. That buried detritus, though, never quite disappears. Whether or not Freud's model is actually true of the psyche, it seems to me to ring true for the American city. We repress conscious recognition of our garbage, as well as garbage itself, sending it to the unconscious realm of the landfill.

We're said to live in an era of "late capitalism," but a late friend of mine, Adam Krims, riffing on the term, used to call it "latte capitalism," which seems more accurate to me, and not only because I see no signs of capitalism nearing its end. Latte serves as a perfect metonym, or representative exemplar, for what Marxist theorists would call "mystification" and "commodity fetishism"—the way we desire and consume things like coffee while keeping ourselves protectively ignorant of the conditions of their production. In late capitalism, the economy is maintained by consumers' constantly reproduced desire for the new and the even newer: a cultural logic of disposability. Mystification works to protect ignorance not only toward conditions of production (as Marxists have long maintained) but also conditions of postconsumer destruction. The whole system depends on our repressing the ultimate costs, both to people and to the environment, of such continuous disposal and replenishment.

Latte capitalism is alive and well here at my wooden table. The conditions of the production of coffee and of its postconsumer wastes are mystified away in this "urban rustic" ambience, with its green walls and wooden windowsills. Not only is the trash rendered invisible; even the garbage can itself is invisible, hidden tastefully under a granite countertop over a wooden cabinet. It's not even labeled TRASH, but sits silent and unmarked. We don't see it being emptied, much less where all its mermaids go thereafter: their long haul to the landfill, some finding their way to the ocean, where these disposable mermaids fail to swim; each holds her split-tailed fins in her hands, until she, waterlogged like Millais's Ophelia, goes under. Meanwhile, the true water creatures, the ones who do swim, compete with this swarm of disposable mermaids and their polystyrene lids, stir sticks, and straws. I remember with horror that viral image of the sea turtle with the straw in his nose, and that continent-sized landfill in the ocean so euphemistically referred to as the Great Pacific Garbage "Patch." ("Sludge" might be a better term.) And these are just the visible, spectacular disasters of the mostly unseen sea world.

The problem with the repressed, though, is that it has a funny way of returning. As our vast schools of Frappuccino cups decompose in their great oceanic garbage patches, the fish who manage to survive ingest these plastics, and then we eat the fish. And not just fish. Even vegetarians eat thousands of microplastic particles—enough in a month, it's been estimated, to comprise a credit card. As microplastics slowly line our bodies, we become the waste we thought we'd thrown away.

But these mermaids in front of me, with their Mona Lisa smiles and flowing hair, tell me a different story, one of green-backed adventure in a world beyond human reach. Their green outlines and green milieu suggest that they are part of nature, or at least ecofriendly. I prefer this story in front of me to the one out there somewhere unseen.

Recently, overwhelmed by my own waste footprint, I bought a (plastic) reusable cup. I suspect I'm merely purchasing the illusion of waste reduction. I'm buying smugness and absolution the way, in the Middle Ages, some Catholics bought indulgences. I can have my coffee cake and eat it too. Now that I keep this cup nestled in my car's cup holder so as not to forget it, my own private mermaid stares blankly at me, stirring new hungers and thirsts on my way to everywhere. She stares at me now, at this lacquered wooden table. But individual action can only go so far in a culture set up to render the true environmental damage invisible.

Indeed, plastics are mystified from start to finish. It's sometimes hard to remember that the material we associate with cling-wrap cleanliness and transparency is dirty stuff. Most plastic begins as crude oil and ends in debris. Oil is unnaturally cheap because the environmental costs of its extraction are not factored into its price. Nor are the environmental costs of its refinement into ethanol (and other hydrocarbons), its polymerization into plastics, or the disposal of these plastics. These unpaid costs make it cheaper to produce new plastic than recycle used plastic. Most plastic waste that doesn't go to landfills or scatter to oceans is now burned in "waste to energy" incinerators (which tend to be located in underprivileged neighborhoods), releasing carcinogenic chemicals and creating toxic ash that itself must be disposed of.

The biggest problem is with single-use plastics, such as coffee cup lids, Frappuccino cups, straws, and cellophane. These items, used once and then tossed, are made of material designed to last forever. Today we produce an estimated 300 million tons of plastic a year, half of which, turning into single-use items, become instant, everlasting trash. To reduce single-use plastic consumption, we need not only to make the problem and its true costs more visible but also to make their use more difficult, commensurate with those true costs. That requires large-scale action. While the EU has voted to ban single-use plastics by 2021, and other countries have imposed taxes or partial bans, the Trump administration has refused to take action. Meanwhile, it has cut EPA regulations on oil production and refineries, incentivizing plastic production and leaving the environmental and economic burden of cleanup to state and local agencies and to individual consumers. But the problem is much bigger than refillable Starbucks coffee cups. As Sen. Tom Udall and Rep. Alan Lowenthal wrote in a June 5, 2019, letter to the president, "We believe that a well-coordinated and well-funded interagency research plan, coupled with robust investments in our response programs, is essential to address the domestic and global plastic pollution crisis at both a human level and at an ocean conservation level."

Meanwhile, behind the counter, a barista washes his hands and then pulls, in quick succession, one-two-three-four-five napkins from a dispenser that seems to grow them as an ever-renewable resource. Just as quickly, after barely a wipe, the napkins disappear down the black hole of invisibility, along with someone's *USA Today* and its headlines of the administration's latest deregulations and degradations, all shrouding the mermaids below.

Even now, at this late date, it's still not too late to lift the shroud of latte capitalism. We can still hear the mermaids sinking.

Yours,
Debby Thompson

Let Sleeping Wolves Lie

DANA SONNENSCHEIN

Dear America,

Let sleeping wolves
sprawl in the brightness
of summer afternoons,
jaws wide, tongues lolling.
Let them paw down
to cooler dirt and shape
themselves to match
that bowl of shadow
till night rises past the rim.

Let wolves break trail
through snowdrifts.
Let them lope along roads.
Let them circle and curl
through blizzards,
noses nestled in tail-fur,
drifting into darkness
as starry crystals fall
across their flanks.

Let sleeping wolves lie
in mist and morning rain,
guard hairs sinking
toward gray undercoats—
Let wolves dream runoff
along ridge and slope

and wake, rise, and shake
the water from their backs
in a storm of drops.

Let it rain and let the wolves
lick their sleek forelegs,
drinking from the sky.

Let wolves be wolves,
coursers of deer and elk,
and let beef cattle be cattle
as they once were,
big-shouldered, nervy,
all sharp hoof, horn,
and instinct to turn, mass,
and face what hunts them,
to charge a threat, not run.

Let the lowing herds roam,
grazing on ranchland
that someone owns,
not in sheltered basins
where elk winter over,
not in protected thickets
or forests. Let there be
no salt licks near dens.
No helicopters with guns.

Fence in the cows
during calving season.
Flag the live wires.
Send riders singing down
the line as dawn bleeds
through and at dusk,
when hungry packs awaken
and stretch their legs
in the long light.

Watch over those
golden hours, America,
but let sleeping wolves lie.

Lamentations

BARBARA HURD

Dear America,

In times like these, lamentation is what we have for voicing sorrow. It's what Wallace Stegner calls "the conscience speaking," which I might amend to say that lamentation is the conscience *struggling* to speak. Groping hard to make sense of grief, it sometimes first resorts to stuttering facts:

> From the early 1500s to the 1800s, almost 150 species including the dodo bird and large sloth lemur disappeared, wiped out by habitat destruction, pollution, and the natural causes that have kept this world in constant flux for billions of years.

> Two hundred years ago, the Falkland Island wolf vanished, as did the great auk and the big-eared hopping mouse.

> By 2050, if the planet continues to warm at current rates, more than 10 percent of all species will likely cease to exist.

But a list of losses is not a lamentation. The conscience, if it speaks at all, more often wrestles to imagine a voice not ordered but invented, perhaps shaped by rhythm and song.

Think of biblical prose or Giotto's fresco *Lamentation*, Matthew Arnold's "Dover Beach," or Whitman's "When Lilacs Last in the Dooryard Bloom'd."

Think of Martha Graham's masterpiece opening ninety years ago in New York City. In the dance, "Lamentation," a single figure wrapped in a stretchy cloth squirms for four minutes on a bench, leaning left then right, reaching up, bending over, as if she cannot abide what's twisting inside her, as if she's trying futilely to writhe into relief. The dance is not meant to convey particular mourning for particular loss, but to embody archetypal grief itself.

Here's how it feels, Graham seems to say: You do not walk away or deny or give up. You're stuck on a bench, wrapped in a purple shroud that moves with every move you try to make, transforming every distorted thrash into a visible line, a traceable shape.

Or into hair-pulling, clothes-rending keening, as the women of Ur did. Some four thousand years ago, their city in ruins, they wandered speechless, as if their tongues, too, had been stilled. The power belonged to others, along with the orchards and fields. All that had once made them mothers and wives, sisters and daughters had been destroyed. The grief that remained was charred beyond speech. They invented a new language, which screeched in their open mouths like small, rabid crows.

Almost two thousand years later, Plato condemned such high-pitched keening. Let the disreputable wail, he declared, not the decent, the noble. He censored lamenters for the same reason he banned the poets. Both express shadowy feelings that distract from the idealized forms which Plato saw as ultimate truths; both prohibit platitudes, purities, tidy solutions that sabotage the need to ponder the unruly in our hearts.

Perhaps Plato feared that lamentation could provide no protection from the mess of who we are. Perhaps he was right. Lamentation demands, after all, that we feel this death and that death. But this wisdom, too: the "greatest poverty," as Wallace Stevens says, "is not to live / In a physical world, to feel that one's desire / Is too difficult to tell from despair." You can have your grief, lamentation seems to say, so long as you yoke it to the dazzle and drudge of a daily life.

Gone in the last hundred years: the Tasmanian tiger, Toolache wallaby, desert bandicoot, and Yemen gazelle.

In the last twenty: the Alaotra grebe, western black rhino, Yangtze River dolphin, Caribbean monk seal, black-footed honeycreeper, Pyrenean ibex, Spix's macaw, golden toad.

Higher in the last twenty-five years: sea levels all over the world.

Smaller: the West Antarctica Ice Sheet.

Higher: acidity of ocean water.

Lower: chances of avoiding catastrophe.

Lamentation displays. It doesn't petition.

It doesn't allow for bargaining. No *I'll grieve like this for thirty days if you will...*

It doesn't traffic in denial, forgiveness, explanations, hiding, or compensation, which, if it could judge, it would see as obscene.

It doesn't tolerate magic or heart-felt appeals to mythological gods, false prophets, or any other quick-action, result-driven strategies that promise some kind of solution.

In the last five years: Formosan clouded leopard, Japanese river otter, Malagasy hippopotamus, Bermuda saw-whet owl.

No justifications allowed, no payoffs, no talk of collateral damage.

And now, at the current pace: dozens of species a day.

Dear America, some of us here in the early twenty-first century are still pretending the world's not fundamentally changing. Time, after all, is tricky, and loss across slow time even trickier. Some of us try to adjust our diets, accommodate to shrinking beaches, invest in solar panels and in the idea that there's no reason for alarm. Some of us make a different list:

The heat-aversive Hawaiian honeycreeper still has a little cool air left at the tops of the Kauai Mountains.

The South African quiver tree, more and more stunted, manages to keep producing seeds, though they're starting to drift poleward.

Most Adélie penguins are learning at last how to keep their eggs out of the puddles left by melting ice.

Heat-stressed white lemuroid ringtail possums persevere, licking leaf moisture in the threatened cloud forests of Australia.

How do we lament what's not finished dying?

Maybe what we need now is not merely an updated version of keening and wailing, not just protest art and policy fights or publicly displayed extinction lists of the unambiguously gone. In these times of sped-up climate change, maybe what we also need is a new lamentation that choreographs the ritual even as it conjures up the grief for the still-here-for-now. Stay, it will insist, and mourn what's not yet gone. Straddle the space between what you can bear and what you cannot until you know not only what's on the verge of vanishing but the price you'll eventually pay. That, it seems to me, is what a new lamentation might do: give form to what it simultaneously elicits. Shape language and image and dance from the raw heartache we're not yet sure we even feel.

A new lamentation won't be a path or a door. It won't go anywhere or open up new vistas. Think of it, America, as a hopeful act of preservation, not of what's on the verge of vanishing but of the shame that remains. Think of it as preserving our ability to grieve what we're doing.

Yours,
Barbara

Swallows: Common yet Declining

CATHERINE STAPLES

And yet you'll see them everywhere—
    on telephone wire or fence rail,
        diving the swale between dunes
    riding the sunbaked meadows
uphill through aerials drifting on wind.

Swealwe, suala, swalue, swallow—
    they swoop loose of syllables, the ancient
        names that called them down.
    Iridescent blue and black, masters of the long
glide and liquid reverse. How slowly they go

from hayfield and sea-cliff, so slightly diminished
    we hardly notice a few less arrivals.
        For still they build in barn rafters
    knock the nest, they'll build again.
If ever once you've seen them, shuttling by hundreds

over sea swells, they shake the water from
    their wings, they skim
        the bright forever—
    the drop-off, the flyby, the see-able truths.
How the mind hoards beauty and resists the new

news about neonicotinoids in farmers' fields:
    the insecticide casing of seeds
        killing off the bees,
    diminishing a swallow's ability to breed.
Who will hear what can't be heard—
    gap in the whirr of singing—another silenced spring?

What Will Keep Us

DEREK SHEFFIELD

for Katie and Kelsea on the Save Our Coast Hike

The coast is never saved. It's always being saved.
PETER DOUGLAS

Every pack-heavied step over sand hoppers
        and weed-slicked rocks, through driftwood scatters
and the chill of tidewaters, over wooded headlands
        as wildfires blaze north, south, east—every step says
stay. "I know mermaids aren't real," Kelsea says, "but Daddy,
        look," holding a whip of bull kelp whose lightbulb face
is a brown-green eye under ribbons of translucent hair.
        We trudge our miles, stepping over oscillating
anemones in sunlit pools to pause at Hole-in-the-Wall
        and let their tentacles tongue our dipped fingers.
And what's this holographic sheen? Not the oil
        we would keep from this shore, and not plastic,
we see, just a rainbow's iridescence beaming
        from a plant. Over teeth of barnacled rocks poking
from pools of sand crabs and sculpin, through foamy
        maroons, emeralds, violets—tangles of surfgrass
and lettuce cushioning our steps—we hike, flies parting
        briefly for our ankles as we take in the gleaming curve
of the otter's tail as she rises and dives into clear
        shallows, a pliable needle threading us and them, water,
land, and rippled sky where the numberless legs
        of sandpipers twiddle their skittery flocks always
just ahead. For even the reek-slap of rot from a carcass

too far gone for ravens or gulls we hike, for our own
place among the eaters and the eaten pricking at us
     as we see how wide the jawbone, how long and curved
the fangs. For the piping stutter of a crow-mobbed eagle
     landing on a shaggy bough, for the lightest touches
of day mist on our skin and our headlamps
     in the night lighting the tracks of slugs silvering up
every spruce trunk's loom. We hike for what will keep us
     if we keep it. On a bare stretch of sand ahead, a boulder
splits into two bear cubs whose dark heads swivel our way
     before they turn as one toward the woods and lope
out of sight, to go on in the multitudinous dream we need
     to be beyond our reach. Out past the breaking lines
of waves we can just glimpse through binoculars,
     where the rounded humps of humpbacks slope one way
and gray whales the other, sixty-some otters floating
     on their backs have knit themselves into a living net—
weft, warp, leg, paw—kelp blades fixed by holdfasts
     to the deepest rocks. What is it they catch
in their drift of sleep amid mists and rolling webs
     of stars? Far enough where, if we fail, the drills
will rise. And what now as they ride day's swells in
     and out of sight in the rhythm of our own breathing?
Our hike ends at the beginning of what the map calls
     Wedding Rocks, where people of the Makah long ago
carved the round faces of sun and moon among fishers
     and fish, a whale, an orca. What feelings
spilled through them as they knelt in these same
     unceasing sounds of waves, chip after chip falling away?
We trace the grooves with our fingers, five centuries
     of wind laced with the wet snorts and hunger cries
of passing animals. Kelsea kneels over some new swirl
     of shell and exclaims. Katie says not a word, drawing
with her stick something in the sand we can't yet see.

In the Garden

TODD DAVIS

When the last pollinator fluttered its wings and folded
into itself, like newspaper as it catches flame,
we'd already buried the skeletons of the remaining
hummingbirds, the husks of bees, what little was left
of the antennae of moths and butterflies, the tiny corpses
of the penultimate wasp and ant, the sting and bite
of these small lives no longer a threat. Nothing had to be done
for the scurrying beetles who burrowed into caskets
of their own making, but some of us hung the now still
bodies of swerving bats from lampposts, while others gathered
them in nets, making pilgrimages to caves to lay them to rest.
At a museum in Washington, D.C., small brass plates named
each creature, explained their place in the vanishing taxonomy.
Underground installations housed seeds for plants and trees,
and we collected an example of each species
that played a role in fertilization, pinned them to a board
with elaborate charts that identified body parts
and their peculiar uses. We were most interested in
their mechanical efficiency and wished to recover
the ways they conveyed pollen from anther to stigma.
We brought in theologians who revised the sign of the cross,
a version that emphasized reproductive organs
and the importance of fecundity. Even the scientists believed
resurrection, grown in a petri dish, was our only chance:
stigmata marking the wings of a swallowtail or monarch,
each of us longing to touch the holes we'd help to make
in the colorful fabric. This was our prayer to unburden us

of doubt, and despite our lack of faith, we ached for a peach
at the end of a branch, a plum or apple, the honeyed pears
we greedily ate in August, juice dribbling from our chins,
fingers sticky with our own undoing. The few scientists
who were not already living off-planet began to create
new designs for our children's hands and lips,
working to enhance the ridges in the brain that help
to discern and process olfactory signals. They wrote code
while the future slept in its fleshly rooms, reprogramming
the cells for stunted growth, perfectly proportioned
for the work that lay ahead. Where some might have seen
deformity, we saw beauty: sons and daughters walking
orchard rows, crawling between cornstalks and vineyard grapes,
scaling almond trees whose cupped blossoms waited to be filled
with our answers. The children stopped at each bloom,
stooped with fingers shaped like paintbrushes, caressing
silky petals as grains of pollen caught against their skin,
enough static so this precious dusting wouldn't fall away
until they delivered it to a flower of our choosing.

A World Departs

SHERWIN BITSUI

Flames, thirty degrees
warmer, become leaves
rustling in an autumn
dream. We rename

sharpened shadows
with shadow light, climb
beads of gunshots backlit
on clifftops, then dive

into our hands holding
our teeth back, when
butterflies drizzle, spit,
and float out our ears.

We trace a hearse
breathing up through
our footsteps, the plastic
wrapped moon's jaw
locked around its sweating,
    never again snow-peaked.

Stone Age

ANDREA COHEN

I could—with one
stone—kill two birds,

but then I'd dwell
alone with a blood-

stained stone, one
too morose to build

a stone house with,
and nothing overhead

suggesting a way to fly
outside myself.

She's Going to Be Beautiful

TODD BOSS

She's going to be beautiful as she goes,
isn't she? Gorgeous plumes of cinder
blooming rose in dying light. She's going

to give a stunning show. The melting ice,
the slow decay of zones. Our drones
will play it all in full HD, and lavish insult

on the injury. All the satellite imagery.
The National Geo photography. She's
going to be calendar-worthy stuff

if ever again a calendar there be.
Like forcing someone to disrobe
and wishing you don't want to watch.

The moon will touch her everywhere goodbye.
An elephant—the last—inelegantly,
will pass in a savanna gleaming gold.

The cloud formations no one's ever
seen, in towers shimmering with ash,
we will no longer wonder to behold.

Coastal cities under sea. She will be
beautiful, of course she will. And
devastatingly.

Geographies
of Exclusion

Assembly-Line Justice

FRANCISCO CANTÚ

Dear America,

Every weekday at the federal courthouse in Tucson, Arizona, where I have long lived, dozens of men and women are gathered in a courtroom and made to face the high pulpit of a judge like shackled parishioners. Most of them are young, wearing T-shirts, sneakers, and jeans. Called up in groups of five, they are each asked the same incantatory set of questions: Do you understand the rights you are giving up? Are you pleading voluntarily and of your own free will? Are you a citizen of the United States? Did you enter southern Arizona from Mexico without coming through a designated port of entry? How do you plead? *Culpable,* the defendants all say one by one. Guilty.

Using a stopwatch, I once timed the proceedings: in less than four minutes, each group of five was convicted and sentenced to prison terms of up to 180 days. All in all, the court can adjudicate the cases of as many as seventy-five migrants in as little as an hour and a half.

The dogged rhythm of the proceedings means that any deviation is conspicuous. I notice when defendants pause for too long, when they interrupt the judge's questioning to admit they don't understand, when they tremble at the microphone as they say, "I had to leave because they wanted to kill me," or "The money in my country isn't enough," or simply "Thank you, I'm sorry." I notice when a man from Honduras refuses the black headset that relays the Spanish translations from the court interpreter. He has three children born in the United States, his lawyer explains; he has made his life in this country. The man answers the judge in confident English, as if to assert, *I belong here.*

This grim daily ritual, known as Operation Streamline, began well over a decade ago, in 2005, a year in which border apprehensions climbed above 1.1 million. The program was conceived of by the U.S. Border Patrol and the Department of Justice as a way to reduce recidivism and alleviate the overburdening of southwestern courts by sentencing undocumented border crossers en masse. After a few years, Streamline was reserved for "repeat offenders," migrants previously deported from the United States who thus faced felony charges of reentry in addition to the misdemeanor of "entry without inspection." Under the program, defendants agreed to plead guilty to the misdemeanor and waive their constitutional right to appeal in exchange for the dismissal of the more serious felony charge and its associated court fees. Attorneys who represent migrants differ widely in their assessment of the program—some consider it a good deal, but many others believe it silences their clients in the name of expediency.

For a brief moment in time, in early 2017, it seemed as if Operation Streamline had perhaps outlived its supposed "usefulness," even in the eyes of those who had long helped sustain it. After trending downward for years, undocumented crossings reached their lowest point in decades, and there were days when no more than six migrants passed through Tucson's cavernous courtroom. Many attorneys and judges questioned the necessity of the operation—it had become a mass hearing without the mass.

But then, the incoming Trump administration announced its intention to "bring the full weight of both the immigration courts and federal criminal enforcement" down on undocumented immigrants. U.S. prosecutors were directed to once again pursue conviction for first-time entrants, expanding the pool of prosecutable border crossers and giving Operation Streamline the numbers boost it needed to survive. By procuring misdemeanor convictions for first-time entrants, the program could effectively dole out more convictions among the dwindling number of arrivals, saddling them with criminal records and a history of deportation.

Many here in the borderlands are quick to remind us that changes like these must be understood as an extension of what came before them. When I asked one federal judge about the "Trump effect" in their Streamline court, they conceded quite plainly: "It was already awful." Many attorneys and judges doubt that hard-line immigration prosecution even deters would-be migrants in the first place. "They don't fear

American prisons," a career public defender named Joel Parris once told me. "They fear violent existence, a life without money and opportunity."

One summer, I committed myself to spending an entire week in Streamline's immense courtroom. My overwhelming impression was of assembly-line justice, of a vast machinery quickly and dispassionately grinding away at the lives of men and women who were forgotten as soon as they were named. "It's the same thing seventy-five times in a row," one judge confessed to me. "Sometimes it's like an out-of-body experience, and I don't remember what I'm doing or where I am or what I said."

Such proceedings desensitize us to the humanity of those with an unwavering hope of becoming part of the fabric of our nation—in many cases, even dispatching with those who are already American in every way except on paper. "We are being made to look at everyone the same," Joel Parris told me. He is certain, dear America, that such a structure would never be tolerated were it designed for people we consider our own. To stand by as policymakers perfect a mechanism for rejecting outsiders, he warns, is to become blind to the individual lives of those it condemns. Thus, it falls on us now more than ever to gaze without blinking at what is being wrought in our name, and to act swiftly against it.

In hope and solidarity,
Francisco Cantú

History Kids

DAVID HERNANDEZ

These kids, these kids in tents, white tents
in camps in Texas. These brown kids who trekked
miles with parents, deserts and mountain passes
with parents, days of scorch and nights with parents
with flashlights, stars with mama's voice soothing
kids with moon-blued skin, with closed eyelids
and dreaming, with high-noon shadows and humming,
the land sliding into hand-me-down shoes,
laceless, rubber soles worn thin. These kids
now in chain-link pens, trapped in, wrapped in
thermal blankets, in synthetic shine, flashing together
like stars, the ones you don't see, hidden
by distance, by degrees below horizon, by these
government tents, these canopies of white. In pictures
they blur their faces, they vanish anguished eyes
we see anyway, anyway we imagine, which shade
of earth, which hue of helpless, specks of gold
or green like mica in stone. Oh America, your own
kids shimmer this summer, this season of turning
hydrants to fountains, mailboxes to scrap metal
thanks to fireworks, waxy vines on kitchen walls
thanks to crayons, thanks to kids, but that's
how they are, that's what they do. They're just
kids. They're just kids.

A President, a Travel Ban, and a Playdate

BOB FERGUSON

Dear America,

Thank you for your letters—thousands of them.

When sitting down to write about the Trump administration and this dark chapter in our nation's history, I realized no one describes what America represents better than you—so I decided to share a few of the letters you recently sent me. One of those letters is especially meaningful. But I'm getting ahead of the story...

Shortly after taking office, President Trump signed the first Muslim travel ban. It was not a surprise. He had repeatedly promised to institute "a total and complete shutdown on Muslims entering the United States." It was an applause line during his campaign.

The travel ban separated families, divided employers from employees, and prohibited students and professors from resuming studies in the United States. In addition, many individuals lawfully residing in our country were denied the right to visit family members abroad or travel for business.

As attorney general of Washington State, I decided to challenge this un-American and unconstitutional action. My team worked around the clock to quickly craft our legal arguments, and I immediately filed a lawsuit challenging the constitutionality of the travel ban. A few days later, a federal judge, appointed by President George W. Bush, granted our request to halt the ban nationwide.

The best moment of my professional life was being in the courtroom when Judge Robart issued that restraining order. We knew it was an important moment—but I underestimated the emotional impact of our successful lawsuit on the American people.

Thousands of handwritten letters began pouring into our office. Americans from every corner of our country shared their stories. Their letters eloquently connect the ban to historical moments when injustice touched them and their families. They convey how the ban represented a betrayal of our American values.

> I am the daughter of a Jewish refugee from Nazi Germany who was grateful for the chance to immigrate to America in 1939. Yet many of my relatives did not manage to escape Hitler. They were still waiting for approval of their visa applications to the U.S. when they were deported to death camps in Poland.
> TOBY, BELLINGHAM

> We immigrants know how precious our rights are as Americans because we know what life can be like without them.
> PHILLIPA, RICHLAND

> This executive order recalls another time in our history seventy-five years ago when President Roosevelt issued Executive Order 9066. My parents, grandparents, and aunts were incarcerated at Tule Lake because they were Japanese, and not because they had done anything wrong. We never wanted this to happen again to any other group.
> TONI, MERCER ISLAND

The letters are also optimistic and hopeful. Americans express solace in the work of my legal team and the message sent by the court—that even the president is accountable to the rule of law. They appreciate that we successfully used President Trump's divisive language against him in the court of law. They express a rededication of their patriotism.

> Refugees need us, and we are not the greatest country if we are afraid.
> MICHELLE, SEATTLE

> The people of Washington State believe in the American values inscribed at the base of the Statue of Liberty. We are strengthened, as a nation, by our diversity, and we have a moral obligation to provide safe harbor to those whose lives and families are at risk due to political repression and widespread violence.
> AMY, OLYMPIA

Thank you for protecting the Constitution, and thank you for showing us that truth and justice still matter very much.

MIN, LAKE FOREST PARK

I decided to send handwritten replies to Washingtonians. It was a time-consuming process, but it seemed the least I could do for the inspiration their letters provided to me and my team.

One evening I was working at our dining room table with my then nine-year-old daughter doing her homework beside me. Katie noticed a drawing on one of the letters and asked me about it.

The letter that caught Katie's eye was from an eight-year-old girl. Her family is from Iraq, one of the countries included in the first travel ban. A colorful drawing of me, done in the obvious handwriting of a child, grabbed Katie's attention.

I read the letter to my daughter. The girl wrote, "If you did not stand up, I would not be here."

Up until that point, my wife, Colleen, and I had not discussed the travel ban in any detail with our young twins. The kids did ask why I was working so much, and I simply said, "The president did a bad thing and daddy is trying to stop him."

But when Katie listened to that letter, it put the travel ban into a language and context she understood. This child was her age and could be her classmate, her friend. That letter was not only a powerful message to me; it helped my daughter understand something important happening in her country, and she wanted to know more.

Katie asked if she could add her own note to my letter and decided to write replies to all of the many letters I received from children. It became a wonderful evening ritual for us. In addition to a note, she drew a picture on each one—a horse, a butterfly, sometimes a rainbow.

President Trump lost his appeal and eventually rescinded that original travel ban. I made the federal government send a check to the State of Washington to cover our costs in responding to their failed appeal. It wasn't very much money, but that wasn't the point, was it?

This was our first court victory against the Trump administration, but not the last. As of this writing, my office has filed fifty-four legal challenges against the Trump administration. Our record stands at twenty-four victories, zero losses. Fifteen of those cases are finished and cannot be appealed.

Many of our victories involve environmental issues. For example, we defeated the administration's efforts to delay a rule regulating emissions from new oil and gas facilities, another delaying air-quality standards for ground-level ozone, and still another attempting to restart a program to lease coal-mining rights on public lands without updating its nearly forty-year-old environmental impact statement.

And that little girl who wrote to me? She and Katie had a playdate. I'm not suggesting we can solve all the world's problems with playdates, but it's not a bad place to start, is it?

Thanks for writing.

Yours truly,
Bob Ferguson

Red Sky

PEGGY SHUMAKER

List
everything
you've lost.

Ars poetica
of heartbreak.
What's possible

to replace. What
never is. The sky's
memory, smoke.

Say a wall of flame sears
inside your eyelids every time
you close them.

What wish
floats on streams of ash?
What sky remains?

■

In the waiting room, on the never-off
TV a river of poor people
draws near the line.

The talking head's scarlet lips
say officials can process only a trickle
each day. Thousands gather.

Next to me, woman with a fistula
mature &
swollen, woman

with her upper arm Saran-wrapped,
woman with a beatific smile, says,
"Why process them? Just

send them back."

■

Say a girl knows early.
Knows as a doctor
she wants to improve

world health. Say this girl
hears along the way
what girls can't do.

Say she laughs.
Say she prepares herself
to laugh a lot.

■

Say this season
coyotes sleek & shiny
gorge—plenty of rabbits.

Surefooted
javelina brush by
creosote's tiny yellow blooms,

nip new paddles
of prickly pear.
In their burrows, whiptail

lizards, shedding
rattlers, scholarly &
deliberate Gila monsters

repose, patient as earth.

The Earth Was Once Water

LINDA HOGAN

Dear America,

I knew a ragpicker who created stories about his items. People paid for the stories more than for what they purchased. One evening he sold me a leftover bag of items. Inside I found a slab of amber containing a small tree frog. I felt terrible sorrow for the frog. Whether it was real amber or a human creation, I felt its last desperate moment for breath.

James Baldwin said people are trapped in history and it is trapped in them. I know our tribal nations feel this most keenly because we have been locked and held inside your long-standing desire for gold. It has ruined much of this land and broken the lives of our people who retain knowledge of ecosystems, and who cherish the beautiful breath of water in each form it takes.

America, you haven't cherished this element, water. The Yellowstone with benzene, the Kalamazoo pipeline rupture, the Flint River running with lead, the Mayflower oil rupture, Exxon flooding an entire town. Oil, gas, chemical spills; slaughterhouse waste. Our waters are polluted with lead, mining waste, and agricultural runoff carrying female hormones that diminish the ability of male animals to reproduce. The Animas River, flowing yellow-orange with sludge from the Gold King mine.

Then came the Dakota Access Pipelines from the Canadian tar sands, a countries-long *black snake*, an extraction of entombed animals, trees, and plants of long-ago earth. In what became one of the most politically significant events of the last century in Indian Country, numbers of people arrived at Standing Rock, the Missouri River, and Lake Oahe to protect the water from this pipeline.

Tribal chiefs arrived from across the country in full regalia. Native and non-Indian supporters came to protect the enormous Missouri and Lake Oahe and stop the pipeline from crossing beneath the river. Indigenous leaders from other continents joined leaders here, as did paddlers from the Northwest Coast—all to support the living waters of the Missouri.

We know water is the mother of life, yet in the midst of this peaceful stand came one more war against both water and people. Our Native presence threatens you, America. It always has.

Standing Rock is a story still raw to tell in ordinary language. Elders spoke of peace, both on loudspeakers and at quieter campfire rings. Yet police shot protectors with water cannons in below-zero cold, bombarded them with tear gas and rubber bullets that broke ribs, legs, arms, and cheekbones—aiming first at medics, journalists, and Natives. Private security workers used dogs and pepper spray. In one night alone almost two hundred people were injured, many intentionally shot in the eye or groin. A concussion grenade destroyed a young white woman's arm. At night, planes sprayed chemicals, leaving sediment. Women were stripped naked and placed in dog cages. The elderly too, even with medical needs, were locked in small dog cages.

During the day, young men were chased by law enforcement and the private army using ATVs, their horses shot as they rode. Grandmothers were maced in the face. Burial grounds were bulldozed by corporate employees, ceremonial items defiled by their urine.

Warring America, I am an Indigenous elder, and I tell you that the story of one Native human is as long as the story of blood and earth. We are different because we don't want to be like you. We want to hold to our own nations and languages and knowledge, our own countries from the ancient beginning.

We know each tree holds water and cares for those around it, offering what it can in dry times. Water: mother of all life, each life a creation of beauty, carrying its own intelligence, different from all the rest but still equal.

Linda Hogan
Great-Grandmother

20,000 Pallets of Bottled Water

JUAN J. MORALES

September 20, 2018

On a runway in Celba, under blue tarps pulled taut,
FEMA's water shipment still sits, one year after Maria.
Against a backdrop of the people boiling river water,
the agency apologizes for *distribution issues,*
officials promising to test each bottle
though everyone knows it's as foul as their island support.
In the gaze of the aerial shots—pallet after pallet—stretching out
like a crumbled runway, the tallies of the dead jump from *64* to *3,000,*
    and
the mainland president tweets congratulations to all
on a *job well done.* The island is a dry throat,
a voice in the eye of the aftermath, hissing words
unspoken elsewhere: *commonwealth, statehood, independence?*

"Virtually Uninhabited"

SCOTT WARREN

Dear America,

The law enforcement ranger escorted us out of the Cabeza Prieta Wilderness for having driven our pickup on a road open only to law enforcement vehicles. He also suspected that we had left behind jugs of water and cans of beans, or, to put it another way, that we littered. Not quite sure what to do with us, he took our information and said that someone from the refuge would be in contact. After months of silence, I was served a summons to appear in federal court on misdemeanor charges of "abandonment of property" and "operating a motor vehicle in wilderness."

Since this incident I have reflected on a recurring dream that I had while on backpacking and camping trips when younger. In the dream, we hiked for miles into some beautiful and remote mountain valley. But once we arrived we were shocked to find that instead of pristine wilderness there were 4x4 vehicles, roads, and industry. One time, while on a backpacking trip in the Sierra Nevada with my dad, I woke from a version of this dream feeling defeated and depressed, until I realized that the wilderness in which we slept remained safe from actual assault.

I was first attracted to the Cabeza Prieta by those who had written about it. Its desert mountain ranges and valleys comprised one of the remaining wild places of the lower forty-eight, and when combined with the adjacent Organ Pipe Cactus National Monument and the Goldwater Bombing Range, it made a larger expanse of unbroken Sonoran desert that was about the size of Connecticut.

One of those who wrote about this place was Edward Abbey, who worked as a seasonal ranger at Organ Pipe and loved this part of the desert. Abbey's environmental writings about Organ Pipe and Cabeza

Prieta decried the intrusion of copper mines and ranchers whose cattle overgrazed the desert. But he also wrote racist passages about nonwhite people, especially Mexican immigrants, whom he feared contributed to overpopulation and destruction of America's wild places. His approach to curtail immigration and "secure" the border was quite troubling. In a 1980 letter to the editor of the *New York Review of Books*, he argued "most of the border runs through flat, wide-open, sparsely vegetated terrain" and "could be easily patrolled and easily 'sealed' [by] a force of 20,000...properly armed and equipped." In the urban areas he called for a physical barrier that would be "watched and guarded."

Abbey proposed this in the 1980s, a time when the informal migration of workers between Mexico and the United States was both routine and a source of anxiety for many Americans. Images of migrants running across the border in San Diego and El Paso populated media accounts of the region. By the 1990s, with anxiety increasing over the pending North American Free Trade Agreement, the United States government unveiled a new plan to "seal" its southern border.

The plan was to deter migrants from crossing in the first place by imposing new hardships on them. Chief among these would be the natural environment. In the minds of government planners, the rugged, remote, and "virtually uninhabited" deserts and mountains of the border would form a natural wall, stopping most migrants before they even set out. Those who did brave the wide-open deserts would be easy to spot and apprehend. Better to chase them around in the desert, according to the government, than around downtown El Paso. So they built walls and beefed up security in cities and hoped that the desert would enforce itself.

Instead, tens of thousands of people who had once crossed in urban areas now crossed in rugged and remote areas. As the years wore on, thousands of migrants died while crossing harsh landscapes. And it became clear the strategy also relied on mass suffering, disappearance, and death as hardships, even as it failed to deliver the objectives. The government now argued that Border Patrol needed reinforcements to respond to the security and humanitarian crises unfolding. Ironically, each boost in border policing strengthened the hand of cartels in Mexico, and the tangled, arms race–like escalation between the forces of smuggling and the forces of interdiction gave rise to a new kind of border industry.

Abbey's plan has materialized: there are walls, watched and guarded, in every urban area on the border. About twenty thousand well-armed and well-equipped Border Patrol agents maintain line watch, staff checkpoints, and conduct roving patrols. Those walls, checkpoints, surveillance towers, tire drags, high-intensity enforcement zones, and tens of thousands of miles of new roads and tire tracks laid down by the Border Patrol are the industrial scars left behind in the Cabeza Prieta and other protected areas. The border industry now threatens these wild, protected places in the same way that copper mining and unfettered grazing did a generation ago.

Most troubling is the myth that undergirds the government's use of Cabeza Prieta, Organ Pipe, and other protected areas for border enforcement. The deeply held American myth of "free" and "open" land is one of the core tenets of colonialism and conquest. In the border region this history is not ancient but rather recent, and it pervaded the creation of the wilderness in the first place. In the middle part of the twentieth century, Native, Mexican, and Anglo farmers, ranchers, prospectors, and woodcutters were displaced from this part of the desert to create protected reserves. In the 1950s, for instance, the National Park Service razed the homes and orchards of the Orozco family and the Hia-Ced O'odham Native community in which they lived in order to make the desert appear more "natural." Both the wilderness mystique and the government's rhetoric of "virtually uninhabited" serve to make this place an eerily blank slate.

According to his wishes, Abbey was buried somewhere in the Organ Pipe and Cabeza Prieta wilderness. His friends rescued him from the hospital and brought him to a final resting place in the desert he loved so much. No doubt many thousands of migrants have passed his grave on their journeys north, and hundreds of these—perhaps a thousand or more—have died in the same wilderness in which Abbey now rests.

For several years I have gone into these places as a humanitarian volunteer to leave water and food for migrants, to search for those who are lost, and to recover those who have died. Like the Sierra Nevada of my childhood, the Cabeza Prieta to me seems big, wild, and wide-open. But I have new dreams about the wilderness. In these dreams, an unknown vehicle approaches at night, driving with its lights off, while I sleep in my tent. A helicopter descends on our isolated campsite and blows hot embers from the cooking fire into the night sky. Saguaro are silhouetted on a mountainside by incendiary flares. Migrants, in desperate need of water, stumble into our camp and report the bodies of others who have died nearby...

Since the 2016 presidential election the government has undertaken the task once again to "secure" the border. The new plan is to build an even bigger wall. Public land managers who are charged with protecting these places are unlikely to protest this new industrial intrusion into the wilderness, as they have shown more interest in ticketing humanitarian aid volunteers and working with Border Patrol and the U.S. attorney's office to prosecute those who offer food and water to migrants.

Before this desert was a high-intensity border enforcement zone, before it was a protected wilderness, even before it was a geopolitical borderland, it was Hia-Ced O'odham territory. These new land uses are but layers on top of a persisting native landscape. Abbey's idea that conservation could find common cause with border militarism is misguided. Instead, conservation in the borderlands, if it is to succeed, must find common cause with humanitarianism, human rights, and Indigenous rights.

Sincerely,
Scott Warren

Club

CHRISTIAN WIMAN

Rich men whose souls are silos
from which their lives have long ago been launched
squeak as they sink in deep embosoming chairs.
How they love their nooks of oak and nineteenth-century light!
They do not mind the golden rule, as it is called,
not to speak of business here. They do not need to.
Even now, out in the screech and lurch this peace
obliterates, money, immunity, metastasizes.
Attended by brief embodiments, shadows with hands,
living whispers, the rich men nod their needs.
And when they've downed one dusk, they have another.

Invitation to the NSA

NAOMI SHIHAB NYE

Feel free to scrutinize my messages. Welcome. Have fun fanning through my private thoughts on drones, the Israeli Army chopping down olive trees, endless wars in Iraq and Afghanistan, horrific from the get-go, and we told you so, but no one listened because there was a lot of money and oomph in it, so feel free to listen now. Bombs have no mothers. That is an insult to mothers. See what I think about Bashar Assad vs. the children of Syria, pass it on, please, or weapons in general, the George W. Bush Library in Dallas, which I refused to drive my mother past. I like the sense of you looking over our shoulders, lifting up the skirts of our pages, peering under my fury at how you forget Palestine again and again, forget the humble people there, never calling them the victimized innocents as you call others. You forget your promises, forget religion, *Thou Shalt Not Kill*, and yet you kill, in so many ways, so what do we care? You might as well see what we say.

Song for Long America

ALLISON HEDGE COKE

Dear U.S./The States/Estados Unidos,

America is long, so long, Inuktun to Yámana, America. Inuktun to Yámana. Something fluttered sail-white into blue wideness, oceans, opened outbreak, annihilation, postured presence, pressure, cut hands, heart, feet, heads, hearts, cut America red, blue, cut her, cut the body for resource treasure, still is on, still takes. Still vanishing, still missing, still defile, still murder, still disappear women, children, still steal, still invoke-elemental-control-for-white-profit for posturing for posing upon the long, long place with long memory and longer soul   survives.

America is long. Long, long, so long—the continent sans canal U.S. cut at Panama. Cut the body to channel flow Pacific and Atlantic. Cut the lungs manifesting monied passing. Cut belonging. Captured, whipped, bought, sold. Ship sails wealthy fleet economic, always economic.

Look at it, this long place. Ocean bound, rivered blue.

Look at this blue, complicit Statesian, these people, these children, Indigenous, caged.

Look at this blue, complicit American Statesian. These parents, these grandparents, Indigenous slaughtered, bloodied.

The States

Look at it, this long place. Look at it, this blue. Look at this blue.

Star-spangled night vault shielding earth with universe exploding rockets flare empty display. Complicit   *The States*

Firing assault rounds into romance, into Back to School, into music, into hope, into families, friends, kinship communities, into heroes, into saints, *into loving arms that hold you*, into faces, necks, breasts, bellies, backs, torsos, legs, feet, hands, heads, cutting life from the husk hold, cutting life cold, cutting life.

The States

Extermination, all the beautiful. The continent kept in killing. Kept in chokehold strangle, I-can't-breathe momentum. You are killing me momentum. Kept in plastic, crude oil product, plastic waterfowl massacre, water life massacre, microbead disaster, oil pipeline malady, gas fracking tragedy, heating up drowning, immolation burning, sacrificial for funding. Kept in guns. Kept   *Complicit*

She rests in her glory, glorified, glorious, glaring at all who challenge her destruction. 45's thumbs up smiling with Melania's capture hold of El Paso massacre orphan.   Lost bird

The States

The stolen, the removed, the separated in the very short history of *The States* scooping Indigenous/Latina children away from their parents from sea to   Mississippi

Where is the love?

Solid trust, repose on forest floor, up mountains, in deserts, on plains, riverside, in ponds, lakes, streams, in oceans wide and beautiful, in the world, in the world.

Hush, Baby. Singing you to sleep, now. Singing you back into yourself, into the long long long long America. Away from the lonely tantrum you became, *The States*. Away from your anointing the original people as constitutional *merciless savages,* far away, into a miraculous mature vision of yourself   knowing. Sing you into yourself, sing you back into the long America into the place before America was misnamed, to the America of longer memories names into the place of cranes, the place of shallow waters, the place of cloudy waters, the place of good earth, the place of bad earth, where he split the butte, where she walked, where they ran through fire, where they appeared, where they rested.

Singing you into yourself from the self-destructive madness you have entered. Singing you back into reason, back into

song slaying fascism, slaying extermination, slaying inconsideration, slaying monetary gain, slaying hate, slaying the sacrifice-of-all-others for resources.

Singing you away from destructive habit, from hatred, from cruelty, from any tantrum you may throw and beyond that gleaming wealthy teenager you've become on backs of those around you, into a surer self-of-these-lands, these waters, these leaves, this fur, feather, the whip-poor-will cry seldom heard anymore. US you are killing us, killing us, killing us, killing us. *The States*

Singing you into love of land, abundance, life, respect, reason. *Sing*

Look at this blue, beauty, abundance, river, ocean, life, us. Look at this blue, murderous destruction, hatred-filled U.S. grief, blues. Look at this blue water healing, sky swallowing up union in the sacred blue bowl of intricate design, water, sky, life, us. Look at this blue, America, all long of you, look at this blue, specific. Look at this blue song, blues song, blue singing you back to reason, reality, respect, relation, resonance in blue letter addressed to you.

Sincerely—

Dear America, Sanctuary of a Posthuman Exile

KAREN AN-HWEI LEE

Dear America,

Everything here is carnal, souls vetted to survive
fire bombings, night raids, annihilations of love.
Whom shall we trust, what camaraderie exists?
Truth or dare. No one creates beauty here; desire
nothing. War is no beautiful thing. Not a curative.
Truth: girl once said to me, your body is designed
to heal alone. Algal sea fog rolling every noon is no
remedy for nostalgia. No, this is not a pleasure—
nothing is holy in this world. Dare we inhabit
the posthuman, a fractal ebb and flow of lymph
and laser. Bless our given bodies without reprisal
or regret: borders we crossed as youth, invisible
at a distance when the fog lifts: no longer home.
Toxic compass rose of exile, carcinogenic, blooms.
The land under our soles exudes a bluing perfume,
notes of a failed paradise, of undocumented flight
from zone to sanctuary: exiles fleeing to the allure
of citizenry acquired by sea, by flood, by fire, by war.

Aperture: A Photoless Photo Essay

TRACI BRIMHALL

Image: A white clapboard house with a black sign that reads *Hospital*. The shadow of a tree rubs the siding. In the window, several blinds appear stuck or broken at the height of a woman peering out to see who might be visiting—a soldier, a patient, a friend.

Caption: This is the first photo I see when I click the link in the email. My friend is doing research on her family interned at Gila River in the 1940s. She'd gone looking for pictures of life there, of her family's incarceration, and what she found was my name. Top of the photo lists the image's provenance: The Brimhall Archive, a part of the Densho Digital Repository cataloging the visual histories of incarcerated Japanese Americans. Although I research the ancestry sites, I cannot find how I am related to this nurse and teacher who worked at the Gila River concentration camp. But there is my surname on a photo archive. There is my friend's surname. There they both are, years before either of us is born, over a thousand miles away from the city where we become friends, together at a camp where our country imprisoned Japanese Americans, taking away their homes and livelihoods, confiscating contraband: radios, weapons, cameras.

■ ■ ■

Image: A field of sunflowers grown and open. The ray florets look soft and silky as the inside of a cheek. The rows of corolla—a bright astonishment beneath the aching blue of a summer sky. Puffs of cumulus animate the frame of the photo. From the left and extending to the horizon is, Dear America, the dark smear of your border wall, its individual bars blurring into a solid line.

Caption: My friend tells me she took this photo in McAllen, explains why the sunflowers are there—it's public hunting land. The bossy brightness of the sunflower serves as a temptation, a feast of seeds to draw hungry doves from the other side of the border to be shot.

∎ ∎ ∎

Images: (1) Rows of barracks and a dust storm moving through them. Dust through the floorboards. Dust through the broken windows. Dust through the unfurled American flag straining at the pole. Dust through the clothes of the two Japanese Americans running through the dust roads between the barracks. The mountain behind guarding half of the sky. (2) A father posed with his family. A tag looped through his coat buttonhole. The child next to him, tagged. The child in front of him, tagged. And the other child. And the other child. Each one staring unsmiling except the smallest child who watches someone the camera cannot see. Their bags labeled with their surname and a symbol to reunite them someday.

   Caption: The War Relocation Authority asked for the pictures, and when Dorothea Lange submitted them, they were impounded, sent to the National Archives until they resurfaced in 2006. It seems odd to me that a government would ask for its unethical acts to be documented, but supposedly it was so that they could defend themselves against accusations of mistreatment. They must have believed it was true, that their actions were just, humane even. When they realized the photos were sympathetic portrayals of Americans moved into horse stalls, standing in line for hours for food, weaving camouflage nets to help the war effort, the WRA realized the images must remain unseen. Dear Unlooking America, it embarrasses me, but when a mirror teaches us who we are, do we ever believe it?

∎ ∎ ∎

Image: A stuffed dog on its back, the white fur of its belly exposed, all four fake paws up in the air as if waiting to be petted by a trusted hand. Its plastic eyes hidden. The pink underside of its felt tongue slipping from the mouth. The suggestion of a red and black collar with a name that could be called, perhaps a tag with a number, an address, a way to help it find its way home.

   Caption: A former janitor for the Border Patrol collected discarded items seized from migrants crossing the border—CDs, water bottles,

Bibles, cigarette lighters, cans of food, blankets, toilet paper, sticks of deodorant. He saved the items in friends' garages and then arranged and photographed the objects. Only the photo of a seized and thrown-away stuffed animal remains simple, unposed. He called his collection of confiscated items *El Sueño Americano*. I'm glad we know about this, that toothbrushes and toy dogs are taken from children. But I also don't know why it needs to be art for us to see it. Why did someone curate other people's suffering? Is that what white Americans need to make us look? A little beauty to make it all bearable?

∎ ∎ ∎

Image: A line of children outside a tarpaper barrack labeled "Toy Loan Center." Not an orderly line, but still one of order, though one girl stands to the side with a jump rope, one holds a wagon askew at the back, one boy stares out with a kaleidoscope on his eye watching the colors move and reorganize themselves. A boy watches a girl who stares at an unopened door. Their bodies make little dollops of shadow on the desert sand.

Caption: Although the War Relocation Association seized every-one's camera, photographer Toyo Miyatake managed to smuggle a lens and film plate holder into the concentration camp at Manzanar. A car-penter built a box for the lens and a former client snuck in film. At first, he took photos in secret, wanting to document life at the camp, but eventually the ban was lifted. He was designated the official pho-tographer of Manzanar. He created portraits of people resting against buildings, children huddled in play or gazing through barbed wire at the mountain, infants in the orphanage pulling themselves to standing by the crib's even bars.

∎ ∎ ∎

Image: Application form from the Gila River Indian Community. Lines for name and address and phone number. A form of identification. A claim for right of entry. A box for "Internment Camp." A box for an explanation of the request.

Caption: When the United States built the Gila River concentration camp, they built it on a reservation. A prison on a prison. Fort Sill in Oklahoma has served as a relocation camp for Native Americans, a boarding school for Native children taken from their parents, a concentration camp of Japanese Americans, and now, Dear America, there are plans to use it to house detained migrant children. I don't enter the Gila River Indian Community. I choose not to find out how or if the Brimhalls there were my family. It's still my history, even when I choose not to know it. My privilege lets me look away.

· · ·

Image: Green marker on canvas in a grid—the shaky hand of a new artist, the way a child draws lines for a game of tic-tac-toe. In the unmeasured rectangles of green are not X's and O's but children with arms outstretched like butterfly specimens on a spreading board. Covered in wrinkled blankets, their heads face the bottom of the frame as if they are upside-down ghosts. Guards in baseball caps stand at the single door and at the center of the room's panopticon. At the hip of one guard are two dark lines. A mistake perhaps. Or the L of a gun in its holster.

Caption: Three children released from Border Patrol detention facilities are sent to a respite center, given markers, and asked to draw their experiences. They are about ten or eleven. Their names, unknown. They can only stay at the respite center for twenty-four hours before being transitioned elsewhere. I don't know if they are reunited with their parents, their siblings, someone whose touch and voice are the codex of their history. The Smithsonian expresses interest in acquiring their drawings as artifacts. I'm disturbed that this is collected and curated for a museum, this expression of suffering they did not consent to make public. I am disturbed that we need images to make us pay better attention. The Smithsonian also owns combs, razors, and toothbrushes left by migrants in the desert. They own a Border Patrol uniform. They own an old piece of the border wall. They're trying to show you as you are, America.

· · ·

Image: Also in the Densho Digital Repository from the Gila River Camp: Lilla Brimhall holding her son on the steps of the white house that is also a hospital, her face turned away from the camera as she studies his quizzical expression at something out of view, his outfit's tiny buttons, the soft rolls of his baby thighs, his curled toes kicking inside frilled socks.

Caption: She got to do it. She got to hold her child.

Still Birding While Black

J. DREW LANHAM

Hey America,

Was out birding a while back, black as I am and have always been, checking out my white-crowned sparrow honey hole, absorbing one of my fave winter birds. Fully engrossed in their melancholy leftover Northwoods songs and snazzy namesake stripe-headed plumages, I wasn't expecting to have my identity challenged as I was identifying them. In the face of the daily "how can we insult the people of color Oval Office challenge," I was trying hard, America, doing my own nature-loving, bird-adoring thing, watching and reveling; escaping as it were, when this old farmer approached to tell me in this very odd, one-sided, pickup window–to–pickup window exchange, that he thought the world was a better place with "niggers knowing their place and picking cotton." Really? Right there in the middle of my ornithological reverie, a brontosaurus-sized macro-aggression complete with racial pejoratives and a couple of unveiled half-threats of shooting trespassers who didn't know their place thrown in for good hatemonger measure? Well, America, I took the old man at his word and left. Whatever that bitter-slick taste was that welled up on the back of my tongue was warning enough that maybe I should find another place to watch birds. So much for nature's respite and free-roaming choice. To have someone come at me with threats and hateful ideas of revisionist history like that was, in my mind, a forewarning to a wishful lynching. I guess the old man was feeling his impunity oats and making his personal contribution to a great-again nation. A racist affront on a country road, birdwatching in South Carolina seems like a long way from 1400 Pennsylvania Avenue, but I guess there's a shortcut to being emboldened when the "right" to spew such rhetoric comes from on high.

Can't say some horrific consequences of birding while black anywhere in 'Merica don't cross my mind more often these days. Caution trumps life-list. So I traded sparrows in for a loggerhead shrike—an appropriately black-and-white feather-miscegenated bird. I seek my birds in places where white supremacists are less likely to abound. I consider my range now changed.

Regretfully,
J. Drew Lanham

The Red-Bellied Woodpecker's Tongue

ELLEN BASS

Dear America,

I've always wanted to tell you
about the red-bellied woodpecker's marvelous tongue.
Maybe you already know.

Or perhaps you're not interested. There's so much
that requests your attention these summer days:

sweet corn ripening in its humid silks,
    the rim of salt on a margarita, the 100 best-
        selling items on Amazon—Curtain Rods, Stroller Gloves,

Dog Jerky Treats. And then there are hungry children in cages.
This morning I looked at a photo of one girl,
a strand of dark hair blown across her cheek, stuck there, damp.

She could have been any little girl crying—
    there was no barbed wire,
    no piles of shoes, no gold teeth mounded—
but she wasn't. Maybe no one knows

how long she's been crying. America, if you're quiet
    enough you can hear her.

I'm old now, the age of children
whose parents almost—but didn't—perish
in Dachau or Buchenwald. My grandfather came here, America.

The plan was to send money back to his wife and children in
    Germany.

But he was too slow.

I've never known
hunger—I don't mean when I didn't
have time to grab a bite on the way to Concourse G. Is it wrong
    to still be thrilled by a bird's tongue? I believe

you're exhausted, America. You work two jobs. The baby's
teething and your father died. Someone backing up
        in the hospital parking lot just cracked
                                    your taillight.

But maybe you'd spare a
    slow exhalation to consider the fleshy organ of this small citizen.

This high-tech appendage—almost as long as the bird's smoke-gray
    body—
must somehow be packed inside its head. So

the cunning tongue forks in the throat,
    one side wrapping around the jaw, up and over the brain,
and then the halves rejoin and circle the eye socket.
Really. So

when the hungry woodpecker taps into a tunnel (dug by a beetle),
    it contracts the muscles of its jaw, propelling the tongue to slither
                        through the galleries and skewer a grub.

Then it relaxes its jaw and the tongue winds up like a
retractable clothes line.

It took a lot of time for the kingdoms of DNA
    to dream up this flying shred of existence
that weighs as much as a fat letter
    sent from the Late Oligocene. Fossils

of small birds, diminutive engines mounting
and amending as the centuries surged. And now

do we speak about extinction? Should we rattle the numbers?
The million species that 145 experts from 50 countries tell us
may be doomed in the next few decades?

Or do we abide with the sumptuous
    tongue of the bird—reveling in its brilliant elaboration? I'm
    terrified.
Maybe you're terrified too.

But for the space of the poem, could we allow ourselves this swath
of elegance and purpose, a moment

to recline into the joy of description
so we can observe that the belly of the red-bellied woodpecker
    isn't really red, not nearly as red

as its scarlet head. Its belly is more like a slight blush,
    like a creature that's modest about its riotous beauty,
its riotous success. Oh, it might say

if it could talk (and if it bothered to),
    oh this old tongue? It's nothing really,
just something I picked up a few million years ago.

Climate Change
and Science Denial

Come November

DEBRA MARQUART

                         come
cold eye corrective, come pendulum
take wrecking ball to venerable walls

come cerulean wave, come
typhoon earthquake tsunami
blow the gentlemen from

utahiowasouthcarolinakentuckymaine
back to higher ground
or (better yet) homeward

to the distant shores
that spawned them
washed up   jobless   uninsured

come classic EF5 tornado
good ol' midwestern tradition, come
barn-splintering wedge of gale force winds

come vacuum up this mess of a land
rip the flimsy scrims from the chambers
where black-robed justices

work their corrupted levers   these days

it's tempting to curse biblical—
to call down pestilence, plague, a pox upon
both houses & the thundering hooves of horsemen—

instead, embrace November's wintry grip
november come inevitable
november come early & often   listen

can you hear that ticking
like fingertips of sleet
upon window panes—

it's the clicking of check-marks
in ballot boxes
the coming blizzard
of millions.

The River between Us

KURT CASWELL

On October 9, 2017, at about 8 p.m., a nineteen-year-old student at the university where I teach was escorted to the campus police headquarters for a welfare check. Once inside the building, he pulled a handgun, killed the campus police officer leading him in, and fled on foot. Campus, city, and state police, along with county sheriff's deputies and a SWAT team, captured him in about two hours. The morning after, the university community was on edge. Police sirens sang all over campus because everything, everyone, every twittering leaf looked like a bomb about to explode.

· · ·

The shooting on my campus followed the then-deadliest mass shooting in U.S. history in Las Vegas, which followed other shootings in schools, in public places, and in private homes: *this* shooting, *that* shooting, *whatever* shooting. Meanwhile, our united states have endured unprecedented wildland fires in the West, frequent and destructive hurricanes in the South and East, and massive flooding in the river lands. And these events parallel the latest newsworthy scandals—for example, Hollywood's Harvey Weinstein, for decades of sexual misconduct. And then come the lies from his famous friends and colleagues in order to distance themselves from him—"I had no idea!"—initially, the Clintons, Meryl Streep (a self-proclaimed champion of women and the oppressed), and Judi Dench, followed by many, many others. They all knew and did nothing because it was in their interest to do nothing: money and power, fame and fortune, keeping it for them, keeping it from us. And the champion headliner of all time, President Trump, exchanging threats with North Korea, then later, Iran, tossing about words to seed a garden in hell.

To live in America in the twenty-first century is to live inside a bubble flush with oxygen while someone goes around distributing matches.

∎ ∎ ∎

The United States is not the greatest country in the world.

∎ ∎ ∎

The president of the United States is not the leader of the free world.

∎ ∎ ∎

And the American Dream—if ever it was alive at all—is dead.

∎ ∎ ∎

We all know these three truths, and still our politicians, our corporations, and our media spoon lies down our throats to keep us, the citizenry, doing what is in *their* best interest: buy, spend, consume, keep your mouth shut.

Dial it out a few hundred miles into Earth orbit, and note that these problems are human problems: human created, and of concern almost exclusively to humans. They are distractions, merely, from real problems. They are as petty as we are petty, and while we all champion our special causes on Facebook and Twitter, another disaster beats us flat.

Trump is not the problem, nor is he the answer. His tactics of chaos and obfuscation are a distraction, merely. No matter your position, you and I, all of us contributed to the cultural, economic, and political climate in which Trump was elected. Everything you love or despise about Trump is a reflection of us, which means it is a reflection of you. So then, *you* are the problem. And *I* am the problem. *We* are all the problem. And the problem with our problem is that it puts us off the real problem, the biggest problem of all: global climate change, and the mass species extinction even now unfolding on Earth.

In his essential book *Learning to Die in the Anthropocene*, Roy Scranton spells out the future of humanity in this world we have created. He does not offer a possibility of climate change impacts if we don't take action now; climate action is the impotent cry of the establishment. And he does not mourn the bunnies and bees of our special time on

Earth. The Earth will be just fine without us, just as it was before us, and just as Mars is fine, perfect and beautiful, even, with no life at all. What Scranton is willing to say, and what we all know is true but are unwilling to accept, is that climate change will lead to the collapse of our civilization and all its wonders. "This civilization is already dead," writes Scranton.

Things are going to look a lot different from here on out, and you and I are powerless against it. Trump is powerless against it. Monsanto and Exxon and Amazon are powerless against it. The United Nations is powerless against it.

■ ■ ■

My father gave thirty-four years of his life to working for the U.S. Forest Service before he went to work for the state of Idaho, and then to Washington, D.C., to direct the Bureau of Land Management under President Bush. Mine was a boyhood in wild places, a collection of government houses around a district office in the mountains in Oregon. There I roamed freely among the trees and creeks, caught lizards sunning on the rocks, fished from a canoe in the lake near the house, and attended a school of just over thirty students, kindergarten through eighth grade. To me, in those days, the world was a wilderness with a few scattered cities, none of which I had ever seen. It wasn't until high school, or even after, that I realized that while fossil fuels are flowing, the world appears to be just the opposite: a sea of cities whose influence pushes into the few remaining and scattered wildlands. And this is so, more and more each day.

There is no solution to the problem of global climate change. Democracy and its capitalist economy will not fix it. A dictator and a communist economy will not fix it. A culture war between us and them will not fix it. A race war will not fix it. A gender war between men and women will not fix it. I recycle, avoid driving, and turn off lights and electronics in my house that I'm not using, and even if everyone in the world does so, too, the Earth's warmer future will still arrive. It is here already. And what is left for us to do is: cope, adapt, endure.

■ ■ ■

I lived and taught school for a year on the Navajo Reservation in New Mexico. During that time and after, I read widely about Navajo history and culture. In the Navajo creation story, there is a time when women and men come to such odds that the Creator decides the only solution is to separate them by a river. The men are forced to live on one side, the women are forced to live on the other. Time passes, and the people begin to complain. The women miss what the men have to offer, and the men miss what the women have to offer. Each discovers that men and women are not the same, and they are not equal; men and women are complementary. Women possess attributes that the men do not have. Men possess attributes that the women do not have. In the Navajo story, the lamentations of the women and men finally prompt the Creator to put them all back on the same side of the river, and they live together with their differences, as before.

In the warmer future we have created, human beings—all of us, everywhere—are going to face real challenges, challenges that threaten even our species' viability. The extinction of *Homo sapiens* is not a Hollywood movie script only; it's a real possibility within the next century. There is no more time to publicly honor all our private wounds. Instead, we must honor our strengths and our differences. Then, one group of people with similar beliefs and values (a kind of tribe) may use their strengths to help another group of people with different beliefs and values. Globalism is not the answer because its underlying mission is to further consolidate wealth and resources, a system designed to ensure that most of us serve a few of them. The answer, or perhaps our best chance, is some form of cooperative tribalism, which brings together the best of what each group has to offer to benefit the whole. And groups would cooperate with one another because we have a common enemy: global climate change, which is to say, ourselves.

In the warmer future, women and men are going to need one another. Indigenous people and so-called non-Indigenous people are going to need one another. People with darker skin tones and people with lighter skin tones are going to need one another. People whose lives are guided by the Qur'an and people whose lives are guided by the Bible are going to need one another. In fact, we need one another now.

If we can't all come over to the same side of the river, and then walk together onto higher ground, it is the river that will inundate both sides and wash everything out to sea.

Please Do Not Spit Everywhere

CHRISTOPHER MERRILL

Dear America,

On Memorial Day weekend in 2018 I attended a forum in Nanjing that drew sinologists from around the world for discussions about the influence of Chinese literature on national literary discourses. The subject interested me, but since I cannot speak Chinese and my translator was unable to render into English much more than the odd phrase or two, my attention in the morning sessions drifted. In other circumstances I might have checked Twitter or Facebook, or read the *New York Times*, or googled the writers under discussion. But the "Great Firewall of China" censoring the internet had grown ever taller in the months since the National People's Congress had declared Xi Jinping president for life—a development that drew praise from Donald Trump, who said at a fundraising event, "Maybe we'll have to give that a shot someday." Think of China as an authoritarian's dream—and a nightmare for anyone seeking to discover the truth about, well, anything.

I had traveled to the ancient cultural capital not on a fact-finding mission, strictly speaking, though I intended to use my invitation to the World Historical and Cultural Cities Expo to gauge the viability of Nanjing's bid to join the UNESCO Creative Cities Network as a City of Literature, but to gain some distance from America to gather my thoughts on the many ways in which Trump daily, even hourly, debases the world's oldest democracy and threatens to undo not only much of what made this country a beacon to people in every land but the entire postwar liberal international order. (That this order was created largely by American statesmen and has served us well for seven decades—the span of an individual life—is one more truth lost on the president.)

In Nanjing, the shortsightedness of Trump's isolationism and transactional approach to the presidency struck me with sudden force. His doctrine of America First coincides with China's determination to be the guarantor of a new international order, the signs of which are everywhere on display: in the construction of bridges, roads, high-rises, museums, and shopping centers; in the strategic thinking of the Belt and Road Initiative (a $1.4 trillion development plan to establish a Silk Road for the future, linking sixty countries via infrastructure corridors from Oceania to Central Europe and Africa); and in the palpable energy animating nearly every encounter. Here is a nation on the rise, in sharp contrast to the Trump administration's leave-taking from the global stage.

I prefaced my remarks on "The River Merchant's Wife: A Letter," Ezra Pound's version of a poem by Li Po, with an assertion that from my experience in coordinating Iowa City's effort to become the third UNESCO City of Literature, and from my work with stakeholders in Baghdad and Durban, who put together successful applications for the Creative Cities Network, it seemed to me that Nanjing met the necessary criteria to become a UNESCO City of Literature—with one critical exception: a commitment to the free flow of information and freedom of expression that are not only central to UNESCO's mission but also essential to any enduring creative enterprise. This drew an audible gasp from the Chinese members of the audience. But this is the shape of things to come: Trump's announcement that the United States will leave UNESCO at the end of the year, like his decisions to withdraw from the Trans-Pacific Partnership, the Paris Agreement on Climate Change, the Joint Comprehensive Plan of Action, the UN Human Rights Commission, and other multilateral organizations, reduce his leverage in every forum, not to mention American standing around the world. William Matthews concludes his poem "Wrong" with a question: "who is by himself except in error?" We are just beginning to register what this error in our electoral ways will mean for the future of our country—and the planet.

After the forum, I went for a walk across the Nanjing Eye, a cable-stayed pedestrian bridge erected over the Yangtze River for the Youth Olympic Games in 2014. I stopped under both pylons, which looked like open eyes, to gaze at the twin towers of the Nanjing International Youth Cultural Centre, which housed delegates to the expo. Designed by Iraqi-British architect Zaha Hadid, the complex includes a hotel, concert hall, theater, and shopping plaza. I had circled it a couple of times on my first day in Nanjing to photograph its fluid contour, which in one writer's words creates "a dynamic transition from straight to curved lines, from plane to cambered surfaces." Hadid's futuristic vision for the center was inspired by sailboats, and from my vantage point above the river I had the impression that at this juncture of the maritime and overland routes of the ancient Silk Road, China was embarking on a journey that would leave us far behind. It was quite hot, and I had sweated through my shirt before I made it to the park on the other side. A barge was riding at anchor under the bridge, and in the flower beds were signs with English translations that matched my mood: *Please do not spit everywhere. Please do not play combat.* What did Pound write? "The monkeys make sorrowful noise overhead." Call it the music of our time—music fit for memorializing the decline of a Great Power, if not the death of the Republic.

Yours,
Christopher

Our Climate Future

DIANA LIVERMAN

Each summer, as temperatures ascend in Tucson, I pack up the car and, to the dog's delight, take him along on a road trip to the west coast of greater California. We visit friends and walk beaches from Baja to Santa Cruz, and I get time to think and talk about my hopes and worries for people and the planet. This summer, things feel different. People I meet are talking about climate change, anxious about our climate future. My friends are angry, really angry, about what is happening on the border—children taken from their families and held in cages and the arrests of humanitarian workers. They are mad about the reversals of environmental protections and opening up of public lands for mining and fossil fuel development, and depressed that Britain and Brazil are accompanying the United States into racism and right-wing politics. We discuss signs of hope—border activism, the youth movement, the legal experts who uphold social and environmental protections, the cities and states that are acting on climate change—and wonder what more we should do.

My career and research have focused on climate change for more than forty years. I came to America from England following a searing drought across Europe to study how communities became vulnerable to droughts and other climate hazards, yet not thinking that climate itself would change. In the 1980s, only a few people were writing about climate change, and no one was doing anything to prevent it. But I was fortunate to get a scholarship to study at the National Center for Atmospheric Research in Colorado, where scientists were starting to model global warming and its impacts. My research there on how a warming climate would affect food security really got me engaged and worried and led to decades of study and action on the human dimensions of global environmental change. I fell in love with the American West and was lucky to land a university position that granted me a green card and eventually led to citizenship.

Now I study a wide range of climate topics, including the risks of tipping points in the climate system and the effectiveness of policies to reduce greenhouse gas emissions and adapt to the warming already underway. The discussion of what is now being called a climate emergency is everywhere. But we are not yet acting as if there is a real crisis. Global greenhouse gas emissions just went up again, after a few encouraging years of slower growth, heat waves around the world are breaking records, and every week scientific journals and news media report another ecosystem at breaking point. Last month it was melting ice sheets in Greenland, this month the Amazon is on fire.

The last couple of years I have contributed to a series of ever-more-frightening reports on climate change. In the so-called Hothouse Earth paper "Trajectories of the Earth System in the Anthropocene" appearing in the *Proceedings of the National Academy of Sciences*, we warned that global warming was starting to trigger feedbacks in the earth system that could result in temperatures more than 5°C (9°F) and sea levels thirty-plus feet higher than today. I was the optimist on that paper, identifying signs that human actions were shifting to a more stable scenario, but media reports focused on the apocalyptic scenario. In interviews I tried to talk about the hopeful trends, saying that "hothouse Earth was not our destiny," but journalists wanted me to dramatize the cascade of melting ice, shrinking forests, and leaking methane that would end life as we know it.

A few months later, the Intergovernmental Panel on Climate Change released a report on the chances of limiting global warming to no more than 1.5°C (about 2.7°F). As one of the ninety lead authors, I read dozens of papers over eighteen months as we worked to assess how near we were to the 1.5°C limit, what could be done to stay under it, and whether 1.5°C would prevent significant losses compared to higher temperatures. We met with government delegates for a grueling week of negotiations in Incheon, Korea, to get the report approved. Whether it was anguish about the report results or plain exhaustion, I wept on the plane home.

Our message can be reduced to a few key points: the world has already warmed by 1°C, threating sustainable development; every bit of warming matters, as 2°C will cause much more damage than 1.5°C; and to have a chance of limiting warming to 1.5°C we must cut greenhouse gas emissions by almost 50 percent by 2030.

Perhaps it was the relatively simple message that occasioned another media frenzy—including headlines that we only "have twelve years to save the planet." As one of the few U.S.-based authors, I spoke to everyone from my local to international media, and with every interview grew more forceful and created more anxiety about the messages.

One of my messages for you, America, is that if you think 1.5°C seems okay that it is more in Fahrenheit (2.7°F)—and is only an average with greater warming, up to 6°F, over land, near the poles, and in drier regions. We have already warmed by more than 4°F in parts of Alaska and Arizona. The *Fourth U.S. National Climate Assessment*, released at the end of 2018, described the impacts that climate change will bring to America: steep declines in water supply in the American West, losses in ecosystems such as the Everglades and Sierras, fatal heat waves in our cities, damage to coastal infrastructure, fires, and disruption of supply chains that sustain our economy and food security.

I was embarrassed when the U.S. administration ignored and even tried to undermine the IPCC and *NCA* reports, and I tried to save face for America by talking to people and the media about climate action and awareness in states like California and Florida and in many cities, including Tucson. The 2018 elections brought the Democrats to power in Congress and a flood of hearings on climate change. I was invited to testify before the House Committee on the Climate Crisis and tried my best, in the five minutes allowed, to convey urgency and options for action. It was hard to condense the science and the solutions into such a short time, and the hearing was mostly a chance for the politicians to make their points.

Afterward I felt drained and depressed. I think mostly because I had stopped believing that we actually could and would limit warming to 1.5°C, not just because of political inertia and opposition, but because the ask is so big. In the United States, our fair share of the IPCC-recommended reduction in emissions is much more than 50 percent because we are responsible for a large share of historical emissions, and carbon dioxide remains in the atmosphere for many years. The fossil fuel lobby is still powerful, low-carbon technologies need to work better and be more affordable, and we overconsume food and other goods.

I'm just not convinced that we can switch away from fossil fuels, change our diets, and protect forests fast enough. My own summer road trip and all those flights that I took as author of those papers and reports drove my personal carbon emissions through the roof. When I decided to out myself as a frequent flyer to my students, they were horrified at my lifetime flight miles, and although I swore to change my habits I continue to be tempted by invitations to conferences and my desire to see the wildlife and landscapes of the world. Chile, Iceland, Antarctica, and New Zealand are on my bucket list—the irony in dreaming about long trips to see disappearing glaciers and species before it's too late.

■ ■ ■

This summer, as I drove across the West, I spent a lot of time thinking about overshoot—how we could get through the period of much warmer temperatures that I think is coming. I do think we will start getting those emissions down—just not fast enough to stay under 1.5°C. So I'm thinking we will have to get through peak warming, maybe 6 to 10°F in parts of the Americas including in Tucson where I live. I want us to spend a lot more time and money on adaptation; on how we plan to protect coasts, food systems, cities, and protected natural areas; and on helping the most vulnerable cope with heat waves and the higher costs of water, food, and energy. I admit an intellectual fascination with the overshoot scenario, the same way I am captivated by disaster movies and science fiction. I want to know more about when that will be, how long it will last, and who and what will thrive or survive. But there is also dread: Who will die? Which species will go extinct? Will there be conflict? What does it mean for current youth and future generations? And can we figure out how to help people and ecosystems adapt to this warmer world?

I'm sorry this letter is a bit of a downer. I wish I could be more optimistic about how fast we can respond to the risks of climate change. I want America to do more, I want to do more myself, and I want, more than anything, to feel more hope. I want us to elect officials who understand and will act on climate change, I want America's great innovators to throw all our resources at a low-carbon future, and I want a society that ensures climate justice by providing for the vulnerable and empowering the excluded.

Diana Liverman
August 2019, 106°F
Tucson, Arizona

Science under Fire

ANITA DESIKAN

Dear America,

Long before I became a scientist, I worked behind the counter of a pharmacy in San Diego. It was fall 2007, and the Witch Creek Fire had erupted across the region. Fanned by the powerful Santa Ana winds, the fire forced hundreds of thousands of people to evacuate their homes. I worked close to one of the affected regions, and on the day after the city ordered mass evacuations, one of the first customers I served told me their house had burned down—and their medications with it. Another told me they had evacuated and could not return home—they only had the clothes on their backs. Over and over I heard similar stories. I nearly broke into tears. But I took comfort helping fill their prescriptions, providing them with a needed service.

In San Diego, it is not earthquakes that we fear but fires. It was once a well-established fact that fire season occurred only in late summer or fall. But climate change has shifted that. Wildfires are now a yearlong potential horror, and they grow increasingly destructive. Every year, more people lose their homes; more people breathe in that terrible concoction of soot that leaves you gasping, wheezing, out of breath. The higher frequency of catastrophic wildfires in California has certainly been noticed by insurance companies, which are starting to hike prices or cancel homeowners insurance outright.

As a public health researcher with a keen interest in air pollution, science policy, and environmental justice, one of the most impactful lessons I have learned is that science has the power to improve both public health and the environment. When the best available science is incorporated into policymaking, it can deliver powerful benefits to the health and safety of our people and environment. So it was with a certain amount of horror that I witnessed the Trump administration turn its antiscience political machinations toward California's incessant wildfire threat.

At first, the administration only wanted to spin wildfire tragedies as a way to bolster President Trump's own agenda. In August 2018 the Carr and Mendocino fires raged across Northern California—some of the worst wildfires ever experienced by the state. In the middle of this crisis, rather than speaking words of condolence, President Trump tweeted a message of hate toward environmental safeguards, blaming them for the severity of the fire by allegedly restricting access to water for firefighting purposes. And in this "tweet-to-policy" administration, Commerce Secretary Wilbur Ross decided to take the president up on his words. Ross ordered the National Oceanic and Atmospheric Administration (NOAA) to sideline water-management procedures supported by the best available science. Specifically, NOAA's Fisheries division was ordered to go against its own mission statement of regulating activities that might harm threatened or endangered aquatic species like salmon and instead divert water for firefighting efforts. Reality was thrown asunder—firefighters and state officials kept declaring in no uncertain terms that the state of California has enough water to fight these fires— and the pain and suffering of my fellow Californians were milked in order to declare war on endangered fish species like the Chinook salmon.

In November 2018 the Camp Fire struck, ravaging the town of Paradise and causing over a thousand people to go missing. This time Trump placed the blame solely on California's poor forest management (in actuality, the U.S. government owns and manages a majority of California's forests) and threatened to cut off federal funding for firefighting efforts altogether.

But here's a part of the story you may not know: in December of that year, Trump quietly issued an executive order that once again challenged the science underlying the wildfire threat. Apparently, the Trump administration believes that the best way to fix California's wildfire problem is through logging. No joke. The executive order declared that, in order to prevent future wildfires like those that had struck California, the Department of Interior and the Department of Agriculture must harvest more than four billion board feet of timber that will then be put up for sale—an increase of 31 percent from 2017. While it is true that increased logging may help quell a small percentage of the fires that occur near homes, it can do little to halt large-scale wildfires or stop the fires that are fueled by nonloggable but flammable plants, like chaparral shrub brush. It is hard to foresee with certainty the ecological impacts of the increase in logging, as it is dependent on how federal agencies implement the executive order. However, since market conditions of timber sales are required to be considered during the process, the most robust scientific evidence on how to safely and sustainably reduce trees that pose a fire hazard risk has the real possibility of being sidelined in favor of timber sales.

These actions by the Trump administration are downright dangerous because they mask the real problem at hand: climate change. Scientific research tells us that climate change acts as a threat multiplier by decreasing rainfall and increasing the temperature in the western United States (i.e., it can make California into a tinderbox). Since 1972, wildfires in California have grown 500 percent larger thanks mostly to climate change. In essence, global warming acts like a dose-response curve—for every degree of warming, larger and more frequent fires will result. Scientists and political officials from across the West have urged federal officials to adopt evidence-based measures to reduce the threat of wildfires, including cutting greenhouse gas emissions linked to climate change. But the Trump administration pursues few if any actions to prevent climate change, and the Union of Concerned Scientists, where I work now, has documented numerous cases in which federal scientists were directly censored or felt no choice but to censor themselves on the topic of climate change.

I became a public health researcher to use science to find evidence-based ways to improve the lives of others. I can't help but think back to that day at the pharmacy when I listened to my neighbors' stories about the wildfire that had threatened or consumed their homes. I believe that they, like all Americans, would have wanted proven, science-based policies in place that could have reduced the threat of fires. I doubt they would have supported policies that take away water from endangered fish or cut down large swaths of the forest as distractions from the very real existence of climate change. This is why I find the administration's denials—and silencing—of the science so unsettling. We rely on science because it is the best method we have available to protect the health and safety of people, and of this land we call our home.

Sincerely,
Anita Desikan

Letter from a Concerned Scientist

JACOB CARTER

Dear America,

I'm a former government scientist who investigated ways we can adapt toxic sites to future flood risks so they don't leach cancerous chemicals into your neighborhoods. My research was near completion when the Trump administration came in and asked me to leave the agency I worked for, the Environmental Protection Agency, telling me I could no longer conduct this research. I also was going through several personal issues that made this time a living hell for me. Here's my story:

The night of the 2016 election I was home alone. I had a bout of strep throat, and my journalist roomie was out of town to cover the returns. As a climate change scientist, postdoctoral fellow at the Environmental Protection Agency (EPA), prior intern at the White House Office of Science and Technology Policy working on President Obama's climate action plan, and gay man, I was heavily invested in Donald J. Trump losing the election. I don't recall exactly when, but after several swing states swung red, I headed to bed. I knew that what I thought would never happen had happened. But I couldn't sleep. I cried. I cried a lot. I couldn't shut my brain off from worrying about what my country would look like under Trump.

His campaign was marked by blatant racism, sexism, homophobia, xenophobia. Did I live in a country where most people supported these awful things? Trump's constant lying... Were Americans okay with a president spewing misinformation? Did no one care about the truth anymore? What are we going to do on climate change? Going backward on the progress we had made in the Obama years—I knew the world couldn't afford that backtrack.

I felt so awful the next day that I texted my ex-fiancé seeking comfort. Russ and I had ended our relationship about three months before. "I wish we could be together right now," I texted through tears. "I know," he replied. We chatted more than we had in a long time.

I didn't go into the office the rest of the week so that I could take some time to heal—from both my strep throat and the election. But I'd stay awake worried about droughts, famines, extreme natural disasters on scales that humans have never experienced. I'd think about the people who'd suffer the most. Then I'd worry about my own situation. I knew the Trump team would likely choose not to renew my contract, which meant I had little time to find other work. But what if I couldn't find other work? I couldn't move back home—my parents had disowned me for being gay.

I chatted more with Russ. Ah, sweet comfort.

Near Thanksgiving, I got the expected news from my boss. "I'm sorry, but I've got some bad news for you. It'd be wise of you to start looking for another job." I got up from my cubicle, locked myself in a bathroom stall, and cried some more. That stall on the fourth floor at EPA headquarters would become my crying place for many weeks.

Russ was no longer available for commiseration. He had met someone, and they were in love. Alone and somewhat new to Washington, D.C., I'd have to support myself through this tough time.

Throughout December I applied to several jobs and got a handful of phone interviews. Jobs were available for climate change science experts, but funding for these jobs became uncertain after Trump's election. For other positions, I was either underqualified or overqualified. Climate change science—science that was desperately needed, especially in the policy world—was no longer important in Washington.

I sank further into depression. I went to bars, I drank, I smoked cigarettes, I had sex with strangers. I got sick. One day, my lymph nodes were swollen, but I didn't feel sick. I went to the doctor. He asked, "Do you think you could've been exposed to HIV recently?"

The adrenaline raced through my veins. "No. I'm always safe," I replied. But I hadn't been safe some nights.

"I ask because this is a symptom of seroconversion of HIV. If you think you've been exposed, we can start you on an antiretroviral drug."

"No. I don't think I've been exposed." But having been promiscuous for the first time in my life, I was tested for HIV.

Sleep became more difficult. I was lucky to get two or three hours. When I did manage to fall asleep, I usually woke up covered in sweat—another sign of HIV seroconversion. I was convinced that I had the virus. I stopped going out with friends. I stayed at home playing video games to keep my thoughts about the world at a distance. The night sweats got worse and didn't go away for another month, even after I learned that my HIV test was negative. I had the doctor test me two more times. When I came back a third time, he told me, firmly, that another test was not necessary unless I thought I had been exposed.

Work was difficult. I didn't feel like I belonged to the EPA any longer, even though I loved my climate change research at the agency. I felt my work would truly help people. That's very different from what I felt as an academic. Sure, in academia your peers read your papers and you contribute meaningful scientific research, but at EPA my work was going to be applied to a global problem.

I spent the rest of my time at the EPA mostly applying for jobs. In December, I had finally landed an interview that I saw going somewhere. It was with the Union of Concerned Scientists, a nonprofit group that did research and advocated for science-informed policy. I'd never heard of them, but many of my friends and colleagues had. "They're a really good group. You're fortunate to get an interview with them," my boss said. It was my first glimmer of hope.

Just before Christmas, the Union of Concerned Scientists offered me the job. I accepted immediately. After working so many temporary positions, I had finally landed a full-time job with good pay, benefits, and work that I was passionate about doing. Life was getting better. I found new meaning in work. I joined a rowing team and a kickball team. I made new friends. I started dating again.

But the thoughts that swirled in my head on election night haven't gone away. They have gotten worse. I see every day the rollbacks on climate change policy, on policies that ensure we have clean air and water, on policies that protect workers from harm at their jobs. And I know that the people affected most are those with the least amount of money in this world, those who are struggling to afford necessities. I hear the stories about having to choose whether to buy groceries for the week or an inhaler for a child with asthma—a gamble I know has resulted in at least one mother weeping over her daughter's burial casket. I know, too, from years of studying climate change that such situations will only get worse.

Election night of 2016 and the months thereafter were tough for me. But I'm still alive. I live on the East Coast where there's an ample water supply. I'll be okay as the impacts of climate change intensify. But others will not be so fortunate—people who have been oppressed for years by systematic racism and poor policies will be hit hardest. I like to feel like I've made some difference for those people by doing climate change research and being a policy advocate. But is it enough? Will I ever be able to do enough?

So I still don't sleep well at night. And unfortunately, I'm not the only government climate change scientist who has gone through this experience—many others have now been pushed out. My suffering has strengthened my conviction that science must be the backbone of our policy decisions, because that's one good way we can protect our loved ones from harm.

Still working hard to keep you and your loved ones out of harm's way.

Sincerely,
Jacob C.

To Think Like a Mountain

Dear America,

In 2015 a lawsuit was filed by twenty-one plaintiffs against our government. All under the age of eighteen, the plaintiffs asserted that our government's failure to act on climate change is a violation of the public trust doctrine and of the constitutional rights to life, liberty, and prosperity of generations to come. The case, *Juliana et al. v. the United States*, is still active.

What, dear America, will be the outcome? How do we begin to understand, let alone resolve, this conflict of interests? As an undergraduate I, like many young people, am acutely aware that my goals and dreams hinge upon whether or not we are able to bridge this divide. As a result I, like many Americans, am trying to figure out how we can leverage our power in this democracy to make the necessary changes.

More and more I think that, for change to be possible, we must learn to perceive time differently.

Those who would dismiss the suit claim that because no harm is *currently* being done, there is no legal issue. This reflects clearly our present view of time on a human scale, measured by the variations of clocks and daily circumstances. On this scale, the natural world changes slowly; we do not see significant signs of alteration in a day or, historically, in a generation. Time, however, has other scales—measured by variations of rock layers and extant species—that we have yet to fully understand.

"[We] have not yet learned to think like a mountain," Aldo Leopold wrote more than seventy years ago, and it seems many of us *still* haven't. As a result, the land is often treated as a passive thing. The earth, however, is not passive. It is as sensitive and dynamic as we are. This concept is far from new to us—we know, from an early age, about the cycles of nature. We know the water in the river today is not the same water that will be in it tomorrow. Yet too often we act in response to what occurs in a small area or a small amount of time without considering what our actions might mean for the future, without acknowledging that we may be toying with systems far more intricate than we could possibly imagine. I think of the story Leopold tells in *Sand County Almanac,* about a great bear living on the mountain Escudilla. In the end, the bear walks into a set-gun trap and shoots itself. It's only after this that those who acquiesced to the setting of the trap begin to question if doing so was really progress. We, like Leopold and his comrades, are playing by the rules of economic growth without questioning. We strive for gain but neglect to acknowledge the cost of that gain to the systems our lives depend upon.

Lauret Savoy, in her book *Trace,* augments Leopold's call for a broader perspective and more inclusive ethic. "The pace and degree of such environmental changes are unprecedented in human history," she writes. "Yet the embedded systems and norms behind them in the United States, the most energy-consumptive nation, are not. Their deep roots allowed and continue to amplify fragmented ways of seeing, valuing, and using nature, as well as human beings."

Such problematic deep roots are not easy to accept, nor are they easy to deny. Though the Constitution was established to "secure the Blessings of Liberty to ourselves *and our Posterity,*" our current policies reflect little interest in securing anything for future generations. The Declaration of Independence decrees it to be self-evident "that all men are created equal, that they are endowed by their Creator with certain unalienable Rights, that among these are Life, Liberty, and the pursuit of Happiness"—nevertheless, as Savoy points out, "without backing belief or means, 'rights' become limited and limiting to legal form and process rather than a moral imperative extending from heart and spirit."

Savoy, recalling her family's trip to Point Sublime on the Grand Canyon's North Rim, writes that the moments there "illuminated a journey of and to perception, another way of measuring a world I was part of yet leaving behind." Throughout her life, she has remembered that day. "It's impossible to step into that bright summer morning again," she writes, "attentive to it, to parents alive, to an intact family drawn by hope and promise."

We, too, are standing at Point Sublime, in awe of what is before us without fully acknowledging the meaning in those layers of rock or the direction we are headed. The difference is that for us, the bright summer morning has not yet slipped away. The sun is progressing across the sky, but we still have time to change the road we're on.

A mountain's moment ago, thirteen colonies declared independence from a king who had plundered their seas, ravaged their coasts, burnt their towns, and destroyed the lives of their people. He had refused his assent to laws "most wholesome and necessary for the public good," and "forbidden his Governors to pass Laws of immediate and pressing importance." Those colonies proclaimed that governments are instituted to secure the inalienable rights of their people, and that "whenever any Form of Government becomes destructive of these ends, it is the Right of the People to alter or to abolish it."

Now, we plunder the earth's seas and fill them with plastic. We ravage the coasts. Floods destroy homes by the thousands while droughts lead to wildfires that burn our cities to the ground. Though we are a nation built upon and made strong by diversity, and although the challenges we face demand greater understanding and cooperation among people of all nations, we are cutting ourselves off from the world. Science, which the founders of the country held in high regard, is denied.

We cannot declare independence from ourselves, but we *can* declare independence from an unsustainable way of life. This is the demand of *Juliana et al.*, and it is more than an issue for the courts. It is a demand that a country with the means to create positive change also summon the will to act. It is a demand that we at last learn to think like a mountain because, for a future to be possible, we must.

"America was ingenuity," Ray Bradbury wrote. "It still is and could be."

Dearest America, let us remember what we could be.

Yours,
Sarah Inskeep

Whirling Disease

R. T. SMITH

in memoriam, John Montague

Who are the men and women who deny
the damage, who say the earth, the sky,

the waters are beyond our powers?
I have seen brownies in the Rockies

swimming in circles like hounds by the fire
or a sycophant polishing a lie

for profit or the cold thrill of mischief.
The parasite behind the whirling disease

savages cartilage and skeletal
tissue in fish, dazes, bewilders

akin to senility, twisted circuits.
The victims can no longer feed

efficiently and make easy prey. Now
afflicted specimens have been witnessed

near Foscoe and on the old Watauga,
the rainbow trout likely to infect

brookies, and our own shameless species
spreads the damage, sportsmen dispersing

the lethal cells on their waders and flies,
for we are never so clean as we claim,

especially when we swear no harm
comes to the earth from our passage.

In a pool downstream of the Maury's bend,
I once saw a young trout curling round,

spores on his scales, fins torn, the shimmer
of his glamor giving way to shadow,

and with all my stealth I edged closer,
parted weeds and reached into reflections,

fingers spread, easing till my hands were
beneath him, then crossed creel-wise

that I might lift him from confusion,
his worst dream, and leave him to swim

deftly downstream with the current
and his own kind. Now it's clear he could not

be rescued, and I shiver at the thought
of those who claim nature immune

to our meddling. Glassy-eyed with greedy
smiles, they spin. May the waters close over

them, may they choke on their empty
victories, may the snelled hook still

glistening and with no mercy catch deadly
in their throats, ripping at every syllable,

delivering, justly, mischief's cold thrill.

Memories (Imaginings) and Other Americas

An American Question

LAURET SAVOY

To my country:

An old and perhaps unanswerable question has troubled me since childhood. Now it won't let me rest.

The Revolutionary War had entered its final years, still undecided, when J. Hector St. John de Crèvecoeur asked, *What then is the American, this new man?* Most of the soon-to-be former colonists would probably agree with his response, published in 1782 in *Letters from an American Farmer.* "*He* is either an European, or the descendant of an European,...who leaving behind him all his ancient prejudices and manners, receives new ones from the new mode of life he has embraced, the new government he obeys, and the new rank he holds." He makes "a new race of men, whose labours and posterity will one day cause great changes in the world."

So many *others* were excluded from this definition: women, Indigenous peoples, as well as one-fifth of the population of the fledging United States "whose labours" had driven the economies of all thirteen colonies. Slavery and its profits—whether from tobacco, cotton, sugar, or rice—buttressed the new republic. National prosperity would continue to depend on exploiting cheap labor and exploiting land once dispossessed of its original inhabitants. Part and parcel of this "new mode of life" were adaptive prejudices: concepts of race, whiteness, and white supremacy. The social and political community imagined as the new nation by the founding property-holders had to be carefully guarded.

Although recent assaults on this country's civil society might seem unprecedented, de Crèvecoeur's question has always been contested ground.

Any expanding membership in the imagined community of "we the people" was answered time and again by tightened boundaries. Radical Reconstruction, for instance, defined and broadened the reach of U.S. citizenship with the Civil Rights Act of 1866 and the Fourteenth and Fifteenth constitutional amendments. Those (men) once enslaved could now, in principle, enjoy equal protection under the law without regard to race. They could own land. They could run for office. They could vote...until the surge toward justice fell with the compromised presidential election of 1876.

A retrenching racial hierarchy promised white redemption, and not only in the South. It would take the 1964 Civil Rights Act to make into law again what had been gutted when Reconstruction was abandoned. And the era of Jim Crow would also see immigration quotas. In spring 1882 Congress passed the Chinese Exclusion Act, the first major federal law restricting immigration. That statute (with its extensions) would stand in force for six decades in the name of racial purity.

As a child I stumbled over "with liberty and justice for all," wondering if there was an elastic limit to realized citizenship while my schoolmates recited the Pledge of Allegiance. These six words seemed at odds with the ceaseless media images. TV news alone brought into our home each night footage of war, assassinations, and protests by people who looked like me. I came of age doubting claims of incremental progress yet still wanting to believe in expanding tolerance if not equality.

But I wasn't so naïve as to believe the nation had entered a postracial, postracist age with Barack Obama's presidency. Not when white-supremacist and hate groups have proliferated in the last decade. Not when an opportunistic presidential campaign in 2016 could exalt ignorance, suspicion, and fear to feed racism, xenophobia, and misogyny—and win. Not when many white voters, of all economic classes, perceived that campaign's promise to be redemption.·

In the age of Trump the clock has turned back yet again on civil rights. The rule of power and profit reigns supreme. White nativists vilify Muslim, Mexican, and other "nonwhite" immigrants as alien. A nuclear arms race and other military threats escalate. Environmental regulations and protected lands fall prey to oil and gas plunder or mining. Climate science and language are censored despite global changes more rapid than predicted. Perceptions of race cut sharper, more divisive lines.

Taking back the country to "make America great again" can mean many things. One, of course, is the monochromatic need of whiteness to believe this nation is what it never was, except in the minds and rhetoric of those longing for it to be so. Their public memory requires amnesia and selective erasure of different peoples and cultures long part of the American experience.

It is tempting, here, to exhort. To warn, to urge, to insist: *We* must... *We* should... *We* need to.... But changing any situation for the better requires knowing what it really is. And key to this, I believe, is comprehending how forms of *othering* have always been central to the democratic project that is the United States. The seeming paradox between an American creed of liberty and justice for all and the realities of an American promise denied to members of marginalized groups is, instead, a malignant symbiosis.

Transgression in word and deed—the root meaning of *outrage*—has occurred each day in the polarizing age of Trump. One step toward confronting and defying injustice begins with grasping the paradox and contradiction in the heartwood of this society.

Innocence is not an option. Neither is hopelessness.

The first documented arrival of Africans in the English colonies on mainland North America took place in August 1619. Four hundred years later I don't know if we the people can acknowledge, with honesty, our intercultural past-to-present and thus admit many varied responses to "Who is an American?" I had hoped, though, that more than half a century after the assassination of Dr. Martin Luther King Jr. this nation might see itself more clearly.

Yours,
Lauret Edith Savoy

Duplex

JERICHO BROWN

I still believe in God. What else keeps me
From slaughter? Who else holds the butcher's hand?

Sweet slaughter. Though I'd pray, *Give me butcher's hands,*
Matthew baked me cakes as if I could be saved.

He baked spice cake, humming as if we were safe,
As if this weren't the land of milk and money.

We can't survive this nation of white money,
Says the black man as his excuse for malice.

What black man needs an excuse for malice?
Why mask the salt? No sugar is that sweet.

My pressure's high. No sugar could make me sweet
If he came back today, if he forgave me.

Since he won't come back, won't forgive me,
I believe in God. Who else would keep me?

Left to Themselves They Tell Lies

AMANDA GAILEY

Dear America,

Our dubious monuments are everywhere—sometimes carved from stone, sometimes woven into stories, and sometimes hiding behind heroes.

The town of Tecumseh, Nebraska, was named after the great Shawnee warrior who led allied tribes against American forces in a desperate attempt to establish a sovereign nation for Indigenous people before they were effectively exterminated.

But really Tecumseh was named Tecumseh because the county it sits in was named for his killer. Richard Mentor Johnson, U.S. hero of the Battle of the Thames, ran for vice president with the nickname "Old Tecumseh" and the slogan "Rumpsey Dumpsey, Johnson killed Tecumseh." A frieze in the dome of the U.S. capitol depicts the moment the top-hatted gentleman from Kentucky shot two balls and buckshot, the story went, into the warrior's heart. With Tecumseh died any hope of an Indigenous homeland.

Except Johnson probably didn't kill Tecumseh, according to many at the battle, and Johnson himself was strategically coy on the subject. "A tall, good-looking Indian approached me with his tomahawk ready for a throw," said Johnson, who had been wounded and trapped under his dead horse. "I pulled out a loaded pistol from my holsters and shot him. They say it was Tecumseh I shot. I care not, and I know not; I would have shot the best Indian that ever breathed under such circumstances, without inquiring his name, or asking the ages of his children."

Johnson had a hard time getting elected vice president because race issues plagued him. Not the killing of Tecumseh or the owning of slaves or his sexual relationship with one of them, Julia Chinn, but the fact that he openly called her his wife and expected polite Kentucky society to accept their two daughters. Julia was ten years younger than Richard, the daughter of an unknown white man and a woman owned by Richard's father, and grew up at his childhood home. These facts raise the question of whether Julia may have been Richard's sister as well as his legal property, his "wife," and the mother of his two children. Julia remained Richard's "wife" and legal property, but also his plantation manager, until she died of cholera in 1833.

Except Julia did not merely die of cholera. She died of cholera on her owner-husband's estate along with nine Indian boys wiped out in an epidemic at the Choctaw School on "Old Tecumseh" Johnson's property. Two decades after killing or not killing Tecumseh, Richard was running a school for the education of Indigenous children, to train up the next generation of Native leaders in "the habits and arts of civilization."

Except Richard really opened the school because he was drowning in debt and wanted to siphon government funds meant for the upkeep of students into his own coffers. For years he fretted that too much of the money earmarked for the boys was being spent on the boys, and that his creative bookkeeping would be discovered. He instructed the schoolmaster how to cram small boys into rooms as tightly as possible, feed them as little as possible, and clothe them as cheaply as possible, and how to write invoices and checks so they could divert funds to Richard without being traced back to Richard. Richard was legally forbidden from making the boys do hard labor, so he put his slaves to work running the school, cooking the food, washing the laundry—human property upkeeping human assets, the more assets maintained the more cheaply, the more money for Richard to pay off his debts. Richard told his schoolmaster to carefully monitor letters the boys wrote home.

He explained: "Left to themselves they tell lies."

Richard wasn't worried about all visitors, because the official inspectors were in his pocket. But a visit from a Choctaw or Cherokee delegation could be disastrous. If the boys did not wash when visitors were coming, Richard told his schoolmaster to "give them the lash"; if the slaves did not keep the environs clean when visitors were coming, Richard told his schoolmaster to "give them the lash" too. Richard was paid to provide the boys with medical care, but doctors were expensive, so he put Julia on the task, only finally hiring a doctor when cholera ripped through the ranks of the weakened black and brown bodies producing his wealth. Johnson told the schoolmaster not to report deaths or runaways until the quarterly stipends for them were collected.

But one group of runaways got prompt attention. Two years after Julia's death, fifty-five-year-old Richard had a new romantic interest, an enslaved teenager named Cornelia Parthene. The interest was not mutual. That summer, after two young men from the school ran away, Cornelia and Julia's niece ran away to meet them, intending, as two couples, to get to Canada. Richard's brother caught up with all four in Ohio. A judge released the young men, but according to the Fugitive Slave Act, the two young women "owed service or labor" to their master, so Richard's brother locked them in a hotel room, and after they jumped from the second floor window to get away, he was able to catch only Cornelia, whom he brought back to Richard. He sold her as punishment.

By the time Johnson County, Nebraska, was named in the 1850s, Richard was dead and unpopular. One theory says the county was named for him because early settlers there were from Kentucky, but people in Kentucky didn't particularly care for him. It might have been named for Johnson by whoever named nearby Cass County for Lewis Cass, Johnson's comrade-in-arms when someone killed Tecumseh, later the executor of Andrew Jackson's Indian removal policy, and still later a champion of letting white men vote on whether to allow slavery in Kansas in Nebraska. Or it might have been named for Johnson because he and his brother had invested in the Yellowstone Expedition, which sent a team of soldiers and scientists in a serpent-shaped, metal-clad, Indian-proof steamboat to pierce through the rivers of the vast grasslands all the way to the Yellowstone River. It got as far as the Council Bluffs on the eastern edge of Nebraska, where it added to the massive debt Richard would try to pay off by exploiting Indian boys.

Tecumseh might have found something honest about that serpent-shaped boat, funded by his supposed killer and stranded not far from a site that would one day bear his name. He had once warned Osage leaders that they must band together to fight the Europeans, who had been made too strong by Indigenous charity. "White people are like poisonous serpents," he said. "When chilled, they are feeble and harmless; but invigorate them with warmth, and they sting their benefactors to death."

Today, the town of Tecumseh, Nebraska, has about 1,600 people. That's not counting the population of Tecumseh State Correctional Institution just to the north. Black people comprise less than 5 percent of the state's population but 27 percent of its prison population. Tecumseh State Correctional Institution houses the state's twelve death-row inmates, nine of whom are black or Latino. Native people now make up less than 1 percent of the state's population and don't register demographically in this sprawling facility wreathed in razor wire on the grassland, named for a man who it's hard to imagine would want to lend such a place his name.

In 2015 the state had been admitting far too many prisoners and not paying to keep enough guards at Tecumseh. What staff there were created two classes of prisoners, one made up of favorites who were given the best jobs and time in the yard, and the others who were deprived. They were easier to manage that way. Some of the prisoners planned a peaceful protest and wrote a list of grievances that they tried to present to the warden from the yard. But resistance spread quickly, some of the prisoners got out of hand, and chaos broke out. One of the petitioners was shot and wounded. Two prisoners were beaten to death, probably by other prisoners. Two guards were injured.

Afterward, there were investigations. The Department of Corrections released an early report that said the riot was spontaneous, coming from too much free movement for too many prisoners. Any rumors of grievances, it said, could not be confirmed. A later report, by an independent team, concluded that long-simmering grievances were clearly at the center of the riot, and that video showed the protesters holding the list of grievances in plain view at the beginning of the protest. A third report, kept secret by the director of prisons, came to light only when a prison employee accidentally let its existence slip. It blamed the riot on rampant mismanagement and anger among prisoners that many of their sentences had been miscalculated by the Department of Corrections.

When asked why he had concealed the report, the director of prisons said that it is "essential that certain information remain protected."

Left to themselves they tell lies.

Sincerely,
Amanda Gailey

Look at the Ways We Work upon Them

ANNE P. BEATTY

Dear America,

It's first period, standard ninth-grade English, and Michael is late as usual, because he's in the hall finishing his federally funded breakfast, some beige, molded grain product in a package labeled Educational Cereal Treats. Michael reads at a third-grade level, according to the tests in the scripted literacy curriculum purchased by the school district for $13 million. He writes poems about his older brother with AIDS and people he knows who have been shot. Each day he gets into it with a rotating cast of other boys. The tussle begins, always, with one of them slapping another on the back of the head en route to the pencil sharpener. Every time the teacher asks the class to write a poem, Michael cheers. He loves to read his work aloud. In other classes, his case manager says, he sleeps and fights, sleeps and fights, like a dreamer cycling in and out of REM stages. Sometimes he sleeps in English too, but when he wakes up, he writes, *We don't talk about my brother being sick. It's like we're little and still playing the silent game.*

Teachers, along with ER doctors and public defenders, know that the work of the world is done up close. Like hospital rooms and courtrooms, classrooms distill the shimmering brocade of policy and theory into pixelated humanity. Such a refocusing makes teaching a daily exercise in humility that I'd recommend to anyone suffering from an inflated sense of her own influence. Teachers are forced to look closely instead of squint, which means they see students who live in a country where the largest predictor of academic success is household income, and where our schools have become more racially segregated, not less, with each of the past five decades. In schools are the contradictions of our country incarnate, shoving each other's backpacks out of the way and jostling to get their journals from the bin.

Take Haley, who sits down the hall from Michael in a tenth-grade honors class, her lacrosse stick under her desk. Its dirty net lies slack against the scuffed tile as she tries to remember what she read last night when she googled "*Othello* Act 3 summary." For breakfast each day she brings Chick-fil-A in a red-and-white bag that broadcasts *I don't ride the bus. I drove myself to school, in my mom's hand-me-down Lexus.* She pops chicken bites into her mouth furtively, the greasy box hidden in her lap. She turns in her vocabulary words on time. She turns in her literary analysis essay on time. When asked to write a poem, she turns in a grammatically polished piece that dies on the page. Every line is end-stopped. Every line rhymes.

Or Ari, who does not want to be called Arielle anymore, and doesn't understand why the science teacher insists on calling them by their given, feminine name. Does he innocently forget? Willfully refuse? Why do people still see them as a girl? The hair can't get any shorter. Is it the eyebrows? Not bushy enough? The voice? Too high? The teacher separates the class to play a review game. "Boys over here! Girls over there!" Ari stands uncertainly in the middle, then shuffles to the girls' side. The teacher either doesn't notice or pretends not to notice. Only three more years of high school, Ari thinks. When I get out of here it will be different. But during English next period, in a discussion on marriage equality, nearly every student says a version of "I don't care who people marry. They should marry who they love." The teacher thinks, *This is different than when I was in high school.* She knows a few students sit in silent dissent, but it seems no longer permissible to speak out against LGBTQ people's right to marry in a public-school classroom. This is a rule the kids made. At the end of class, Ari has tiny air bubbles inside their chest. So does the teacher.

In class the next week, students are discussing the American dream. Is it dead? Only some white students say no. Someone says, "Everyone can get ahead in American society if they work hard. Everyone's equal here." The teacher asks, "Is that true?" In the honors class someone says, "Well, it's *supposed* to be true." In the standard class people guffaw and scoff and talk over each other to testify to the death of the American dream, except for one white boy in the corner—only a few white students in standard classes—who wears cowboy boots that leave pale curlicues of dried mud on the floor, like empty parentheses. When he says his papaw worked for everything he had, the teacher remembers he lives with his papaw because his parents are gone.

A consultant from the literacy program flies in from Florida to meet with the teacher during her planning period. The teacher's stack of essays sits, ungraded, between them. The consultant, who has a reptilian handbag, knee-high boots, and a paper cup of coffee, crosses her stockinged legs and asks, "What's *your* power goal?" The teacher evades the question, asking instead about the purpose of the script in the four-hundred-page teacher's guide. "It's not a script," the consultant says with a cold, molten smile. The teacher points to page after page with the word *SAY:* followed by italicized lines. "That's a framework," the consultant chants. "It's not a script. You don't have to say those exact words in that exact order."

The teacher meets with Michael in the weekly one-on-one conference that she must hold while the other twenty-eight students read silently at their desks. She is supposed to enter the results of the conference into an online software system that color-codes reading levels and assigns goals. "What's your power goal?" she asks Michael, though the words clank like marbles in her mouth and she wants to spit them out. He is supposed to say "look up words I don't know" or "reread sections I don't understand" or "make predictions about what's going to happen to a character." He says nothing. The teacher asks, gently, if he's been reading at home, the easy chapter book with the blatant white sticker branded on its spine. He ducks his head. The teacher asks, "How's your brother?" He begins talking.

Before first period, Haley comes in with a Styrofoam cup of sweet tea. She heard Parkland survivors speak in D.C. and wants to organize a protest against gun violence here. The teacher agrees to help. On the day of the walkout, students wearing orange T-shirts hand out flyers with statistics about how much money various North Carolina lawmakers receive from the NRA. (Hint: lots.) In the afternoon they flow out of classrooms to the front lawn, holding their posters aloft as they give impassioned speeches to each other. The principal watches from a distance, arms crossed, a silent god. All week leading up to the protest she has fielded angry phone calls from parents, most of whom say yes when the pediatrician asks, "Is there a gun in the house?" The principal says, "This isn't a political issue. It's a school safety issue." Still, she refuses the students' request to line the road where parents' cars queue for pickup. "We'll be silent," they plead. "We'll just hold our signs." She shakes her head. Later she tells the teacher, "I was worried what the parents would yell at the kids." This seems overly cautious until one of the protest organizers shows the teacher a tweet in which a classmate's father called her, a sixteen-year-old, a retarded asshole.

When a student who immigrated from Nepal reads her poem about a childhood memory of a man on fire in her village, a boy across the circle looks up and sees her for the first time all year. "Wait, where are you from?" he asks. She says, "Nepal," in a tough, you-got-something-to-say-about-it voice that no Nepali teenager would use to speak to a peer in Nepal. She has learned this in America, how to talk to other teenagers, especially if your English pronunciation is as woolly as a yak's winter coat and you are in all standard classes, where people tend to be more honest, less polite. The teacher adds, "It's in Asia, between India and China." The boy considers this fact, then asks, "Do you eat dogs?" The remark, less mean-spirited, perhaps, than ignorant, makes the girl's face flame. The teacher stops the lesson. They move from poems to offensiveness to stereotypes, then crawl their way back to poems.

There are as many causes for hope and despair in our schools as in our country. A student says to his Latinx classmate, who was born on this soil, "You're going to be deported anyway, so what do you care?" But the next day another student hands in, as a satire project, a picture of a detained child at the border. Written below it in Magritte's restrained cursive is *Ceci n'est pas un enfant.* In our schools are all of our looks and languages and prejudices, and the idealism and ethics to make us a better country, something closer to what we pretend is true of us. These are our kids, America. Look closely at what we give them. Look at the ways we work upon them.

Sincerely,
Anne P. Beatty

First Picture Day in America

DIANA BABINEAU

for my Haitian mother

The photographs are proof she's found an angle
where the camera can't quite catch her squarish jaw,
the width of her nose, or her low-boned cheeks
above which two dark pupils stare emphatically.
A side-glance, one brow slightly higher than
the other, raised in perpetual judgment of—
well, no one meets her standards nowadays.
She counts the seconds down—*a flash*—it's done.
Her face relaxes, smile recedes, then feigns
indifference as the next set of features
—blue eyes bright against a rosy white—
fill the frame; and more after that.
Later, in darkish hands, she turns the photo
over, exposing its colorless sheen,
and folds it into herself, until she's part
of that ivory gloss, that perfect blank.

Dear America / Dear Motherland: An Essay in Fractures

LEE ANN RORIPAUGH

1.   When I die, I want to become all *aperture*, all openness to the rush and heave and teem of the world: the August confetti of the Pleiades spilling down night sky's onyx in a fizzy glitter; the wispy plumes of breath vortexing out from the beaks of small birds' predawn songs; the shape-shifting narratives clouds murmur to the sleeping forms of mountains.

Of course, aperture can also be a kind of rawness, a vulnerability. Lately, each day feels flecked with shrapnel, until it sometimes seems difficult to feel the complexities of one's emotions, only the instinctive animal pain of *woundedness*: images of crying children in cages; photographs of dead whales washing up on beaches in apocalyptic pods; footage of emaciated polar bears stranded on melting ice floes; a car-struck rabbit with a crushed hind leg painfully flailing on asphalt.

Sand chafing raw the tender mollusk within its shell. Grit scraping raw the tender eyeball.

Sometimes I wish to close my eyes and shut everything out, but hypervigilance is both my gift and my curse.

And right now, dear America, you make me want to shutter the lens, close my eyes.

2.   My mother's brain is coming undone from dementia, like a clipped thread of yarn unraveling the complicated cable stitching in a handmade sweater. Some days, I arrive at her apartment to find her in pajamas, fuming, speaking only Japanese. Some days she thinks I am her sister. Other days my father. On many days she claims people are listening to our phone conversations because they want to *snitch* her

money. And every day without fail, she tells me how my stroke-addled and wheelchair-bound father *snitched* all of the money she'd hidden at the assisted-living center and gave it to his new girlfriend.

She is *penniless*, she insists, even though my father has left a lifetime of careful savings to her, even though everything was already owned jointly between my parents. In one sense, she's not entirely wrong about her vulnerability: immigrant, nonnative speaker of English, Japanese, elderly, woman. At the same time, she's always been taken care of, has always insisted that it's her *right* to be cared for by someone: her father, my father, now me.

When she's finished excoriating my now-deceased father for *snitching* all of her money, my mother usually turns to me and says, *You even worse than your father!*

3. This complex, toxic family narrative makes people uneasy. My friends send me emails anxiously peppered with hopes for *forgiveness*. They want a happy ending. My life right now is messy and complicated. It doesn't adhere to the outlines of a nice narrative, and I don't have any control over whether the ending is happy or not.

And isn't *forgive and forget* a paradigm that aligns with a certain kind of privilege? My anger, and my memory, are powerful. They help me process trauma, and help protect me from future abuse. *Forgive and forget* requires exhausting contortions of self-silencing and self-erasure that feel too much to me like *shame*.

I prefer *compassion* to *forgiveness*. I prefer *letting go* to *forgetting*.

And doesn't any sort of restorative justice for cultural trauma, too, rely on acknowledging painful truths, acknowledging anger, and refusing to forget or erase histories?

Because, America, this current political moment is also messy and complicated. I'm scared that we've forgotten and/or erased our own histories to the point that we're doomed to keep repeating them—even at the brink of moral and environmental apocalypse.

4. These days, I can't help but notice how the toxic gaslighting from our current administration bears an eerie resemblance to the toxic gaslighting from a formerly abusive parent with dementia.

According to my mother, I've *snitched* all of her hoarded money from the empty house where my parents live, and given it to my boyfriend.

The truth is that as legal guardian to both of my elderly parents, I de-clared the cash to the court as part of my parents' estate and put it into the bank for safekeeping.

Nothing I do, in the end, will convince my mother that I'm any-thing other than a *snitcher*, a *liar*, a *thief.* When I show her the court documents, or the bank statements, she says, *Blah, blah, blah, such big talking, I don't care about that!* When I give her large sums of cash for her birthday, or to tide her over for spending money until my next visit, she becomes angry that I haven't handed over the entire estate to her, in cash, to keep under her bed at the assisted-living center. A few days later, she will deny that I've ever given her any money at all—claim that she can't even go shopping for shampoo, because she is *penniless.*

Your father so upset when I tell him you snitch all my money and give to your boyfriend! my mother hisses. *That's why he tell you don't come, you no welcome, for Christmas before he dead time*, she says. *He never going to forgive you for that*, she says, smiling a little as she goes in for the kill. *Right before he dead time he* hate *you for do that to me.*

5.   I am driving my mother over the Snowy Range. On Saturdays, I try to coax her from the assisted-living center and take her on outings. As we round the hairpin turns toward the summit—near Mirror Lake and Lake Marie—the peaks, which seem so blue from Laramie, are now, up close, rocky-gray and patterned with tiger-stripes of snow. The sky is a grand battle of cloudage: corpulent blue sea beasts vs. ruffled dragons of ornately carved white jade.

My mother seems somewhat happy, recognizing places she used to visit with my father. But when I suggest we go back again, she shrugs and says: *I been there two times already! Once with your father and once with you. Why I have to go again?*

I'm reminded of driving through Wyoming to summer swim meets. How my mother would insist on clamping towels over most of the Jeep's windows, so we wouldn't get *truck-driver suntans.* I imagine all of the miles of missed canyon and sky and clouds and prairie and antelope unfurling unseen outside those old bath towels. My mother's always insisted on maintaining such a narrow aperture that it makes my heart sick—and now, instead of being a beauty to open her eyes to, the world will only continue to become increasingly narrow for her.

6.   An iconic memory of my mother: We are on a plane, on our way to visit my American grandparents in Arizona. I am maybe four or five years old. A flight attendant comes around with a basket of candies and offers the basket to each of the passengers. My mother scoops her hands deep into the basket and comes away with both fists full of candies. The flight attendant, however, makes her put them back, says she can take only one. My mother is visibly disappointed—agitated and irritable for the rest of the flight.

Our house in Laramie is filled to the gills with just this type of hoarded treasure: stale candies, stale tea, stale tins of cookies, expired food, unworn clothes mixed in with trash, mixed in with mountains of plastic bags, mixed in with bill stubs dating back to the 1970s, mixed in with urine-soaked pads, mixed in with an obscene tonnage of mail from the NRA, mixed in with loaded handguns. So many things: unused, unworn, not enjoyed, but mindlessly *accumulated*.

Oh, Mother, I want to say, with as much compassion as I can muster, thinking of the shiny, tightly clutched, cellophane-wrapped candies spilling out of her small hands. *Please let go.*

What a strange foil this all is to the surreal beauty of the Snowy Range. Thunderheads gather on the horizon in the late afternoon, as I haul things out to the dumpster in front of the house—feeling increasingly sweaty, lonely, furious—and sometimes blue-gray spigots of rain squirt down on the mountains from heavy-bellied clouds as if they were leaky water balloons.

It is a beauty that feels increasingly fragile and evanescent. Each day's news brings new reports of climate change and environmental unraveling: more than two hundred reindeer found dead from starvation in Svalbard, Norway; approximately half a billion bees found dead in Brazil, poisoned by the insecticide Fipronil; a memorial held in Iceland for the Okjökull glacier, while all of Alaska's sea ice rapidly melts like ice cubes in a too-warm summer cocktail.

Dear America: I think of all of your greed and plunder, as well as all of the atrocities committed for the sake of greed and plunder.

I think of your sundowning rages when confronted with your oppressive histories.

Oh America, oh motherland, please, please let go.

Not a Good German

SANDRA STEINGRABER

1. Dear America,

My last name, Steingraber, means "by the stony ditch" in German. *Am steinigen Graben.*

It was bequeathed to me by my German American father who adopted me in 1960. I carry it to honor the man who gave me a family.

I want you to start pronouncing it correctly. The *a* is long. Once there were two German dots over that *a*, but they were quietly dropped by some immigrant somewhere along the way to signal loyalty to America.

That's what I was told by my Steingraber uncles. I had seven of them. They all fought the Nazis, and they're all dead now, and I can't verify the story. There is so much about your story, America, that I can't verify.

A. Like the color gray. I'm tired of reminding you every damn time you introduce me at the podium.

2. Dear America,

I'd like you to meet my dad, Wilbur F. Steingraber, who fought Nazis for sixty years.

Will enlisted on his eighteenth birthday, and you trained him to attack Nazi Panzer tanks and shipped him off to Europe. Remember that? The motto of his platoon was *Seek Strike and Destroy*.

What happened to him there was never fully disclosed to me before his death in 2005. I can tell you that he suffered, for the rest of his life, from what we would now call PTSD.

All my friends' fathers had the same problem. We never talked about it. We just tiptoed around our dads, who, we were warned, could blow up at any moment like unexploded ordnance.

3.   Dear America,
Something bad happened in Italy. It had to do with guard duty and war refugees. That's all I know, and I don't expect further details from you. Fine. Keep your secrets.
I do want you to know that Will was never able to take a walk at dusk.
He closed the drapes before sunset.
Our front door had many locks.
Paper bags in the road triggered panic attacks. America, you made my dad afraid of paper bags. Unexploded ordnance.
Here's the point: He flew the flag every day. For you, America.

4.   Dear America,
He taught me to be brave. Lesson from Dad: when you carry around a name like Steingraber, you can't be a good German. If fascism needs fighting, you fight.

5.   Dear America,
Wilbur F. Steingraber was a big believer in willpower.
This is how my dad willed away the Nazis:
He read Rachel Carson and started an organic garden. He made candles. Hundreds of candles. He made dollhouses. Dozens of dollhouses. He took up embroidery. Yes, he did. He embroidered big-eyed children, puppies, and sunflowers, and he hung them everywhere.
He never lit the candles.
He bought yarn in bulk. Also ice cream. He bought a chest freezer to hold all the ice cream. Plus all the organic tomatoes.
He bought chainsaws in bulk.
When the hedges in the front yard became large enough for Nazis to hide in, he chainsawed them down.
At some point, PTSD skidded straight into dementia. I want you to know that my mom and my sister and me feel bad about how late we were in picking up on this. We tiptoed too long.
It was me who made the chainsaws disappear. I also ratholed his car keys. My sister took his rifle.
America, when Julie M. Steingraber attempted to turn Wilbur F. Steingraber's firearm in to the local sheriff, she received a lecture on the Second fucking Amendment. Was this really necessary? At this point,

Will was seeing Nazis in the hallway and wasn't sure how a spoon worked.

6. Dear America,

It's true. My dad stabbed a nurse with a fork. He said it was his duty under the Geneva Convention to escape.

When I called the VA they told me they didn't have facilities for combative patients.

Me yelling *Are you fucking kidding me you made him a combatant in 1944 and he's still fighting Nazis* didn't help at all.

The second-to-last conversation I had with my father took place in a locked Alzheimer's unit—paid for with a lien on my mom's house—on the sixtieth anniversary of D-Day. Dad wasn't sure who I was, but we conversed about Rommel's offensive in North Africa.

In my last conversation, America, my dad pointed at my son and said, *Keep him out of the lane.*

Wilbur F. Steingraber was big on protecting kids above all else.

7. Dear America,

On July 11, 2019, I was arrested in downtown Buffalo and charged with disorderly conduct and unlawful assembly. This was an act of civil disobedience conducted in coordination with the nationwide #Close TheCamps movement.

With my actions—which were glorious and involved shutting down a major city intersection for several hours—I sought to highlight abuses within migrant detention camps here in New York.

Specifically, in Buffalo, my actions were directed at shining a spotlight on the real estate developers who are shamefully leasing office space to the wretched Immigration and Customs Enforcement and the wretched Customs and Border Protection.

From the investigation: "The federal government lease—which covers ICE's Homeland Security Investigations offices and Enforcement and Removal Operations offices, as well as its holding cell in downtown Buffalo—will yield $1,953,161 in rent in 2019."

At the time of my arrest, I was sitting in the intersection of Chippewa and Delaware Avenues between a hospice chaplain and a military veteran. Further down the blockade line: a Jewish activist and a member of the Seneca Nation, who, as an Indigenous child, had been forcibly adopted out of her birth family and raised in a white family.

Left right left right. They ran toward us in formation, the police, bearing their batons like candles. We began singing.

Basically, America, you are a nation of adoptees, some abandoned, some kidnapped.

Are you listening?

8. Dear America,

Civil disobedience arises as an act of individual conscience informed by our various identities.

America, my name moved me to action. The sign I carried at the time of my arrest said NOT A GOOD GERMAN.

I'll explain it again. A good German was a citizen of Germany during the 1930s and 1940s who said that they opposed the Nazis but who, in fact, did nothing to act on their opposition.

A good German was someone who later, when it all came out, claimed they had no idea about the atrocities taking place in the concentration camps or about the deportations of Jews and others named undesirable.

A good German sees and hears no evil. A good German chooses to not go there.

A good German believes the lies.

A good German doesn't believe the lies but substitutes cynicism for action.

To be a good German is to have convictions but not the courage thereof.

To be a good German is to decide that the thing to do is focus on making a really good cup of coffee.

To be a good German is to become the meme dog in the meme flames who drinks good coffee and says, "This is fine."

Edward Abbey: "Sentiment without action is the ruin of the soul."

To be a good German is to be a ruined soul.

9. Dear America,

Thank you for that warm introduction. It's an honor to be here.

10. Dear America,

I saw you in the lane at dusk.

Who is that lying facedown in the stony ditch?

As American as Turning Your Back on the Flag

YELIZAVETA P. RENFRO

Dear America,

It's 1979 or 1980, and I'm running to keep up with my uncle, whose enormous strides move through the throng of people from the parking lot, through the tunnel under the track, to the betting windows. Suddenly, music comes over the loudspeaker, and everyone around us falls still, as though frozen by magic. But my uncle and I—we keep moving. We wend our way through those statue people, some of whom have put hands to hearts, but my uncle's hurried pace never slows, so I keep trotting after him on my short legs, astonished at how conspicuous and powerful I have become. That we can keep moving against the force of this powerful spell seems a miracle. We are saying something, we are getting somewhere, while the world is frozen in a gripping idolatry.

It's 1979, and my Russian grandmother has come to America for the first time, and when we take her to our local grocery store, the Alpha Beta, she is astonished at the plenty, at the shoppers casually making decisions about what type of cheese they might purchase this week. In the Soviet city where she lives, there is no cheese of any kind except very occasionally soft processed government cheese. And even though they were thousands of miles away from the ear of anyone of any importance who might overhear her, she leaned in close to whisper to my mother, "If it weren't for the 1917 Revolution, we too would live like this." And she swept her arm to indicate the entirety of that Alpha Beta in California and the abundance it contained.

My American uncle, the one who took me to the races, was no rebel or revolutionary. He was hotheaded—a drinker, a gambler, just twenty-five years old, someone who might dare the world to stop him from doing something without having a particular reason for doing it. If I had asked him why he walked through the national anthem, I imagine he might have said, "Because this is a free country, and I do what I want." I think he would have seen falling still at the beck of a note as fawning, obsequious—though I doubt he knew the word. His true reason was probably more pragmatic: likely he just needed to get his bets in before the first race.

In the 1980s, after I had gone back to Russia several times, the day at the racetrack became a measure for me: the difference between the United States and the Soviet Union. In the United States, you can walk through the national anthem, you can refuse to say the Pledge of Allegiance, you can turn your back on the flag. In the Soviet Union, the performance of venerating symbols was a requirement—and to refuse to carry out such theatrics was dangerous.

That I am not a native daughter of this country means my love of it—and its symbols—can never be uncomplicated. I am the daughter of a native son and a nonnative daughter. A hostile daughter, in fact, who came to this country because it was the only way she could be with her American husband. My mother and I had green cards, Soviet passports. And even though I claimed U.S. citizenship in my teens, I keep my expired Soviet passport out of nostalgia—for it is my citizenship in an era in history, more than a place. It is my citizenship in an idea—that we can each be many people, have many allegiances, that our devotion to any nation is complicated, fraught with misgivings.

This summer, moving cross-country, as I caught sight of an oversized American flag hanging from a lonely overpass, I felt the old twinge of recoil: the feeling that I would not want to know the person who felt the need to unfurl a flag there. That need carries a whiff of something insular, shut up, slightly rotten. People who hang enormous flags from overpasses are too caught up in symbols, the shiny surfaces of things, simple dichotomies. They are offended to an absurd degree by other people who take a knee during the national anthem, which is but another symbol. We are awash in symbols—the flag, the pledge, the anthem, the elephant, the donkey, the emoticons that express no true depth of emotion. The American flag—which is really someone's need to display it—has become a shorthand for someone I probably don't want to know.

The problem with the flag is that there are other flags. The problem with God is that there are other gods. And both are used as a shield behind which people revel in jingoism, xenophobia.

When I was in elementary school, one of my friends asked me if I believed in God. I told her no, I was an atheist. The next day she said her parents told her she couldn't be friends with me anymore. They said I was going to hell. Apparently, our friendship had no long-term prospects.

Back then, I mumbled the Pledge of Allegiance, and I never said the "under God" part. I wondered why God was even in there, if we had religious freedom. Which meant the freedom not to have religion. And if we had the separation of church and state. Which meant God had nothing to do with government. And if I did believe in God, it couldn't be one who would take my side over that of someone with darker skin or less education or who lacked certain documents. I could not believe in a God who favored our nation over another—or a God who troubled himself with politics at all. "Under God" meant closed-mindedness, provincialism, myopia, blind faith in something unprovable. It meant idolatry. It evoked in me the same feelings as the Soviet hammer and sickle.

After Trump was elected, I talked with a fellow mom at the pool while our kids swam laps. She said she thought Trump was a symbol—or a symptom—of our collective sickness. That included us both, even if we didn't vote for him. Some part of her—the dark, infected part—had elected him. And instead of merely pointing fingers at *those awful Trump voters*, she needed to look into her own heart and rout out the sickness there. The nation has a collective conscience, she told me.

My racist white male relatives—who would deny they were racist, who would claim some of their best friends back in high school fifty years ago were black, but who still use racial slurs when they talk to each other about what's wrong with this country—are on Facebook now. Their feeds are full of inflammatory Fox News articles, *Turning Point USA* diatribes, apologies for Trump. Illegals are ruining this country. Lock her up. Share this picture of a brave one-legged veteran. Trump is vindicated. Trump is not racist. Islam is not peaceful. Stand your ground. Praise the NRA. Share this picture of a brave K-9 police dog. But more than anything, their feeds are full of American flags, flapping their fury on the wind. Bemoaning the loss of an America that, if it ever existed at all, existed only fleetingly, as a dream, and only for them: the white, the male.

Meanwhile, my Trump-loathing friends post of multiple mass shootings committed by angry white males. They post anti-Trump rants. They post their own alternative news. They live in a separate universe of their own facts. They are not prone to posting flags.

My racist white male uncles are the older brothers of the one I went to the races with four decades ago. I don't speak to him anymore. After too much drinking and gambling, he cleaned up his act, married, became more conservative and cautious. I did not stay in touch with him. But I am Facebook friends with his son—my cousin—whom I hardly know, but who is a cocky young man whose racist posts sometimes rival those of our racist uncles. Such things tend to run in families.

And this is why I don't unfriend my racist white male relatives: to deny their existence is to deny a part of myself. I did not vote for Trump, but I can't help but agree with the swim mom: I am complicit. I did not do enough *not* to elect him. And silencing (in my feed) the chirping chorus of Fox News and its ilk is no solution. And waving a flag is no solution. And maybe walking through the anthem or taking a knee during the anthem is no solution either, but the point is, we have a right to these things. The point is: this is not the Soviet Union.

In my Facebook feed, one of my Trump-loathing friends posted news from Montana. A man slammed a thirteen-year-old boy to the ground, fracturing his skull, because the boy did not remove his hat during the national anthem before a county rodeo. That's what made me remember, suddenly, that day at the races: not only did we walk through the whole national anthem, but my uncle had a baseball cap perched on his head the entire time. And we passed through that crowd completely unmolested. I don't remember a single heckler calling us out for our lack of patriotism, our disrespect.

We would not have made it across that racetrack in 2019.

And that's the point of all this. America—and its symbols—is not above criticism or even scorn. To resort to idolatry, to mandatory worship of a song or a place or a piece of cloth or a god, is to make yourself no different from other governments, past and present, that do not give citizens basic rights. It is American to walk through the anthem, to take a knee, or to say *fuck you, Trump*. I can see him still, my lanky uncle striding through that stilled crowd with perfect confidence, perfect freedom. And his reason for doing it—even if it is as trite as getting his bets in before the first race—doesn't matter one whit. He has every right to just keep on walking. I can't think of anything more American.

Sincerely,
Yelizaveta P. Renfro

Each One a Bright Light

LEE HERRICK

Dear America,

I was born outside of you, in Korea, in 1970, a year of upheaval and revolution. I was adopted and arrived in America in October 1971, at ten months of age, on your west coast, the San Francisco International Airport to be exact, where I was adopted by a white American couple.

In the year I was born, 1970, upheaval and change was everywhere: the Vietnam War continued, the shootings at Kent State rocked Ohio and the world, UCLA fired Angela Davis, and Richard Nixon signed a measure into law lowering the voting age to eighteen. In the same year, both Jimi Hendrix and Janis Joplin died. It was two years after Martin Luther King Jr. and Bobby Kennedy were killed. In many ways, it was a brutal time of major change. But beneath the headlines, tragic or sickening as they may be, America's best self was always churning, always evolving. Even when it's nearly indiscernible, I believe that America is, in fact, a beautiful idea. Even in the face of great trauma or tragedy, political distress or economic trouble, America churns forward. The America I love is in the people's heartbeat, the Americans who try their best to overcome or live through what inevitable failures and setbacks will temporarily rattle us.

In May 1975 I was naturalized and became a U.S. citizen. There's a picture of me at four years old, dressed in a dark suit, holding the flag, standing in front of a larger flag. In 1977 my kindergarten teacher played her acoustic guitar and sang "This Land Is Your Land" to the class, and I distinctly remember liking the song and her spirited rendition of it, but I also remember questioning it. It is the first memory I have of feeling unsettled because of race. I was the only Asian American in the class of thirty white children. I would soon experience and continue to experience your particular brand of racism. I would learn that because I was not born in this country, I could never become president. I would not have made a good one, but I can think of some transnational adoptees who would.

I became a student of you. I recently learned that nine of the first eleven U.S. presidents owned slaves. (John Adams and his son, John Quincy, were the only two who did not.) So we Americans have a long way to go, and some hard self-exploration to do. I am a student of your presidential history and did my master's thesis on twentieth-century presidential rhetoric and Aristotelian theory. I also became a student of one of your greatest failures: your inability to grant legal, social, and economic liberty and justice to all people. We can say that progress has been made, and in fact there has been, but then I recall that there are 892 active hate groups in this country and that one of the most notorious recently endorsed a presidential candidate, and he won.

I am hoping your better angels keep churning. There are many who live here who are suffering and struggling, but you know this. You know there are many who do not care about the suffering, and what would you say to them? I wonder how you look at your own youth, at your own breathtaking diversity, at the state of your own disrepair. I wonder if you believe, like I do, that if we are to keep forming that more perfect union, we must evolve, we must keep churning forward, we must welcome the immigrant, the refugee, and the transnational adoptee. We must balance the rapid broadcast of our failures and disgust with the beautiful stories of resistance and the truths of Americans forging new and necessary revolutions.

Division is inevitable with an idea so great as you, and while we may take steps back at times—this feels like one, to be sure—I am certain that you are durable, that your bones are good, that your foundations are solid. Are there limits to democracy's elasticity? We'll see. I believe you when you say that you stand for equality, for liberty and justice for all people, but you're currently far short of the mark. For now, I want to celebrate you. I also want to fight for what is good in you and for the ideas you espouse. There are millions of people who do so every day. There will be more travesties, more fires, and more demagogues. But I vow to keep the faith. I vow to care. I imagine millions and millions of people here in America, each one a bright light, thinking and dreaming like I am, certain about the better days ahead.

Yours,
Lee Herrick

What You'd Want to Remember

Now, daylight spent,
darkness falls before supper,

votives flickering down the long table,
and voices,

someone leaning in to hear,
or back, to laugh or consider,

someone reaching over to touch,
tentative, kind,

not out but over,
across the dark.

It wasn't any one thing
you'd want to remember later,

a story, a gesture, a beautiful face,
animated in the candlelight,

the glasses refilled again and again,
or how late you stayed, talking into that autumn night.

You'd need an old word for what it was,
our *commonweal*.

You'd need that, when you thought back.

The End of the Pier

ALLEN GEE

Dear America,

Over a decade ago I lived within the concrete sprawl of Houston, so to escape I drove south down I-45 to Galveston and veered farther south along the Texas coast to San Luis Pass. There the San Luis Pass pier jutted out like some kind of wonder of the world, stretching over the Gulf of Mexico, the pilings, boards, and railings forming a huge structure that allowed me to walk across the water. I crossed all the way out to the end of the pier, and as I stood and felt the wind on my face and inhaled the salty air, I felt briny and as distant and removed from the strife and complications of city living as any minority could ever be.

What I remember most about the end of the pier was a yellow line that denoted a unique space where no one could remain. You could cross the line and cast your lines and leave your surf fishing rods propped against the end railing, but you couldn't stay there and block anyone from reaching their rods. No, the small square space beyond the yellow line couldn't become too crowded. Because of the existence of that space, people—African Americans, Mexicans, Caucasians, and Asians (some Chinese American, like me)—cooperated in the most communal or admirable and supportive fashion, so that if there were a multitude of anglers, all the fishing rods were arranged in tight rows, resting against the end railing, the lines fanning out, covering the expanse of the Gulf in a broad swath. And if anyone hooked a bull red or a tiger shark or a massive stingray, people would lift their lines to help any fisherman avoid tangling lines, whether the fish ran in one direction or another, and you might see a fisherman loan another a drop net to help retrieve a catch from far below.

One night when I lost a fish that broke my leader, two Mexican fishermen showed me how they crimped their leaders out of wire, beads, and swivels to be stronger, and on another day a Caucasian fisherman showed me how best to hook fresh dead mullet, and I gave him some mullet when he ran out of bait. There was always the sense that the Gulf and the wind and the sun—that nature—without the least amount of effort, were far greater than any of us. So I have not forgotten all the rituals of civility that occurred at any hour, whether in the black depths of the night or under the hot noontime sun, high tides forever waiting for anyone, the fish inevitably appearing, always seeming eager to bite.

I learned recently how William Lee, an accomplished Chinese American lawyer who grew up in the 1950s, was told in Wellesley, Massachusetts, to go back to his own country, before being followed by another car until he pulled into a police station. And I've read reports from the Southern Poverty Law Center about the outbreak of more than ten thousand hate crimes since the 2016 election.

So I recall the space at the end of the pier with a greater reverence. And this makes me consider how my mentor, the late James Alan McPherson, returned time and again for ideological fortitude to our earlier history, when categories and caste systems in American needed to be abolished by Congress, whereby a third, neutral category was created, as McPherson writes, "for the purposes of legal classification: that of citizen of the United States. This hypothetical person, neither black nor white (and now, by extension, neither Latino, Native American, or Asian American) or male or female, would enjoy all the rights of citizenship and would be expected to meet all the responsibilities required of such a citizen. When such rights and responsibilities were assessed, the separating categories of race would be meaningless." This, he continues, was the purpose of Section 1 of the Fourteenth Amendment to the Constitution:

All persons born or naturalized in the United States, and subject to the jurisdiction thereof, are citizens of the United States and of the State wherein they reside. No State shall make or enforce any law which shall abridge the privileges or immunities of citizens of the United States; nor shall any State deprive any person of life, liberty, or property without due process of law, nor deny to any person within its jurisdiction the equal protection of the law.

This ideal of not being able to deprive any citizen of life, liberty, or property, I think, is how our country is *supposed* to be. McPherson was also fond of citing the famous case of *Plessy v. Ferguson* that stemmed from segregation on trains; the case was argued in 1896 before the Supreme Court. He writes in his book *Railroad* how the phrase "Our Constitution is color-blind" was admitted into the language of the law by Justice John Harlan in his dissent from the majority opinion: "The white race deems itself to be the dominant race in this country. And so it is, in prestige, in achievements, in education, in wealth, and in power. . . . But in view of the Constitution, in the eye of the law, there is in this country no superior dominant ruling class of citizens. There is no caste here. Our Constitution is colorblind, and neither knows nor tolerates classes among citizens."

The phrase, McPherson writes, has "shaped the course of legal theory from 1896 to the present." I find it artful and sustaining. The phrase further points toward how the country should be for anyone born on this soil, so I like to keep it in mind. I should add that I was born in 1962 and grew up believing that by the time I reached midlife perhaps our nation's racial problems might be solved, or at least vastly improved upon. But watching President-elect Trump rallying in Ohio, I saw not one person of color seated behind him; I heard chants of "USA! USA!"; and along with this chanting I noticed how the incendiary language of white nationalism ran hot throughout Trump's speech, decrying globalism, insisting on building the wall along the Mexico border, vowing to renegotiate or throw out all existing foreign trade agreements, along with deregulating on a mass scale statutes that protect the environment (as if nature isn't larger in scope than all of us), all the while promising repeatedly to make America great again. Yes, as it's frequently been pointed out, this is simply code for making America "white" again.

So we live now in a culture of escalation, in a confluence of tension between the haves and have-nots, combined with a struggle over concerns for the environment and the denial of global warming, accompanied by the purchasing and stockpiling of guns spurred by the lobbying efforts of the NRA, further complicated by white fear that minorities will soon outnumber them and forever run the country if some sort of grand last stand isn't taken. Many, like Morris Berman, have predicted a crisis of empire, stating that the American dream is simply over whether Trump is in power or not. At the same time I have never seen as many of my graduate or undergraduate students or old friends as upset, or as fearful, and I have never witnessed as many of my colleagues in academia being watchful, wondering if they might be targeted or put on a watch list for expressing "liberal" opinions, as if we have regressed to an era of McCarthyism. I've heard from several of my former business associates in venture capital that they're uncertain about the future, too, while the sentiment of "What can we do?" seems to grow more prevalent.

The San Luis Pass pier, I'm sorry to say, was destroyed by Hurricane Ike in 2008. But I hold onto my memory of the pier, and as I continue to recall the premise of citizenship, a larger part of me takes life head-on, living day to day and in the moment, feeling more present, alert, and sensitive to changes in the air than before.

As a minority who has lived in the Deep South for over twelve years, I am in survival mode. I always have been, in one way or another. Though I wear eyeglasses because of nearsightedness, I have always strived to avoid the Asian stereotype: I drive a dark blue pickup truck and wear jeans and flannel shirts and hiking boots. I have been known to wear a tan Carhartt barn jacket that has *Ruger* stitched in dark brown letters on the right side, so while I've never owned or carried a handgun, when I'm walking on the sidewalks in our small town I'm aware of how white male southerners notice *Ruger* on my jacket, their expressions becoming contemplative, pondering whether I'm carrying a revolver under my coat. I don't mind their believing in the possibility that I'm armed, because so far I've been left peacefully alone, passing as I may be.

Still, lately I have told my students that they should feel that their choice to be a writer—their public identity as a writer—is more important now than during any recent time, since this is when we write our stories and essays and poems to protest and to chronicle the current state of unrest and to express and imagine how we think life should be—in opposition to all the strife, hypocrisy, and amplified hate we see. Yes, writers have always been activists, so we cannot be silent.

And I suppose there is further wisdom that I can offer because of my age. I lived through being young in the 1960s, when deeper strains of racism and more institutionalized behaviors were taken on, and gains were made, some small and others far more significant, and history is cyclic, so we—which is to say, the better, more inclusive ideals of America—shall certainly survive through *this*.

Sincerely,
Allen Gee

Receiver, Achiever, Reliever, Believer

My Dear Friend,

Earlier this summer, I spent a week in Alaska, a part of the country that wasn't even a state when my parents were born. I didn't encounter you among the estuaries and bird refuges, the bear tours and kayak excursions and countless American flags, but I know you were somewhere nearby. And even though you and I didn't cross paths in Alaska, I did manage to spot a moose—my first ever. David and I were walking near the nature center in downtown Homer, rounding a shady part of the trail, and there she was. "Look at that fat horse," David said, not realizing what grazed before us. He'd never been near her kind either, though this was not for a lack of trying. I've made "see a moose" my New Year's resolution since 2009 (before that, it was "set more reasonable goals"). Over the past decade, we've scoured parts of Maine, Vermont, Michigan, New Hampshire, Montana, and Wyoming for a glimpse. I can't remember why I made the resolution in the first place. Sometimes we lose sight of what first prompts our ambitions, buried as they are under the storytelling we inadvertently heap upon them.

More surprising than how long it took to see a moose is the fact that I've never come face-to-face with you in any of the forty-seven states I've set foot in. Unlike moose, which only thrive in a few northern biomes, you've made space for yourself in every American landscape. Crafty and resilient, you require little more than a fresh waterway to reroute and trees to fell with your orange, iron-enriched teeth. While the creatures that look the most like me—with our vulnerable skin and useless dentition—came to this continent only a dozen millennia ago, versions of your miraculous form have shaped this land for over seven million years. One huge variant walked this continent throughout the Pleistocene, tall as a modern bear.

Though the real you has eluded me, I see at least a dozen cartoonish versions daily, since you're the chosen symbol of both the state where I live and the university that employs me. In my town, you're on buildings, ball caps, and yoga pants, but your image can't seem to hold the menace required of most sports mascots, like wolverines, diamondbacks, or raptors. A few years ago, the college rebranded you down to a series of jet-black lines, hoping to erase goofiness with abstraction. Fans hated it, so they reverted to a 1970s throwback image of you in a Gilligan hat and a bucktoothed smile.

· · ·

That moose we met in Alaska was goofy, too, but large enough to take our breath away. A tawny calf trailed behind her, all knees and matchstick legs. We kept our distance from the pair but followed for a long while. So did another couple, who took a zillion pictures. When another hiker approached, the couple whisper-shouted, "Moose!" and the hiker all but rolled his eyes; he was a local. "I had four in my yard this morning," he said, and kept walking.

Despite how exotic the Alaska moment felt to us out-of-towners, I can see how the moose connects to certain core ideas of our country. Even though species from the *Alces* genus roam two other continents, only in North America are the beasts called "moose," a word with Algonquin origins. They are the continent's second largest native species, with bison at the top. In 1780, when a French armchair naturalist assumed that American fauna were punier than their European counterparts, Thomas Jefferson retorted that a reindeer "would walk under the belly of our moose." Jefferson then sent him a gargantuan specimen from New Hampshire as proof.

I also see America in the natural facts of a moose, which is bigger than the largest SUV in a Costco parking lot and famously tough to kill. Unsubtle, yet strong and instinctive, moose kick in all directions—even sideways!—which aligns with the more vindictive expressions of the American spirit. On the other hand, moose are reluctant to attack (except during the annual rut) and prefer wandering alone to vying for new territories. Neither of those practices ring particularly American, nor does the fact that moose are vegetarians.

One could, I suppose, scan the traits of any creature that lives here exclusively and find something that jibes with an American ideal. We might stretch our imaginations to locate the American spirit in the chumminess of the Carolina chicken turtle or the vicious bite of the American alligator. The country we aspire to be, captured in the dog-gedness of the island night lizard or the benevolence of the long-nosed gar. It feels silly to extend the country into these kinds of American bodies, which is unfortunate. I wish we didn't reserve our national identity for only the regal or formidable beasts among us.

■ ■ ■

The part of Alaska we visited isn't just stocked with moose; it's also overrun with bald eagles. The opposite was true thirty-five years ago, after decades of DDT poisoning (which weakens eggshells) had dwindled the lower forty-eight's bald eagle population to a few hundred couples. But they've been removed from both the endangered and threatened species lists for over a decade. According to the Fish and Wildlife Service, nearly twenty thousand live in the contiguous United States, and thirty thousand in Alaska alone. What was once an American unicorn is now as ubiquitous as a woodpecker.

In Homer, David pointed out nests sprawled over the top of a light pole, and I saw an enormous female curb-stomp a fish in the hotel parking lot. We got the sense the birds were everywhere, watching over us when we walked home from the bar at midnight. One Homer resident told me locals were so tired of bald eagles that they've renamed them "dumpster ducks." A guy at the Salty Dog told me he most often sees them dead on the side of the Sterling highway. "And lemme tell you," he said, "they leave a mark."

A few years ago, my heart nearly stopped when I thought I saw your lifeless body along the exit to a North Carolina town called (appropriately enough) Lumberton. But any roadkill that resembles you usually turns out to be the rat-tailed nutria instead—that invasive species imported to America in the nineteenth century after the fur industry had nearly run out of your kind. What lovely top hats, liners, perfumes, and leather you once made. Before chasing after gold or timber or a nice golf community in Scottsdale to spend one's retirement, the first western expansion pursued you. And in centuries prior, the land you cleared prompted humans to walk in your shadow. Whenever you revamp an American ecosystem, carving out deep ponds to keep your nuclear families safe, your work welcomes myriad others. The plains you irrigate attract my new friend, the moose. Your ingenious dams—often hundreds of feet in length—may have spurred behavioral evolution in American fish. As the adage goes, it's you who taught the salmon to jump.

When Congress elected the bald eagle as our national symbol, Benjamin Franklin famously protested, calling it "a Bird of bad moral Character" who "does not get his Living honestly. . . . Like those among men who live by sharping & robbing he is generally poor and often very lousy." But Jefferson, friend to moose and raptors alike, was compelled by the bald eagle's longevity as well as its macho visage. Compared to the eagle's focused, Gregory Peck glower, your face is much more Paul Giamatti, with that weak chin and myopic gaze. But within those eyes lies a gob-smacking vision. Labor is so hardwired into your furry body that the mere sound of running water unleashes your insatiable urge to chew. No animal (other than humans) can match your drive to work the landscape until it changes, for better or worse. And I ask you, How American is that?

I wonder what would be different had Franklin and Jefferson recognized America in your round body and sloping forehead. What I see in you is enough to make me wish your name were a lyric in every national anthem. I just sat for twenty minutes trying to think of all the words a patriotic poet could have rhymed with it—*receiver, achiever, reliever, believer*—because I want to stand up at ball games with my cap over my heart and holler the verses of *that* nation. America symbolized not by a formidable, high-flying thief or a sideways kicking mass with antlers, but by thirty pounds of oily fur and stinky glands. After all, what's wrong with a goofy power if it shows up to work every day?

I want to picture the American dream as embodied in your lodges— ingenious piles of scented mud with multiple rooms and cold storage. I want to pass laws inspired by your hospitality and desire for collaboration. I know it's easiest to paint blunt, self-serving pictures of the creatures we've never met, but I can't stop wishing it was your face printed on my money. Between the moose and the bald eagle and the chicken turtle and all the other animals unique to the land on which our nation was built, I hereby cast my vote for you as poster child. Sorry, dumpster ducks.

All this returns me to the news story that made me love you, from 2006, when you swam up the Bronx River and settled into New York City for the first time in two centuries. You dutifully built your lodge but had no mate to share it. That fall, you were often spotted atop the muddy hut with a muskrat, gazing at the stars. I would sew this image onto our flag as a commitment to welcome into our spaces those who don't look exactly like us, championing the fact that your buildings, though fortified, are not walls.

My sweet, sharp friend, teach me to keep moving even when it feels like my home is rushing out from beneath me. Let me learn how to dredge, fell, and weave this world into something that attracts life rather than stifles it. Help me irrigate what's underneath me to keep future fires at bay. Show me how to bring the animals of my mind closer to the ones who find me on the trail. And remind me when I get lost in the simple or cartoonish that there is too much work to do to spend my day planning attacks.

Please, dear friend, take me—and the raptors, the moose, and all the other creatures of this country—onto the roof of your lodge. Let us sit with you all night, considering the swell of work that's just downriver. If we place you in the center of our heart, will you warn of what's to come with a hearty slap of your tail? If we swim toward all that you've built, can you teach us how to jump?

Fondly,
Elena Passarello

Drowned and Reborn

JASMINE ELIZABETH SMITH

after Clyde Woods's *Development Drowned and Reborn*

when the lower 9th ward levee broke
in 1961, we prayed
we might become the slipknot of black water
snakes. & because we had no hands,
    our venom bites fastened—
    bayou rocking our babies, fettering
    them to pirogues, our fugitive bodies
    safe in maroon settlements of *cipriere*.
& because we no longer had homes,
    we took shapes of swamp gulls, scavenging
    the officers' lapels of badges, what was left
    of bloated, altering nests—
    driftwood, plastic
    bags, the bloated bodies of idling
    government vans.
child, that year, the watershed
reached over four feet on Claiborne Avenue in Tremé—
fourteen in the parishes of St. Bernard and Plaquemines.
hundreds us became alligators,
    belly crawling the muddy
    velvet bowl of bayou St. John
    when prices of bottled water, gas,
    canned peaches rose.
& because we had no tongues
to speak, our rows of teeth grew longer,
sharper with expression. some say, we ate

what remained of our dead,
    our hunger desperate. imagine our opening
    mouths, our chorus-snagged jaws, devoid of song—
    how a dirge might sound to some a kill.

To the First of Getting Longer Days

CHRIS DOMBROWSKI

I felt unsettled driving northeast in the dark
up what the Salish called the Road to the Buffalo
long before my tribe struck its camp of cul-de-sacs
though some still speak the Road's name in Salish,
further evidencing my aforementioned sense
of self-importance inherited from forefathers who also
wanted more and newer things such as cars without
fender dents that don't burn motor oil at a slow
if determined pace, such that checking the level
seems necessary every few hundred furlongs,
but then again I own it, even if the gasket job
cost roughly what the car was worth, and even
if I'd put repairs on a Visa—this line of thought
continuing as dawn stretched her blue shawl
over the Scapegoat, which is to say I felt the guilt
privilege affords and justly since I was driving
with my setter to hunt pheasants, chiefly a sporting
endeavor so removed from horseback and buffalo
jumps—the NPR station fizzled into white noise
and twenty miles from the next gas station I had to
relieve myself. What a flock of warblers was doing
so close to the mountains on the winter solstice
and chattering in the dark as the falling snow melted
flake by flake into my forehead, not even the most
learned ornithologist could have determined,
but they called assuredly from a slope of sage

as though they had always been calling, and I finished
pissing though perhaps I had always been pissing,
and men shouldering full quivers rode up the road,
one of them glancing to regard not traveler but song
as the light arrived, or kept arriving, as it will.

Crayons

RHINA P. ESPAILLAT

for Miss Conroy, late of P.S. 94

When the child learning English joined your class,
You gave her crayons—a whole box, to keep!—
and said, "Now draw me something you remember."

Windows were trimmed—it was early November—
with toothy pumpkins. What your student drew,
though, was her narrative: figures, afloat
on spikes of parrot green meant to be grass,
waved out to one lone figure on a boat
tilting, precarious, in a roil of blue
meant to be sky and sea, both very deep.

The next day, Miss Conroy, you unrolled,
laid out and tacked up on the bare back wall
eight yards of oak tag. From the far left end,
each artist-classmate worked to illustrate
the nation's past.
                        History would unfold
there every morning, early, day by day,
until we reached our time, then almost lean
into a future—more desire than scene—
you wanted—no, assigned us—to create.

First, Pilgrims landing, done in shades of gray—
weather, weapons, clothes, The Rock itself—all
equally severe. Then, to befriend
those somber strangers, others, bravely red

and brightly feathered, above words you said
to print in colors: *Welcome* and *Homestead,*
Sowing and *Harvest, Hunting, Hut* and *Fish.*

In memory, the scripted scenes are clear:
Arrows in flight pass safely overhead,
missing the *Settler,* bringing down the *Deer;*
crops in the *Field*—rendered in tan and gold—
to feed the *Worker, Farmer, Soldier, Priest.*
Nobody dies except the very old;
even the smiling *Turkey* on its dish
wears a corsage of *Carrots* to the *Feast.*

What simple tales we learned, early, from you
who may well have believed them, though your own
immigrant forebears found them less than true!
Your name, like mine, rang with departures, roots
severed, replanted here in fields of stone
less welcoming than crayons make them seem.

Homelands are not acquired by pure dream.
They may be stolen, and their crops denied
to true owners, to slaves who tend their fruits,
whose claims are honored after they have died—
if ever—and whose names the years erase.

How tempting now, Miss Conroy, to include,
though late, their portraits in our wistful view,
if only out of shame, or gratitude.
But let their absence say we haven't run—
only crept, at a slow, uneven pace—
toward justice; let it say we're not yet done
with your assignment, work we're pledged to do.

Ambient Violences
and Misogynies

American Studies

JOSÉ ANGEL ARAGUZ

November 22, 2016

My wife tells me of reading the *Dear
America* books as a child, those stories told
via the diaries of young women who lived

during difficult times in American history. In these
stories filled with suffering were the facts behind
the suffering. Her favorite involved the RMS *Titanic*,

the unsinkable ship that sank. I ask if
trying to imagine what it looked like was
what captivated, and she says no, says only

one book led to another, until she realized
she could never see it nor accept it.

■

After the election, my friend explains he feels
he could manage here, but not his children.
He explains he spoke to their school director,

who comforted by talking about police presence. But
if there's police, he asks, before anything happens,
what will happen when something does? American algebra:

Everything is *x* until proven *y*. Dear America,
if *x* represents what my friend feels thinking
about the police, what language do you imagine

he worries his children speaking publicly, and what
language are we speaking now? Show your work.

∎

Another friend writes: Here's a verse I think
about a lot: *And maybe the mirror of*
the world will clear once again.* She shares

she's been sick since the election, as I've
been. I imagine our voices trying to commiserate
between coughs. In physics, energy can neither be

created nor destroyed. What American physics happens here
as I read and hear her voice behind
the verse she sent? Are you, dear America,

afraid as I am that our faces will
no longer be there when the mirror clears?

*Faiz Ahmad Faiz

Somewhere I Have Never Traveled

somewhere I have never traveled
E. E. CUMMINGS

Dear planet, dear hemisphere, dear tree.
Dear whitetail buck, dear dirt, dear stone.
Dear crack in the stone from which a wildflower
called scarlet gilia rose and blossomed last summer.
Dear scarlet gilia, now desiccate and gray.
Dear everything that dies.
Dear sky, dear clouds. Dear citizen fly
dying on the windowsill. Dear windchill,
dear midautumn snow, dear woodstove,
dear split of firewood undoing itself inside.
Dear nothing which we are to perceive in this world.
Dear intense fragility. Dear nation undoing itself.
Dear equality. Dear eyes deeper than all roses.
Dear worshipped god, dear dollars, dear
sense of decency, dear home of the brave.
Dear everyone, dear dead in the war
and the peace. Dear peace. Dear piece of ass.
Dear waterboard, dear enhanced interrogation,
dear euphemism. Dear water and air. Dear detainee.
Dear rage, dear fear. Dear queered
in the myriad ways of queering.
Dear others, othered. Dear other countries.
Dear mother country. Dear tired and poor, etc.
Dear documents, dear "all men," dear women, etc.
Dear etcetera—you know who you are. Dear you-

know-who-you-are. Dear drones. Dear nonvoters.
Dear inalienable rights, dear aliens, dear Natives, who hardly exist, etc.
Dear registry, dear dead majesty, dear internment,
dear slavery, dear mass incarceration, dear prisons
and hospitals for the purpose of dear profit. Dear planet,
which will not die and will not mourn us if we do.
Dear two-by-two, dear ark. Dear sea level.
Dear Pacific Garbage Patch. Dear itch
to destroy, dear boy become a man
no good man would recognize. Dear maximize,
dear capital, dear nobody, not even the rain.
Dear America, rendering forever and death
with each breath. Dear Klansman, having got
exactly, so far, what he wants.

The Woods and the Weeds

DEBBIE WEINGARTEN

Dear America,

In third grade, I discovered that some of my relatives were exterminated—a word that made me think of rats. They were rounded up like cattle, stripped naked, pried from one another, marched in the snow toward the gas chamber and the incinerator, where they were piped out a chimney as glittering dust.

For years after that, I would stumble upon Anne Frank's words, over and over again, scrawled in secret in the dark: "In spite of everything, I still believe that people are really good at heart."

How? I wanted to ask her. I was angry. *How could you possibly think this?*

■ ■ ■

Dear red clay on my bare feet. Dear white farmhouse and smell of horses. Dear shiny pennies, buckeyes in my pocket. Dear stick-on earrings, skinny girl legs, shag carpet, the beige landscape of a station wagon. Dear red plastic sled. Dear sensation of flying. Dear hedge apples, found in the snow, hucked at one another through the trees.

■ ■ ■

Just after the election, I drove up to my favorite mountain pass with a new love. We sat and stared at the saguaros and the muted sunset sky. We felt the wind on our cheeks and watched the cars creeping up the hill, their headlights switching on one by one. We sat on a boulder so big that it felt like our very own country.

How is it that life simply ticks onward? we wondered out loud to each other. *Even on the eve of destruction?*

On Election Day, we had gone canvassing. We had begun to feel worried that more people were going to vote for Donald Trump than anyone thought. We drove my Subaru through roundabout streets, a neighborhood girdled against Davis-Monthan Air Force Base. We stood in a driveway just over the chain-link fence from the plane yard. Their metal bodies gleamed in the sunshine.

It was the middle of the day, and most people were at work. But in one house, an elderly woman looked up at us through a fog of dementia. *It's Election Day,* we said, and her daughter smiled at us politely, but shook her head a little. In an apartment, a young mother came to the door, a baby on her hip. Two toddlers in diapers looked out from behind her legs. *It's Election Day,* we said, handing her a pamphlet, and she shrugged. *It's going to be close,* we said. Her face said she was as tired as she was yesterday, and the day before that, and the day before that.

■ ■ ■

Dear tired mothers. Dear grandmothers shot with rubber bullets. Dear Black men gunned down by cops at traffic stops. Dear farmers killing themselves. Dear mothers and fathers and children on boats. Dear hundred-mile crack in the Antarctic ice shelf. Dear babies born in the desert. Dear families on planes being turned away. Dear brave people in the streets.

■ ■ ■

I have been writing the same essay over and over again like a bad dream. It's got arms like octopus tentacles, and all of them are depressing, and all of them seem not to say anything other than *this shit is depressing.* I keep wondering if I owe the reader some amount of hope. Do we? Do we owe each other hope?

I stay up writing at night, trying to manifest hope. I try to wrangle the tentacles in twenty-two-minute installments while my children watch *Paw Patrol.* When my writer friends ask what I'm working on, I sigh and say something like, *I'm just really in the weeds.* I figure that at least the excuse contains some imagery.

I have fantasies about running off into the wilderness. Someplace where the fish and bears and lightning bugs really just don't care about Donald Trump's tweets, or Russia hacking the election, or how terrifying Steve Bannon is, or the disintegration of our democracy. Someplace where I can sit in a tree and scream-sob and fixate on the stars.

What would happen if I stayed out there—made a bed out of leaves, lived on pond muck and the marrow of cattails, roasted a squirrel over a fire? What if I refused to engage, to finish my essay? What if I stayed in the weeds?

■ ■ ■

Dear fat hornworms fed to the turkeys. Dear glassy-eyed gopher in a trap. Dear javelina shot with holes. Dear baby deer I could not save. Dear truck bed of suffocated chickens. Dear all of the morning glory I have killed, entire arbors of blue-throated flowers that I have ripped from the horse fencing, their tendrils like thread. Dear all of the roofs I have climbed to gain perspective: houses I've lived in, my own once-upon-a-time Arizona barn, a three-story building in North Carolina, and on and on.

One winter, when we were teenagers, a friend and I scaled the roof of a church. We crawled past the steeple on our bellies and peered over the edge. Baby Jesus had been disappearing from the Nativity scene, and all of the newspapers had been covering it. We thought it was funny, but we also thought that with enough perspective we could solve the mystery. So we waited, keeping an eye on Replacement Baby Jesus from our perch, but no one came. Not burglars or drunk teenagers or rival church members like we'd joked.

We were unseeable. From the road came the sound of cars driving through the slush. The moon rose through the branches of a big pine tree, and the stars came out, and maybe snow even fell in our eyelashes.

■ ■ ■

Dear Dangerous Leader,

Have you ever laid belly-down on a roof in the moonlight and felt snow fall in your eyelashes? Have you witnessed the beautiful resilience of birth? Have you mussed the roots of a new plant with your fingers, stumbled upon a fiddlehead unrolling in the middle of the woods, smelled rain in the desert? Have you spent a whole night rocking a feverish child? Have you felt a great loss? Have you seen someone die? Have you cried until you felt as though you were a small, empty box on the floor?

Have you known the exhilaration of sprinting until you collapse in a fit of laughter? A best friend? A lover who makes you so happy that it stings in your chest? Have you followed a trail of ants and marveled at how they stop, each one, to deliver messages to one another? Have you napped in a cow pasture or smelled the musty breath of goats? Have you known the glorious strength of a woman? The infinite imagination of a child who has not yet begun to contain her thoughts? Have you flown a kite, sledded down a hill in new snow, picked wild sunflowers from the side of the road?

Dear Leader, *Have you not known love? Have you not known joy?*

■ ■ ■

After Anne Frank wrote the thing about people being good, she wrote this: "I simply can't build up my hopes on a foundation consisting of confusion, misery, and death. I see the world gradually being turned into a wilderness, I hear the ever approaching thunder, which will destroy us too, I can feel the sufferings of millions and yet, if I look up into the heavens, I think that it will all come right, that this cruelty too will end, and that peace and tranquility will return again."

Dear oil companies without souls. Dear politicians without shame. Dear blustery man in your golden tower. You will not win.

■ ■ ■

We stayed at the mountain pass until we could not see the saguaros anymore, and then we clambered down, skidding awkwardly on rocks in the dark. We drove toward the gleaming city, toward the TVs and the radios and the newspapers, toward this precarious future.

Dear America, may we all climb down from our perches. May we come out of the woods and the weeds.

Love,
Debbie

Something Like Tenderness

AIMEE NEZHUKUMATATHIL

I was born a snapdragon—from a burst of seeds knocked clean
by a rabbit escaping a fox. When our skull-shaped seed pods
are crispy and ready to shake, they spit seed. And when the fox
had his catch by the neck—I could do nothing but grow tipped
to light in a bit of blood rain.

America, I am your good, brown friend. For many of you—I am
the only brown friend you have. How I love being your good, brown
friend. Very good. Very brown. Many of you tell me you don't see
color, as if we're colorless, transparent, or rather—as if we're clear
like Zima, Pepsi Clear, hair gel, a varnish, seltzer, a gloss.

A few years ago in Florida, my (Catholic) Indian father had a full can
of pop thrown at his head from a pickup truck while the driver
screamed, *Go Home, Muslim Terrorist!*

He has lived in America since 1969. Longer in America than India,
his birthplace.

1969.

Other people in the parking lot just stopped and stared.
Some hurried to their cars or inside the store.

The next day, my parents went out and bought flag decals to plaster
all over their cars.

America—for over forty years before he retired as an award-winning
and patient-favorite respiratory therapist, my father has helped mostly

white geriatric folks, and white NICU babies breathe. He's missed
some of my sister's and my birthdays, plays, concerts, and tennis
matches because he was helping white people breathe.

He was helping white people breathe.
He helped white people breathe even when his eldest daughter
pouted when he missed yet another one of her tennis matches.

He helped white people breathe for forty years.

America—for over forty years, before she retired from being
an acclaimed psychiatrist, my mother was helping mostly
white people with their mental health, suffering verbal
and sometimes physical assault from her unstable patients.

And still my parents worked those jobs, even when the very people
they were taking care of screeched racist slurs right to their faces.
Yes, my parents received paychecks, but they didn't have to stay
in those often rural places where they were needed most.
They could have stayed in big cities, with even bigger paychecks.
But they love small town America, even when it doesn't love them back.

They love small town America, even when it doesn't love them back.
They love small town America, even when it doesn't love them back.

I know many of you don't interact with many brown people (why
is that?) and I'm one of your only sources of actual lived experience
as a brown woman (again, why is that?) and I'm here to say any
violence or harassment toward me and my family was never EVER
done by someone with brown skin.

Senior year in college:
I had to go to court to get a restraining order because
a white co-worker broke into my dorm room several times.
The last time, I was there sleeping when he broke in. I didn't have
my glasses on so you can imagine my terror. I screamed and
screamed for my life.

O, how I can scream when I need to save myself.

First year grad school:
The two men who attacked me while I was walking on campus
in the middle of the humid morning in Tallahassee during
my first year in grad school were white.

In the middle of the morning.

I was mailing a letter to my parents to tell them I was okay.
It happened on the way back to my apartment, after the envelope
was safely nestled in the blue mailbox with so many other letters
to parents telling them they were okay too.

∎

I sometimes wonder what happened to that letter. Did it fly away?
My parents never told me they received it.

I dropped out the next week and became a waitress in a mall and O–
all the cash I made because I let white men in suits call me honey,
call me baby, call me sugar. So much cash.

So much honey.
But I took it and took it and took it all because I thought I'd never
apply again to grad schools and at least I had fistfuls of cash.

I thought my life in words was over.
I thought my life in words was over.
I thought my life in words was over.

And when I go through the horrible rolodex of awful incidents
in my mind—I have to tell you, all, I mean all—the times I've been
followed or stalked or teased or bullied—have been by white men.
So forgive me if I laugh at your fear and hatred of brown immigrants.
Forgive me when I laugh when you say immigrants are a danger
to the fabric of our country.

Dear America, I am red clover.
Every prick at the edge of the highway makes me consider
my own red highway, mapping out very good blood to me
here in Mississippi. What a riot of joy to say in spite of

where I was scattered, today I am gathered.
I was once scattered and now I am gathered.

I am here, and growing, like a magnolia.

Dear America, I am magnolia now.
Not the white bloom. The sturdy trunk. But I want to start
with the milk. The cream of late spring, so many saucers
spilling in the shadow of the milk moon, the flower moon—
the moon of the fragrant month my oldest child was born.

For once, America—here in Mississippi, I don't look
over my shoulder. It is possible even in this place.
For once, America—I want to pour something like tenderness
back into your hands and your hands and your hands, too.

Fatherland

BLAS FALCONER

The heat not having broken all
month long, we stood

in line and watched a boy
race down the park's tallest slide,

drop into the shallow pool
below, from which he rose

renewed, a look of joy, relief
across his face. My son held

my hand, and looking up,
judged how long it'd take

to reach the top of the stairs.
In front of us, the man, a head

taller, fifty pounds, at least,
more than I, wore red trunks,

his hair, dark brown, short.
I saw the swastika first,

White Power, inked
across his back, the scene:

skeletons climbed his spine
above a sea of flames. I felt

each breakable bone
in my boy's hand, he, who

days before asked to live
with us forever. *Idiot,*

my mother called me once
because, *You think everyone*

is good. The man looked
across the park at no one,

younger than I'd have thought,
and when the line, as if

with one mind, began to move
again, he stepped forward, the foot

or two between us,
perilous, uncrossable.

No One Expects an Answer

ERIN MALONE

The checker at Safeway sings his greeting
in an operatic voice. I avoid his line.
I'd like to just say fine, thank you,

without having to hear his score about
the weather. There's such a thing as too much
cheer. An army of robots is advancing

in the workplace; a woman on the sidewalk
cries quietly. Today a man plowed his car
into a crowd in Charlottesville.

All I want is to buy this chicken, this lemon,
and vodka from the high school girl who lets them
slide past without comment, tearing

the corner of my receipt as innocently as an
afterthought. There are so many reasons

to be sorry. My grandmother is no longer
alive, that's one. And I lied
when my grandfather asked where

she was—he wouldn't remember anyway.
He wanted to go home, but we left him

with the nurses, staring at the bright
songbirds behind glass. Is this home?

No one knows. A woman dead in Charlottesville,
and every day here we are, searching

bins of softened peaches, aisles of jars.

Someone on the sidewalk breaks apart
into her hands, an army advances.
The guilty and the lost among us inflating

our chests, lying and singing, covering up.

The South

LESLEY WHEELER

Once, you knew where you were going:
from winter's unambiguous branches
through flushing eastern redbud
toward the shabby linens of the South
bleaching on dogwood racks. Toward
manly honor and chaste womanhood,
dusted with gunpowder, shaded from heat
by genocidal legacies. Not so fast,
youth I was. Not so neat. Sure, the glass
of tea will sweat where tongues grow cool
and slow as minted bourbon. Sure, some
white shoppers won't stand in the black
cashier's line, allow his wrist's revolution
to float their collards or mayonnaise jars
over a scanner's bloodshot eye. The hate
you'll recognize, thinking you can stand
to one side. An innocent cartographer.

But malice won't sit where you mapped it,
emitting a predictable growl. Stop knowing
everything and look around. Hear,
above your banging pulse, an implicated
tune, weathered and blue, voice of land
pushed up sore, its grudges cold. Those notes
twist down piney slopes, fume into creeks

by whose banks the copperheads sun
like slippery hieroglyphs. They scrawl a tale
that had been camouflaged from you even
as you sang your lines. Now the story holds
you in its lap. Now it's poised to strike.

To Occupant

COLLEEN J. McELROY

it practically leaves me speechless: this retrograde that renders you
    blind
American the beautiful—this happens under your name time after
    time

that's what I am **talking** about
    that's what **I am** talking about

tell me when I can stop on one hand counting black faces
in movies set in the glistening metropolis—tell me why it's normal

    that is what I'm talking about
      that **is what** I am talking about

listen up: I am not *them* or *other* a *mob* or *color*
the only pronouns that fit are: *I* and *me* personally

      that is what I'm **talking about**
        when I want you to hear

look at your reflection in the mirror—own your mistakes
do you have the constitution for it?

        that is what you hear
         when **I'm talking**

say it is not all right (alright) not right to push the laws back
when half of the real story has yet to be told

        talking about that
        talking shade

can you hear me America?—the same old same old
all this chaos and no disorder not for sale

> **can you hear me**
> **talking at you?**

how many died to get us here: boys dead girls disappeared
sheets wearing suits—the rest weeping when the horsemen come

> **I'm talking about**
> **who's not**
> **talking, America**

Obit

VICTORIA CHANG

America—died on February 14, 2018, and my dead mother doesn't know. Since her death, America has died a series of small deaths, each one less precise than the next. My tears are now shaped like hooks but my heart is damp still. If it is lucky, it is in the middle of its beats. The unlucky dead children hold telegrams they must hand to a woman at a desk. The woman will collect their belongings and shadows. My dead mother asks each of these children if they know me, have seen me, how tall my children are now. They will tell her that they once lived in Florida, not California. She will see the child with the hole in his head. She will blow the dreams out of the hole like dust. I used to think death was a kind of anesthesia. Now I imagine long lines, my mother taking in all the children. I imagine her touching their hair. How she might tickle their knees to make them laugh. The dead hold the other half of our ticket. The dead are an image of wind. And when they comb their hair, our trees rustle.

Titration

BRENDA HILLMAN

I. Dear American gun owner,

Several days have passed since the most recent mass shootings. I want to write to you, as a mother, a grandmother & a teacher, about your guns. I don't know you, but I know you aren't all white nationalists. Some of you hunt for your food. Some like marksmanship & shooting ranges. Some go to gun shows to admire the modern technology. Some of you are my relatives.

I've been trying to think about your fear of being without weapons, especially without AK-15s & AK-47s. I feel despair that you are unreachable. It is the lunging inarticulate despair of an adolescent trying to talk to parents when the parents can't hear. Your neighbors cannot reach you. These shootings numb your neighborhoods with sorrow, rage & depression while you remain unreachable. Part of the work is to keep the rage & sorrow alive, not to pursue comfort after these incidents. The country waits for there to be "enough"—as in high school chemistry where something was added drop by drop & the color suddenly changed from pale blue to orange, or orange to blue—titration, it was called.

The weeks after these shootings have a familiar pattern: news outlets describe the shooter; law enforcement searches for a "motive." The immediate motive behind such shootings is usually hatred of people's skin tone, hatred of religious differences, hatred of classmates, loose hatred in an unstable mind. But the motive behind the motive is gun profiteering. Behind the sense of safety & power your guns give you—& what manipulates you into rejecting commonsense limitations on weapons— is corporate money made at the expense of the safety of your children. You who hate government have been made fools of.

Maybe you are a mild-mannered white woman in New Hampshire watching Fox News with a pistol in the oak chest. Perhaps you are in Kansas keeping a fast rifle as self-defense against intruders. Perhaps you're in Texas reading nationalist websites on your phone. Maybe you're a church-going father of three girls who believes the elites in New York are servants of Satan. Maybe you find military weapons aesthetically pleasing & sexy. Perhaps you are a grandmother who finds our current president's sociopathic messaging honest & refreshing after years of political vapidity. A friend in Frankfurt described how his grandmother was sexually attracted to Hitler & killed herself when Hitler died.

Where are your firearms made? Where are the factories? I believe some are in Virginia. I need to research this. When I get to Virginia, I will go with my friend to find the factories. How do workers endure the monotony of assembling assault rifles? Are they like any workers we know, waiting for the lunch break, & what do they have for lunch?

I know you can't give up your weapons, but I'm asking you to support reasonable limits on their use. I'm asking that you give up your commitment to fear. We all have things that are hard to give up. I once loved cigarettes. These things are hard to give up. I ask that you give up your fear of others & your love for these violent endings.

Sincerely,
Brenda Hillman

II. Dear American who doesn't own a gun,

Several years ago, I wrote a poem about selling my father's old World War II pistol. I'd been teaching Dickinson's "My Life had stood, a Loaded gun," a poem about accessing poetic power as if it were a weapon. Dickinson's gun is of course not a physical object but a metaphor. I was meeting my brothers in Tucson to begin cleaning out the family house after our father's death. I had been asked for a poem about gun violence for an anthology. My poem has a flat reportorial style. My brothers & I were trying to get rid of the firearm our father had kept hidden since the 1940s, the mystique of which was dramatized by our lack of knowledge about where & why he kept it. My younger brother carried it gingerly away to a gun shop.

My father's family, of southern lineage, uses pellet guns, BB guns

& hunting rifles; they hunt deer & other wild game. Our grandfather shot rats with pellet guns in the corn barn. I identified completely with the rats. My brothers & I, spending time on that farm in our childhood summers, developed no special eros around guns, though they chased each other around, fake-shooting & fake-dying, plunging to the carpet with loud groaning, arguing about who was really dead. Is the love of the gun shape connected to a Y chromosome? Probably not. Our leader blames mass shootings on video games.

The right, the right. The Second Amendment is a time-specific right, associated with early militias & muskets that took ten minutes to load. The right to bear arms was considered a powerful right by rural settlers; the right wing remains committed to this revolutionary throwback issue. The fierce independence, the fear of being dominated by an outside power; the fear that an authority will hold unreasonable sway over you—all these led to a particularly American defiance. Settlers & occupiers since the beginning of time fear the not-us: protect family; our tribe against *them*; protect property & life. The Second Amendment, made by & for free white men only, assumed militias in the street to guard a particular idea of home as an individual & not a communal space.

Dickinson's poem & the terrified rural right both express defiance toward authority. But those clinging to their guns are physically fearful, holding nothing in common with the ferocity of Dickinson's speaker who writes of the power of her imagination as a loaded gun.

After Sandy Hook & the 2016 election, I signed up for some of the Second Amendment websites so that, like Mithridates VI who poisoned himself a bit each day to prepare for a possible "big poisoning," I could get used to their craziness. I couldn't read them. After Parkland, I decided to turn off all media the moment one shot is fired. Impossible; I can't turn off all movies or "bullet points" in your PowerPoint. Gun eros flows from the corporate world. A poet recently reported (a little proudly) that her poetry reading in an international setting was punctuated by guards firing assault weapons into the air.

According to a 2016 study by Harvard and Northeastern Universities, more than half of the privately owned firearms are by just 3 percent of Americans. Congressman Mark DeSaulnier sent this out: "The United States makes up 4.4 percent of the world's population, but holds almost half of all civilian-owned guns worldwide and the homicide rate is 20 times higher than the combined rates of 22 developed countries. The commonsense reforms we have made in California are working. As the state with the top-rated gun laws, we also have the ninth lowest rate of gun violence in the country. Universal background checks, mandatory waiting periods, and an assault weapons ban are among the reforms that protect public safety while not infringing on Second Amendment rights."

For decades I've participated in demonstrations that have turned "violent"—meaning, protesters end up getting hurt. We are losing patience. In a letter, my hero Rosa Luxemburg says she used her gun to help get a pamphlet printed in 1917. I read this in the context of her time; a gun ensuring speech, not silencing it. When I told an elderly friend that, though I am not an absolute pacifist, I don't think I could shoot anyone, she said, *You never know what you would do in the moment.* She had been in the Polish Underground in World War II & had shot a Nazi soldier to protect another woman. She thought about it every day, she said.

I know my position on guns is possibly a luxury. Though my parents come from poverty, I have the advantage of being white & middle class. I am a teacher with beloved family & friends; I can write my strange poems & talk to trees or the spirit world in great freedom. My participation in street protests is optional—I protest when I can.

This is not Burma or Haiti. If an intruder came through my front door to get my grandchildren, I might lose control. Though he is himself a woman's child, I might hit him with a pan. I might hit him with a dish or a lamp. But I don't believe I would fire a weapon at another human being; that involves planning by having the gun handy, & my inner authorities & my old Christianity say one should not plan to kill, whether under orders or because of hatred or ideology.

That is as far as I've gone in my thinking, America. We need to live so we aren't full of fear. Not doing the wrong thing is on the way to doing the right thing.

Sincerely,
Brenda Hillman

Sentinel

TOD MARSHALL

If a heron stood watch on the bank of that pond
where bluegill bit whatever we hooked to the end of a line
and a curly-q of smoke wrote a last illiterate scribble,
sloppy signature that tried to say *this is our name, this is who I am*

in a wide sky over hills and fields we wandered as children,
then cruelty was the word we learned early: long slow diphthong
at the center like dark clouds in the west, quick *t* at the end
like the sudden swing of a door slapping the siding of a dented trailer,

sly *y* turned *e* like the missing catch that's supposed to keep
the door in check, screen torn, storm glass soon to shatter.
And if, later, we laughed and threw bottles that we found in a man's
    camp
among a grove of trees, if we dumped his water, burnt soiled clothes,

and scattered his bedding, then we were just acting as we'd been
    taught.
Or so I would like to say. The willows swayed and made no case
    against us.
The thorns of locust trees stayed elegant and sharp. Maybe the heron
    launched
into a sky that held birds and smoke in the same blue palm. The
    planks

he'd used for a bed cracked in the fire pit. Greasy blankets in the blaze
put forth a dark smell. We were boys trying to find the easiest way
to *violence, deep class issues,* and *let's brutalize someone worse off than us.*

It's forty years later, and now it seems like the word we learned was
    America,

four syllables owned by only a few. Of course, I never saw the man's
    face
when he came back to his things scattered. We did not watch.
We ran and swam and cannonballed off a rope swing for a few hours
and then half-carried, half-dragged dozens of fish back to the trailer
    park

where we gutted them on porches, hosing everything off before our
    fathers
saw the mess, believing that the sweet meat of those spiny-backs
    would be fried
with butter for dinner, the brilliant blue and bright orange behind the
    gills,
the subtle green flecks like the beginning of a rainbow, oblivious

to how our mothers would throw it all away, the flesh rancid, a lesson
    in language
that takes more than forty years to learn: if you keep them too long on
    a stringer,
metal clips through soft skin under the jaw, they go dry and stiff, eyes
    gray
and black as if they'd never been alive, and then you can do anything
    to them.

In Case of Active Shooter

HEATHER RYAN

An active shooter is defined as an individual who is actively engaged in killing and/or attempting to kill people in a specific and often confined area using a firearm(s). It is unlikely that such an event will occur on campus; however, in the event of such a scenario, it is imperative that you know and understand the following:

- If possible, leave the area. It will, however, be unlikely you will know which way to exit or how to avoid the active shooter.

- The area of a college affected by an active shooter is generally confined, and is referred to as "the zone of immediate impact." It is unlikely you will be in the zone of immediate impact. You should still take cover, barricade all entrances, turn off the lights, cover the windows, and stay quiet if you cannot leave campus. It is especially important all cell phones are turned to silent (not "vibrate").

- False alarms are all too common, as we live in a culture that has decided a heavily armed citizenry is a good idea. You would be surprised by how many, though they typically don't make it this far— "this far" being a full lockdown. Your professor remembers one time at her children's school when a Civil War reenactor parked down the street and was loading his car with Civil War–era weapons.

- Your professor will mention this instance a few moments after the lockdown as a way to calm everyone's fears, including her own. She'll end the story with the phrase, "You can't be too safe, can you?"

- The phrase "too safe," used in a rhetorical question, will be said frequently in case of a false alarm of active shooter.

- In case of the inverse, it will not be uttered once.

- But in a lockdown situation, you cannot be sure. You will hope this is a silly false alarm. You'll hope it's another Civil War reenactor. Or someone going to a costume party, dressed as Arnold Schwarzenegger in *Terminator 2*, or a national guardsman carrying his weapon out of uniform. After all, the armory is just down the block, and you've seen soldiers there, in the parking lot, many times.

- You will cling to these theories—however thinly spun—even as you prepare for the reality that may soon come through the door.

- In case of active shooter or false alarm, it is recommended that you take cover immediately and find items to use as improvised weapons, which include the following:
  - Stapler/mechanical stapler
  - Three-hole punch
  - Lectern or podium
  - Fire extinguisher
  - Books
  - Toner cartridge
  - Hot beverages or water bottles (if full)

- In case of active shooter, this list of improvised weapons is not complete.

- Your professor will direct you to find improvised weapons, and as you grab up the staplers and hole-punches, she will recall the afternoon a group of bullies chased her home, punching her face, stomach, and arms and how her little brother—only eight—came out of her house with a handful of eggs, threatening to pelt the bullies.

- Her brother's threats thwarted those bullies. But your professor is under no illusion that your improvised weapons will work. She believes, though, that gathering them makes everyone feel less small and vulnerable as you wait for this to end.

- You may feel the urge to call close friends and family members. Resist this, as any noise—particularly the half-whispered, frantic, one-sided dialogue created by such a situation—can attract attention.

- You may, however, text your close friends and family. In case of active shooter, it is recommended that you keep text messages brief but sincere. Apologizing for any past wrongs or arguments is acceptable, though be cautious about instigating a lengthy exchange.

- Remember that this is a crisis, and you may have several people to contact.

- Because you're mostly young adults, you may not yet fully understand the weight of those potential last messages as much as your professor does. This is a writing class, and she's committed to making you better writers, but even she—in case of active shooter or false alarm—will stare blankly at the screen of her iPhone, and will wonder whom to text, what to say, and how to say it.

- No course objectives cover composition strategies in case of active shooter. Your professor would argue that all writing instruction covers such situations, but she would also acknowledge that one should never have to consider such rhetorical situations.

- Your professor has three teenagers, and, as it turns out, two of them are on campus today. They are eighteen and sixteen and she thinks, momentarily, that this is the worst kind of luck one can have. They will be the first people she texts, to make sure they are safe and to assuage any fear they may be experiencing. She'll tell them she's sure it's a false alarm, though she's not at all sure. She will tell them to stay away from windows, doors.

- She will hope this is enough to keep them safe. Statistically, she knows it's likely that the shooter will remain in one building, and part of her will wish that the active shooter comes to her building and not theirs, if it comes to that.

- Resist the urge to text your unrequited love a declaration of your affection. No matter the outcome of the active-shooter scenario, you will make more problems than you will solve. Imagine his/her/their response if you do not make it out of the active shooter scenario; imagine your horror if the active-shooter scenario turns out to be a false alarm.

- Your professor will think specifically of the one former love she regrets losing, the one she still wonders about, and still sometimes ponders the slow, inevitable breakup. She will half-construct a message to him, then delete it.

- In case of active shooter and/or false alarm, you may look at your cell phone and wonder how to send the necessary text messages to your family and friends. You may search for a joke to make it seem like you are okay, to make it easier for them.

- You will learn there are no good jokes in a time like this, no words that will be big enough to capture your fear and shaky hope and love. A poet might be able to write such a joke, but you are not a poet. Neither is your professor, so you can't ask her.

- It is recommended that your text messages to family and friends be brief and factual, and include one clear sentiment that expresses the relationship you've shared ("I love you" works well).

- In case of active shooter, your professor will take pains to make sure you are okay. She will smile, even though she, too, is shaking. She will help you move the table in front of the door, stack the chairs into a heap in front of that. She will tell the story about the Civil War reenactor, of course; another about the chemistry professor who blew up a small part of the lab; yet another about the box left outside an office that was "disposed of" by the bomb squad, which is one way to say, "caused to explode in a controlled manner." It turned out to be kiwis shipped from Australia. She will repeat the phrase "no one was hurt" after each story like a benediction.

- In the darkness of the classroom, your professor may come to each of you and say a few words. Perhaps you have not known your professor long—maybe this is the first week or two of the term—but she will want you to be calm. She also doesn't know any other way to deal with her worry over her children, or her friends, or other students. She will wonder at the silence of the building and campus. You may notice her closing her eyes and taking slow breaths. This is a way to control her fears and calm herself. Certainly, she is not conjuring images of the active shooter in her head.

- Though if she did, she might imagine a male, as statistically it is most likely, and she might even conjure an image of his fatigues, his black backpack, his black hat and gloves, the sheen on the gun he holds in his arms, cradled like a dearly wanted infant.

- In case of active shooter, your professor's mind might play out various scenarios that could soon take place. She imagines the risks, the possible need for sacrifice. She thinks of her children, then sends their faces away. This is not the time to think of them.

- In case of active shooter or false alarm, law enforcement response time averages three to four minutes. You might find yourself counting the seconds until you hear the sirens. This is an appropriate response to stress and fear.

- If the sirens do not come for some time, and when you do not hear gunshots, screams, or other sounds of violence, you might engage in quiet conversation. You might show your professor the jokes that your parents made over a group text about whether they should pray for you or not after you told them you were holding the fire extinguisher, which is the best improvised weapon. You explained that you knew the jokes were not entirely for your benefit, that it was also a way for them to manage what might be the last minutes of your life. You knew this because at the end your mom asked how many men were in the room, and your dad said, "No matter what, you do not let anyone through that door."

- Your professor wishes she could thank your dad for that. It made her, momentarily, feel less responsible for the sixteen other people in the room.

- In case of active shooter or false alarm, you may notice the veterans will be the most at ease. One may gently say, "You got this, professor," every so often, in a voice so controlled and clear it may remind you of a beloved aunt or uncle, helping you with some new skill when you were five or six, perhaps hitting the plastic simulacrum of a baseball off a tee, or diving into the deep end of the pool. He will be the calmest of everyone, and will continue doing homework for another class while other students sit on the floor against the far wall looking scared.

- He will tell your professor, in a voice full of experience, "It's a lot harder to kill people than you think."

- Mimicking his demeanor may help you manage your own fear, though it will not completely erase it.

- In case of active shooter, keep in mind that you will probably live and escape physically unscathed. In case of active shooter, remember that this is a numbers game, and an active shooter has only thus far been able to kill fifty-eight people at once. Your school has quite a few more students than this.

- Your professor has made a mental note to check the above bullet point annually to ensure the number is still correct when she revises this syllabus. She has revised it once.

- When you get the word that the threat was an explosion and report- ed gunman close to campus, but that the SWAT team has "deter- mined the campus is safe," your professor will breathe deeply once, twice. She will smile, turn on the lights, unlock the door.

- Later, your professor will sit at her desk and cry—the kind of crying where the body is incapable of speaking. *Everyone is safe*, she will remind herself. *Everything turned out okay.* Her sixteen-year-old son will come into her office and appear shocked at his mother's sobbing. He has already been through several lockdowns in his life.

- At her desk, she will recall the friend who was at Virginia Tech during their shooting, how he lost a student that day, and the arc of grief and fear that determined his life for the few years after. She will think about Umpqua Community College, where a shooting occurred just the year before, how she could have been that pro- fessor, had she not gotten this job. The professor killed there was teaching a writing class she's taught at least a dozen times. He was an alumnus of her own program.

- In the first few seconds of the lockdown, one thought came to her calmly and rationally: *you knew this would happen eventually.*

- It is this thought that will allow her—before the crying at the desk, and the recollection of her friend at V-Tech, or her professional dop- pelgänger at Umpqua—to understand what to do once the lockdown is lifted. She will smile at each of you. She will postpone an assign- ment, change a reading, ask the student who is a parent if she was able to reach her daycare provider.

- Your professor will usher everyone out, and will be the last one in the room, so she can turn off the lights, lock the door.

- She will slowly look over the room. She's taught here hundreds of times by now, and the room quickly became familiar, boring even. There is the printer and the reams of paper stored haphazardly underneath. There is the computer, and the whiteboard, and the projector. There is the collection of remote controls she still has not mastered.

- In the light canting through the blinds, the room will look newly sinister: the collection of staplers and hole-punches at the front on the instructor's workstation, the fire extinguisher set awkwardly back in its mount on the wall. She will notice the windows again: *Why are they so big?* she will ask herself. She wonders how long it will take for the room to look normal again.

- In case of false alarm, you will be surprised at how quickly normality will return. How, within days, you will look for the hole-punch without remembering the way you held it in your hands, tested its weight, and judged it as a weapon. You will again ignore the fire extinguisher on the wall. There will be no fracturing of the class's personality, nor any sense of unification or coming together. You will be bored sometimes. You will make friends. You'll hate the person who sits across from you.

- The texts your parents and children and siblings and former or current loves sent you—the admonitions to fight back, or hide, or the simple fervent *I love you*'s issued under fear and threat of death— will be lost in the inevitable march of other texts to pick up milk, or where to meet for the matinee, or a gif of a man slipping on ice.

- Your professor will marvel at how easy it is to slip back into everyday life, how this will become a story she can tell over cocktails, as though it were the same as other stories of calamity narrowly averted, stories she has perfected: the car hitting black ice and turning, slowly, in perfect, graceful circles until it slumped against a hedge; the $500 deposit she made at the ATM that got stuck in the machine; the RV whose axle broke on I-5, the tire bouncing along the interstate, cars dodging it, the axle sending sparks all over the roadway in dainty arcs.

- These stories are different, she will notice. They are set into motion by natural or technological forces out of anyone's immediate control. Though she will still tell the story, she will laugh about it, laugh about her sobbing in particular.

- It will surprise her how quickly she will laugh.

"My Country, 'Tis of Thee" (arranged for Brazen Bull)

ALEXANDRA TEAGUE

> A Greek device used to torture...the Brazen Bull had an
> acoustic setup that converted human screams into the sound
> of a bull...[through] a complex system of tubes and stops
> MEDIEVAL CHRONICLES

Bellow and bellicose   and the men   and the man's crying
on the stand   red-faced arrogant even in distress   are furnacing
hot new foundries in the news   melting the metals they have
always melted   and women are singing in the burning bronze
and also   and also me and the time I was six   and twenty
and twelve and forty   and I believe   and of thee I sing
of the scared-into and the clamped-quiet woods of shame
bottle shatter and condoms'   spent fireworks' rocket-red glare
in another song   that is not the song the women sing in the key
of keys-spiked-from-fists for the last three blocks   and the dream
of another door   sweet land of liberty   of thee of me   in the burning
beast where whoever stokes the fire and turns the knob
is righteous   is the liberty bell's hard shell   in the land of our fathers
our fathers our fathers   the clapper of the women's laced boots
the women's high heels   the women's bare feet   that do not sound
like bells from inside   that do not sound like singing   but the snorting
of ancient pipes to the tubes to the sky of I don't believe   and she was
paid   and she wants   she only   she   sweet sweet land   sweet lamb
of a girl in the quiet that was never quiet   in the prolonged burning
of the woods and the rills   that is just a pretty word for a stream
where a girl should take off her clothes and the bull will come

the bear will come in his suit of a beast   and will be a prince inside
so the girl should kneel to be pawed   to be eaten   to believe he is
who he says he is   and she should love him when he takes his fur off
and her mortal tongue should wake to sing as it melts   of the pilgrims'
pride   that she's saved for him in the templed hills of the dark
bronze body   that is not her body closed and cast into a form
around her where she cries and it bellows   Great God our king
and our fathers' God to thee and thee and let freedom ring
through its nose   and its breath   and the piped-to-silence
steam of her voice   hot enough inside to break the rocks.

Reply All

SHOLEH WOLPÉ

Dear America,
You used to creep into my room,
remember?

I was eleven and you kept coming,
night after night, in Tehran, slid in
from inside the old radio on my desk, past
the stack of geometry homework, across
the faded Persian carpet, and thrust
into me, with rock and roll thumps.

I loved you more than bubble gum,
more than the imported bananas
street vendors sold for a fortune.
I thought you were azure, America,
and orange, like the sky, and poppies,
like mother's new dress, and kumquats.

I dreamed of you America, I dreamed
you every single night with the ferocity
of a lost child until you became true like flesh.
And when I arrived at you, you punched
yourself into me like a laugh.

Abracadabra

SANDRA MEEK

Asphalt slag: Say a'a lava. A yard's
dank swamp: Say pampas, a sawgrass marsh.

A man at stalk: Glad a man's
at watch. A match's spark: What warms

all dark. Tall grass. A vacant shack.
A gnat-clad lamp's ash star: Aghast, say

at Mass, an all-day's pray at an altar, far
away. An alarm call, a fatal

flaw: A gaff. A lark. A gag.
A gag—a bandana's wad: Say what balms

a gasp. A car's crank, gas, a way
away—a latch that stays.

A frat-chant, *tap that ass*: A psalm's
mantra, a ballad's

track. A lay? A bang? Say that flat—
a gang's attack: A tramp

that asks. Law's task, a warrant's
ask: A grasp

at straws—stall a man's start?
A slap: A pat. Claw marks: A back

scratch—talk, charm; a thrash,
that's all. An arm's

want's wand, harm's arc
at bay—say what was,

wasn't. Scars, flashbacks, stats
that swarm, sad math: Say blank

and blank = blanks. Say abstract art
what chalk-drawn lays: Say

what'll wash away.

The Power of Panic/
The Power of Art

Mortar Shells, Lunch, and Poetry

SCOTT MINAR

Dear America,

My friend Saleh Razzouk sits having lunch in his apartment in Aleppo. He may be working on poems he is translating by Raid Saleh Hussein or Linda Abdel Baki, when a mortar fragment finds its way through his kitchen window. I think we can imagine the crackle of glass, the stinging thud of its passage through a wall on the other side, the shrug of shock he instantly makes, and the quick turn of his head. Saleh does not live in Aleppo's worst neighborhood, far from it. But this is his reality nonetheless. His reality, his life. I think when I hear from him sometimes that the depression is far stronger than the fear. His son has been missing for years, his wife gone to Dubai. He is a secular Muslim educated in England and Poland, a university professor. He grew up in a village in Syria that was half-Muslim and half-Jewish. He has no prejudice; he wasn't raised with it. He writes short stories with a modernist edge: a man is in the Turkish bath recently reopened in Aleppo while his home is burning down. Saleh's character enters the bath to give him the news—the steam, the hot water, the nakedness.

A war zone is a place where people are murdered, where buildings are calved to rubble, where the noise is unbearable. Yet people live there. It is not really a "zone" at all but a place where people live: civilians, the old, children—an artist translating poems and fiction into English because he loves it.

The first of Saleh's translations that I saw was by Syrian poet Raid Saleh Hussein, whom Saleh knew personally and who died at age twenty-eight in the 1980s. He had been exiled to Iraq, imprisoned and tortured by the regime there, and ultimately succumbed.

. . .

I write a lot: poems, essays, some criticism. But none of them is as important as this. I am writing to say there are consequences for our actions in the world. Americans graze on news and events, certainly process our concerns and cares as most people do in countries with significant access to news, generally speaking. We do this at a distance. When the emergency comes to your door, through your kitchen window, it changes things. Saleh Razzouk's life is not the worst in Syria. That would be the sarin gas attacks, the mindless destruction by bombs, the mindful killing from snipers and frontal attacks. But his life is nonetheless tragic by our or any standards. Relativity is useless there. My connection with Dr. Razzouk is through literature and art, as strange as that may sound even to me.

Saleh uses his translations, his correspondence, his literary discussions and speculations, even his own history and story, as a survival mechanism and a purpose for his life in such circumstances. And that, from my point of view, is truly remarkable. To find solace in a thing so ephemeral is understandable, but to find purpose and life there in the middle of death-dealing and despair is extremely hard to fathom. Yet here we are.

Consequences are interesting things. I open my lunch box from Starbucks: half a peanut butter sandwich, sliced cucumber and carrots, ranch dressing, a few chocolate-covered coffee beans. When I write to Saleh about what I am doing, where I go, I am conscious of what I say. I know he can't do the simplest of things: sit in a coffee shop and talk to a friend or colleague, drink coffee regularly. His electricity works three hours a day; water flows sometimes through his pipes. He is alone. Money, his pay, is an issue. Yet we write each other several times a day. He sends poems and stories he has translated; sometimes I make suggestions. We work to publish these in the States, England, and elsewhere. He translates my poems and commentaries into Arabic and publishes these in venues across the world. In all this activity, I can never forget where he is and how he lives. But I want to. It is very pleasant working with him. He is extremely learned and skilled, a superb writer himself. He helps me more than I help him. I think about that.

I started writing poetry as a result, in part, of growing up with Holocaust survivors in Cleveland in the 1960s and 1970s. Eventually, I turned to Paul Celan's poetry, which I felt I understood perfectly past a certain point. But this had nothing to do with those whom I knew growing up. It had to do with my personal experience with despair from another source. Despair can bring us very low, or it can make us smarter and stronger than we have ever been. It is not sorrow, but sorrow's Platonic sphere. In *"Tenebrae,"* Celan writes, *"Bete Herr, / bete zu uns, / wir sind nah."* The lines translate as "Pray Lord, / pray to us, / we are near." This remarkable inversion—that God should pray to us, perhaps ask our forgiveness—is the wise result of despair caused by perceived or actual abandonment. How is this abandonment, Celan's in his poem, effectively different from Hussein's or Razzouk's? Writers and people under these circumstances begin to dig in and push because their feet are on the ground. Technique is not the point, aesthetics are not the point, fame is certainly not. The remarkable achievement of Hussein's poetry and Razzouk's translations for American audiences is to plant us on the ground alongside them and show us where they are existentially, psychically.

Beyond despair, through it, and out to the impossibly tough sunlight and darkness of the other side.

What is the point of literary criticism? Of translation? If not to expand humanity and to succor, then what? Art itself is a balm of remarkable effectiveness. And a purpose, of course. A single human being is a very small thing. We can water our dirt, comfort those immediately around us, try to live for a day and be in the moment. But the circles of our influence radiate. This globalism has positive and negative effects. It is in some ways terra incognita.

The last poem I received from Saleh Razzouk is Riad Saleh Hussein's "A Moon":

A Moon

Everything the shepherd said to the mountain
And the river to the trees
And everything people said or did not say
In dance and in wars and in yards
I told you about.
The girl who was singing behind the window
The gravel that was crushed under the train's wheels
And the grave that is still sleeping happy for centuries

I told you about.
Here's what the shepherd said:
My body's flower: each morning
I harvest it, then throw it out into the street,
Allowing leaders, wise men, and thieves to step on it.
And my body's flower—each evening
I collect its scattered petals for you
And tell you of everything that happened to me.

Can we hear in this poem something of the poet's country? The sound of his voice in his own language would surely surprise and confuse us. Yet the translation reaches across. Whose flower? Whose scattered body telling us everything that has happened?

Yours,
Scott

I Am the Witness:
Accidents in a Time of Trump

JEN HIRT

The story started like so many accident stories: a hurried late morning, the pileup of minor delays, the fateful random decisions conspiring to put me second in line in the middle of three southbound lanes at the stoplight.

First in line was a BMW with bumper stickers: *Trump / Pence* and *This Is Your Brain on Porn*, warning of a shriveled brain in an otherwise empty head. I took a picture. It was February 8, 2017, twenty days after the inauguration. My reaction to such tableaux had swiped through all the filters. Bright Mockery. Muted Despair. Red Anger. Normal.

I might have wished ill will upon the driver of the BMW.

I did wish ill will upon the driver.

The light turned and I wasn't ready because I had two hands on my phone, zooming in on the porn sticker for a second photo. Was it really a shriveled brain? Did people really think that watching porn would shrink your cerebral capabilities? Cars rolled and I tossed my phone onto the seat without getting the second photo. Then I looked up as a red truck plowed through the light and T-boned the Trump car so hard it hit another car and all three spun like disintegrating asteroids.

I stared at the empty intersection, not understanding what happened—my eyes and my brain couldn't put it all together. Smashed vehicles hissed and sputtered in the lanes to the left, the truck way off to the far side and up on the walk. The whole world of traffic was stopped behind me. I put those facts together. Then I added one more: I had just taken the very last photo of that person's car.

Now the first in line, I pulled the wrong way into a reserved parking spot at an insurance agency and grabbed my phone, which had fallen on the floor. It was still open to the camera function and I tapped it closed, embarrassed and guilty and sick to my stomach. I headed to the intersection to help.

The red truck was closest to me. The driver was a young man, and he held his shaking arms wide as he exclaimed, on the verge of tears, about the crumpled front, the smashed headlights, the gush of fluids leaking close to his shoes. I was right there to see him gasp in disbelief over his truck instead of the people he'd hit, who, I could now see, were both women.

The helper in me snapped. Instead of asking him if he was okay, I laid into him with a tirade, without really thinking it through. I'm a quiet person who is called "the voice of reason" as both joke and praise. That day, though, I found the voice of rage. I yelled at him that he'd run a red light and hit two women and he'd almost hit me, and this is what happens when you don't pay attention to your personal space and the important personal spaces around you and ten feet ahead and ten cars ahead and *hell, let's keep going with this*, you are what happens when people can't think ten days ahead or ten months or ten years, you are disrespectful and distracted and dismantling civility, you are driving too fast, you are ruining the mornings of women, you are not fit for this century.

"I saw you run the red light, I am the witness," I insisted, once, twice, three times, and maybe I'm still saying it. And he kept yelling, "This isn't my fault. This isn't my fault." I disagreed in the new rhetorical style of 2017, the one where you have to hold firm about how facts are facts, not opinions, not optional. I pointed for his benefit: there's where I had been watching, here's who I had been behind, how all three lanes on my side had the green light, how he'd had a red light, how it was obvious if you thought about it. I worked a schematic in the air for him. He relented. "My truck was making a noise. I looked down for a second. It was only a second. I thought the light would still be green." *Of course you did.*

Finally, he approached the women he'd hit. I don't know what he said to them. EMTs checked one woman's hip, one woman's back. Both were crying. I didn't know who the driver of the Trump car was. Strangers put arms around shoulders. The guy just stood there. He motioned away the EMTs because, masculinity. The cops arrived and I reconstructed the scene for them: the red truck ran the red light and hit the Trump car who hit the other car.

"The Trump car?" asked one.

"The car with the Trump bumper sticker," I said. It was a red-and-white sticker, brighter than the brain-on-porn bumper sticker.

"You mean the BMW?"

"The huge red speeding truck hit the Trump car." Voice of reason, voice of rage.

"So the Ford hit the BMW."

Don't you see the metaphor! I wanted to yell. *The huge red speeding truck is Trump's administration and they have no intention of helping out or respecting the forgotten lower class or the working whites or the religious right or the wealthy BMW owners or anyone except themselves (and the Russians) that's why "they've" just T-boned one of "their" own and are denying responsibility and the Trumpers aren't even smart enough to see what their president is doing to them.* I didn't say any of that.

And I did not tell them I had the last ever photo of that car. It seemed too hard to explain why I had been taking the photo in the first place: "Well, it's the pairing of the two bumper stickers, the irony that people are still worried about porn altering your brain, literally shrinking it, and those same people have voted for a sociopath who is possibly being blackmailed by the Russians who probably have video of him acting out porn fantasies, and there is no doubt there is something amiss with *his brain*, what with the lies and late-night tweetstorms (is that what we're calling them?), so what we have here, on the back of this BMW, is what's wrong with America."

I didn't even tell any friends about the photo. I told them about the accident, about the guy, about my tirade, but not the photo, symbol of my own complicity.

I told no one and looked at it all the time.

Susan Sontag wrote about startling photos in *Regarding the Pain of Others*. She said, "We want the photographer to be a spy in the house of love and of death, and those being photographed to be unaware of the camera, 'off guard.' No sophisticated sense of what photography is or can be will ever weaken the satisfactions of a picture of an unexpected event seized in mid-action by an alert photographer."

It took me a few days to realize why I was not discussing the photo yet also obsessing over it. It is unsettling because the satisfaction Sontag speaks of is there but not there. I thought I was the alert photographer documenting the unexpected event of waiting behind yet another dumb Trump voter whose bumper stickers displayed no understanding of consequences. I thought it was that simple, that I could then drive on with my day, toss that photo up on Facebook, have a good laugh.

Instead, that photo now represents a different unexpected event, the one I couldn't see coming. The red truck, perpetually out of frame, reminds me that while I was initially trying to capture my awareness that this Trump supporter was "unaware" of my camera and "off guard" to my analysis, it turns out I was unaware and off guard too. In the end, the photo says more about me (smug, angry, uninjured). The photo has a lecture: *Mockery is the airbag, saving you from injury but not from harm.* The photo speaks in portents: *Watch the periphery, because the problem in front of you is nothing compared to what's coming.*

Every few days, I swipe through my photos and think about deleting the one of the minute before the accident. It's not a good picture. It makes sense to no one but me. It is time to move on. But I can't tap delete, because it's also asking me a question, a good question: *Didn't you want this role as a spy in the house of love and of death?*

Poetic Justice

ROB CARNEY

This happened on November 9th
in Salt Lake City

on the corner of 500 North
and Morton Drive,

a spot that used to be in Mexico,
and before that

a tribal footpath, crossing from the mountains
to a million migratory birds.

■

Rewind from there and you'll see mastodons,
mastodons sensing

that the air has changed:
no spring on the way

with its snowmelt grasses,
or violets coming

like the Earth's best secret...violets
they've been waiting all winter to eat.

■

Walk it back more
and it's the home of crabs, sideways stepping

through tide pools,
the corner of 5th North and Morton

on the Inland Sea.
It helps to remember.

    ■

Anyway, after the ballots were counted,
a Somali girl, walking to school, fifth grade,

her head and hair covered as always,
was happy about her teacher,

or noticing the weather,
or thinking that burnt toast smelled too familiar...

like that Red Cross ambulance
hit by a mortar...

when the crossing guard holding his sign out said,
"Enjoy your free flight back to the jungle."

    ■

I don't know what her backpack weighed,
but carrying that moment around all day—

and in her memory
forever—

probably felt like shouldering
a broken moon,

    ■

though that's not the end of the story

    ■

because a dire wolf
(long extinct, but not today)

turned that white man
into red screaming.

Throat gone first. Then his liver.
Then part of a thigh.

    ■

He resurrected.
He had no memory of being eaten.

He stood in the crosswalk, feeling accomplished,
like a star.

Then the ghost of Shakespeare appeared.
He was looking for a half-wit to cast as Polonius.

"Step behind this curtain," he said.
"I need to see

if you're stab-able."
Turned out he was.

∎

The crossing guard
came back from the dead,

this time facing a firing squad.
He'd insulted the daughter of a *hacienda* owner,

and a nun planting corn at the orphanage,
and women from Syria, Somalia,

from Bosnia, Cambodia,
from Poland and Ireland and fleeing

the Confederate South.
He'd insulted the trees who'd heard him.

And the future
for being in its history.

And even the ore taken out of a mountain,
then heated and shaped

into the shovel head
waiting nearby.

∎

When he stood up, lit by the morning,
the bison stampeding him were beautiful,

as if the mountains had decided to run downhill
and out across the valley.

His dying thought while lying there—
a bird's nest

of compound fractures—
was *Where the hell did those buffalo come from?*

But that was wrong; buffalo are in Asia.
His face was in the dirt.

■

He sat up quickly and got to his feet.
His clothes weren't even dusty.

It was post-election Wednesday,
near Meadowlark Elementary,

and all the kids from the neighborhood
were headed his way.

He didn't much care for the black girl's *hijab*,
said, "Enjoy your free flight back to the jungle,"

but instead of sidewalks, or African forests,
there was water... an inland sea.

At the surface above him were silhouettes:
kids' windmill arms, and legs kicking.

It would've been nice to do that too,
but he couldn't swim.

■

He resurrects again,
unaware of drowning,

and a flock of ocean liners flies across the sky,
sounding impossible,

like Salvador Dalí painting with thunder,
a painting titled *Migratory Birds*.

Somehow those huge ships misjudge the distance,
drop anchor

and veer on their wings
two miles before the lake, skid down

atop the crossing guard...barnacled hulls,
and concrete, and him in between.

■

Something quiet flutters now
in the shadow

cast by one of them.
It's a red-and-white fabric sign on a stick.

It says "STOP."

Spell to Be Said against Hatred

JANE HIRSHFIELD

Until each breath refuses they, those, them.
Until the dramatis personae of the book's first page says, "Each one is
    you."
Until hope bows to its hopelessness only as one self bows to another.
Until cruelty bends to its work and sees suddenly: I.
Until anger and insult know themselves burnable legs of a useless
    table.
Until the unsurprised unbidden knees find themselves bending.
Until fear bows to its object as a bird's shadow bows to its bird.
Until the ache of the solitude inside the hands, the ribs, the ankles.
Until the sound the mouse makes inside the mouth of the cat.
Until the inaudible acids bathing the coral.
Until what feels no one's weighing is no longer weightless.
Until what feels no one's earning is no longer taken.
Until grief, pity, confusion, laughter, longing know themselves
    mirrors.
Until by we we mean I, them, you, the muskrat, the tiger, the hunger.
Until by I we mean as a dog barks, sounding and vanishing and
    sounding and vanishing completely.
Until by until we mean I, we, you, them, the muskrat, the tiger, the
    hunger, the lonely barking of the dog before it is answered.

Hasten to Understand

KATHRYN MILES

Dear America,

I want to tell you a story.

Last month, lying in a Jordanian hotel bed, I was awakened by the *adhan,* the Islamic call to worship. It was not yet dawn. The previous day, I and four other U.S. writers had traveled to a humble university just shy of the Syrian border. We were there as cultural ambassadors, sent to build connection through writing and shared ideas. At the school, we were greeted with cardamom-laced coffee served in tiny plastic cups before being escorted to our classrooms. I met with journalism students, many of whom were refugees. They were shy and eager and proud of their work. One of them, a young man recently arrived from Syria, raised his hand. He said he wanted to write about what was happening in his homeland. He knew there were risks. That alone didn't bother him. But he did have a problem—a conundrum he was hoping I could help solve. *How,* he asked, *will I know which of my stories are worth dying for?*

I didn't have an answer for him in that moment. Hours later, lying in that hotel bed, thinking of the students and listening to the distant keening of the *muezzin,* I wasn't much closer to having one. But what I did have was a surprising beatific peace—a joy in knowing that I was surrounded by piety and a commitment to service: a commitment so true that a student half my age, and already far braver than I will ever be, was willing to give his life for it. In that moment, the world felt small and tender and very, very sweet.

I continued to listen to the *muezzin* chant the *adhan.*

حَيَّ عَلَى الصَّلَاة. *Hasten to the prayer.*

حَيَّ عَلَى الْفَلَاح. *Hasten to real success.*

And in the days and weeks following, I've returned to this call again and again.

Maybe the sound of the *adhan* is already familiar to you. Maybe you've heard it as you've walked down a street or as part of an exotic scene in a movie. If you're like me, you've never given it much thought. But just for a few minutes, America, I want you to consider it. To hear this story of my experience and the stillness and love I found on the fifth floor of an international hotel. To think about what it means to live your ideals.

The *adhan* is about spiritual devotion, yes. But it's about more than that as well. The very word *adhani* means "to listen. To understand."

It can be challenging to remember to do either, America. We have been pulling ourselves up by our bootstraps, spurring young men to go west, building and doing and acting so long that I fear we've lost patience for listening and understanding. More than ever, we need to get it back.

This past Friday, President Trump made good on his campaign promise to limit severely the number of Muslims—particularly Muslim refugees—entering this country. It is an unprecedented order and one that has already separated families, denied entry to scientists and scholars, and left visa holders homeless, having sold all their possessions after receiving what they believed was ironclad permission from our country to resettle here. The order detained for hours elderly green card holders, translators for the U.S. military, and young survivors of war crimes.

In the coming weeks, attorneys and organizations like the ACLU and the Council on American-Islamic Relations will contest this order in court. They will argue, as David J. Bier did in the *New York Times*, that the order is illegal, that decades ago our country committed to never restricting entrance here based on a person's nationality.

America, I urge you to listen to what they are saying and to understand what is at stake. I ask you to join in their fight not just because it is the right thing to do on behalf of talented and vulnerable people, but also because it is at the very core of who we are.

We are a nation of immigrants. We are also a generous nation—a nation that has always believed that real strength can only be found in equal parts solidarity and equanimity.

According to the United Nations, we have long since led the world in resettlement of vulnerable refugees. During the Irish famine, we accepted over a million individuals. When xenophobic protesters tried to block the arrival of famine ships, we told them no. Countless lives were saved as a result. Their descendants went on to become housekeepers and shop owners. One of them invented the automobile. Another became one of our most beloved presidents. In 1944, after six years of conflicted policy on Jewish immigrants, President Franklin Delano Roosevelt established the War Refugee Board, thereby saving thousands and thousands of persecuted European Jews, many of whom were resettled here to equal success. Since 1975, we've embraced over three million additional refugees. They have brought much to this country. In Maine, the state I call home, Somali refugees have revitalized depressed mill towns and inner cities. They serve on town councils and operate women's shelters. Their kids attend Georgetown and Swarthmore.

This is the United States the rest of the world knows and admires. It's the America praised by Ameen, one of my drivers in Jordan, who has worked extra jobs since the day his daughter was born so that she can study here. It's the America that had students at that border university want to pose for selfies with visiting U.S. writers and to talk about pluralism and the free exchange of ideas.

It's not too late to return to this best self, America.

Not a single country on Trump's immigration ban, which currently targets Iran, Iraq, Syria, Sudan, Libya, Yemen, and Somalia, has produced a refugee who has committed terrorism on our soil. That alone is not a sufficient endorsement for future immigrants, I know. But here's one: there are already strenuous international safety measures in place. The United Nations Refugee Agency already vets each applicant. We have our own screening process, which includes five discrete background checks and four additional biometric checks, and an additional three in-person interviews. Statewide organizations like Lutheran Immigration and Refugee Services and the U.S. Committee for Refugees and Immigrants assist in the resettling process and provide support—financial, physical, and psychological—when needed.

That system has worked. According to the Center for American Progress, Syrian refugees become homeowners and community contributors. In so many ways, they are already us.

It's okay to be wary, America. It's okay to want to be safe. But we also must listen. We must understand.

Just a few miles from that Jordanian university sits Za'taari, a UN refugee camp currently serving as home to about eighty thousand Syrians. The schools there operate on shifts so that all of the kids can get an education. Even some of the youngest pupils attend late at night, just so they can have their chance. Residents have constructed cisterns to conserve water and gardens to grow food. They've built a main drag where you can buy anything from native spices to phone cards to wedding dresses.

These are not terrorists. They are sons and daughters and grandmothers and grandfathers. They are engineers and entrepreneurs and artists and thinkers. They are that student, willing to die in the name of truth and the pursuit of freedom.

We need these refugees as much as they need us.

America, listen to their stories. Understand their plight. Hasten to do the right thing. For in our treatment of others lies our only hope for real success.

I believe in us. I want you to believe in us too.

Love,
Kate

That Corpse You Planted in Your Garden

ELIZABETH DODD

Dear America,

You may not believe this, but I finished reading Margaret Atwood's MaddAddam trilogy the same week that a corpse flower bloomed on the campus where I teach. My brain clenched its metaphorical jaw as I paged grimly through the days of the Waterless Flood, picturing bodies melting in a hot, apocalyptic landscape where people still texted with cell phones—just like us—until they couldn't. I imagined the stink of it (which Atwood doesn't, actually, describe much): billions of people rotting in their houses, in half-looted stores, in the cars that couldn't take them anywhere far enough, fast enough, to get away. What a glut-fest for scavengers and decomposers. Atwood mentions vultures, and crows, and a bunch of weirdly bioengineered animals, but I've been around enough feedlots to think, my god, the flies. I'm not talking about the handful or two of maggots that one character hoards for pro-tein or to cleanse festering flesh wounds. These would be flies like a 1930s black blizzard, like Orestes's furies advancing on an exponential curve. Flies bubbling up from extinction's debris field.

Meanwhile, back at the Ag School, the fifteen-year-old titan arum in its hothouse pot shoved out a bud the size of a thumbnail, a fist, a football, and then by the end of the week it was a fifty-two-inch-high blossom. The spathe belled like an upside-down Edwardian skirt with a scab-colored fringe along the hem and brandished a wicked-looking spadix like a cross between a baguette and a bloody lance. A friend first shared news of the full bloom on Facebook, but I was offline then, still reading Atwood, chuckling a little over Saint Wayne Grady of Vul-tures, Saint Maria Sibylla Merian of Insect Metamorphosis Day, and trying to decide how to actually pronounce CorpSeCorps aloud.

Corpse flowers don't bloom on any regular schedule, and it takes a decade or so after germination before a plant will be ready for its first inflorescence. Then the flower lasts for only a day or two, so if you want to see you need to scoot. As soon as I saw posts about the bloom, I "liked" everybody, fast, and drove straight to campus. I hurried past the Insect Zoo, past wrought-iron benches lounging beneath an old cottonwood tree, following laminated signs pointing the way. All morning people kept arriving, taking selfies with the main attraction; it was a holiday atmosphere, maybe a little warmup for the excitement in August, when the solar eclipse would lay down a sixty-mile-wide swath of two minutes of weird but manageable darkness.

I had heard of corpse flowers before but had no idea one was under cultivation here, practically under my own nose. The horticultural greenhouses are mostly full of wheat and doctoral students, and occasionally administrators who fight over the space. I'd never been there, even though it's on my route to work, midway between the construction site of the National Bio and Agro-Defense Facility where—I kid you not, America—they plan to study foot-and-mouth disease in a Bio-Safety Level 4 research facility planted smack dab in the middle of the nation's ranchlands, fifteen miles from Fort Riley's ground-zero arrival of the 1918 Spanish influenza—remember that? twenty to forty million people dead and it started right here?—like I say, midway between NBAF and, ahem, the English Department. Compare T. S. Eliot:

That corpse you planted last year in your garden,
Has it begun to sprout? Will it bloom this year?

Man, what a stink.

Last month I stood in the farmers market—this is *Kansas*, America, and we know how just thinking about that can make the head spin; the state has been home to the Progressives, Carrie Nation, Nicodemus, Likable Ike, Despicable Kobach, and Brownback's lax tax law that allows individuals to claim that they're corporations (making their income tax-free)—and I looked around at the friendly faces, the people I buy food from each week, and reminded myself how, out of 105 counties, only two rejected a President Trump, *only two*, and mine—ours—wasn't among them.

But it has been months since the election. We've come to realize we're in this for the long haul, this shit isn't pretty, no one said it would be easy, et cetera and so forth. Human venality and bigotry and cruelty are endemic diseases of the planet, and in case anyone needed reminding, the myth of American exceptionalism was a dream that, if it ever had roots in the soil, got GMO'd into a cash crop years ago.

Atwood's trilogy plays out in a globalized world where the very concept of the nation-state has been bought out by capitalism. The Corporations run the show in the economic bifurcation of Corporation Compounds and Pleeblands. It's all about branding and products, collusive secrecy and distraction. And the Corporations Security Corporation, the CorpSeCorps: they're the gun in the pocket of the man, nothing about law, plenty about disorder. It's easy to see how one brilliant kid—Glenn, who renames himself Crake after an extinct bird—would want to engineer a more perfect hominid and wipe every human face off the face of the earth. It's easy to see how the CorpSeCorps world would—unwittingly—enable his plan. But it's harder to see how islands of resistance move and evolve, and as the trilogy's narrative shifts perspective to retell what has already gone before, it's hard to guess where the story will go next.

In their native Sumatra, corpse flowers are pollinated by carrion beetles and flies drawn to the throat-closing stink of dead flesh. Inside the bloom, the temperature can rise above the surrounding air, so insects may get a sense of putrefaction in the heat as well as the smell. But there weren't any corpse-sipping flies in the greenhouse, flitting from one giant stench to the next. So as the blossom closed in the fetid air, the professor in charge took a little set of tools—a pumpkin carving kit, he told me—and opened a few windows in the base of the spathe. Inside, we could see the individual inflorescences looking like fungus or coral. He'd been hoping the curator of another titan arum would send him pollen he could use to pollinate the plant, but that hadn't happened. Now he was harvesting some from this specimen to set aside, he said, "So I'll have currency. Something to trade whenever it blooms again."

America, are you wondering why I am telling you this story?

"Write when you get work," my father used to say just before I'd take off on some trip: the year I went to Scotland to end up near-hypothermic in a kayak class near Loch Ness, or my first time in Mexico when every word of Spanish I tried to wield came out with a French accent and people thought I must be Canadian. My dad grew up poor in Oklahoma during the Great Depression, a boy who hoed and picked cotton, who had known men so utterly broken and discarded by the nation that they wound up at my grandmother's back door, hat literally in hand, asking, "Ma'am, do you have any work I could do?" hoping to be able to sit down for a hot meal after the job. Years later, he enjoyed the luxury of the joke. It was a sentence, he must have thought, from a world we'd left behind.

"Keep those cards and letters coming," he used to say. But my father doesn't write back anymore. He has shut down, fallen silent, turned to gaze elsewhere.

So, America, I am writing home. I'm writing to you—home from the confounding always-already-otherness that home has become. There's a lot of hard work to be done and a lot of us—honestly—have been reeling around, trying to recapture a sense of direction. We're dismayed and heartbroken and lonely and furious. But I'm never comfortable in the simple algebra of allegory; I'm not offering these paragraphs as a feel-good pep rally or an invitation to snuff out hope in some dystopian sandbox.

A fly has perched on my knee while I've been typing. It does fly-ablutions, rubbing front legs together, then wiping its eyes. It shifts position—crow pose—balancing on its front two pairs of legs while rubbing its body with the pair in back. I think a lot about rot and corruption these days, but the corpse flower was beautiful, really, and during its bloom I went to see it three times. The species isn't listed as endangered, but it's considered "vulnerable," and its existence could become far more precarious with further habitat loss. Which is to say, it will, in the almost-certain future: corpse flowers grow where the most rapid deforestation on earth is taking place.

And shouldn't we assume that is the state of everything we love: vulnerable, and subject to change?

Sincerely yours,
Elizabeth

Reach

ROSE McLARNEY

week of elections, and wildfire, 2016

A fire is near,
the sky smoke-dark.

This day with no dawn,
an end-time come?

The resolution to the blaze
may be no human

intervention, but fire
clearing the land,

burning all possible fuel,
extinguishing itself.

The fuel meaning
what people have built.

Border lines to make
other a side.

Walls, squaring off
in claims to space.

Houses of wood.
I tried to make

our home here.
But have served

in barely a housewife's
smallest of ways.

May not be saved from
fleeing even the plural

just two share.
Running from fire

in the white
of the body's flesh,

not yet stripped free
of this boundary

by any living hand.

In the Wake

ANNE HAVEN McDONNELL

of the Election, 2016

This morning the moon is a ghostbone
in a pale blue sky. Our bodies huddle
for warmth in cold seeps of winter.

They say our whole time on earth
will darken and press into a thin
flaky layer of stone. Even plastic

even bombs even music and cell phones
old churches and skyscrapers and jets
all our bodies and with our bodies

our ideas about the world as ours
our ideas about whales and bees and redwoods and wolves
and the bodies of whales, bees, redwoods, and wolves.

But today, in the wake, I watch
each body pass on the street,
I linger in each stranger's eyes, silent,

listening beneath skin. On the rim
of a canyon, coyotes let loose
an unhinged chorus, lit

on the tip of my tongue. I know
the fires have started. I know
the bodies I will protect, a queer

spring in my step, a shimmer in my
stride. My cry swells like a wave
over lies, shivers down any spine,

dissolves into language of lichen and stone.
I quiver all the way to gone—
then bring it back as heat, urgent

as the purr of nerves quickening, sure
as the lynx who stalks silence
on a ridgeline, her lush spotted coat,
her paws stitching the unbroken snow.

A Great Dawn Chorus

KATHLEEN DEAN MOORE

Dear America,

Here is a small parable from Oregon, where marsh hawks are hunting over flooded fields, even as darkness pools under streetlights in Washington and New York:

My friend, a small woman in Alaska, could not sleep. How can any of us sleep? So much work to be done to save democracy, to save decency, to save children, to save the marsh hawks, for god's sake, and even the flooded fields. We could work all the bright day and all through the night, and still the work would not be done, and how can it even begin? My friend lay awake in a darkened room, one hand gripping the other. Who can let herself fall asleep, when she has not found a way to save the world—because that's the task we set ourselves, each of us. Is this not so?

Every evening, she watched as bare branches and telephone lines sliced the falling sun as if it were an egg yolk, and the day darkened—until one night she remembered that the sun was, of course, not falling. The far edge of the Earth was rising.

As each of us falls into bed at night, exhausted and despondent because we have not yet finished our work, the sun is rising on the other side of the planet, and other people are rising to the challenge of protecting what is flourishing and just and beautiful.

On the rotating planet, there's a great dawn chorus of committed people, millions and millions of them, who rise from their beds or mats or blankets, rustle up coffee or atole or tea, and set off to do the good work of defending the world's thriving. We can hear the chorus if we listen—the rustle, the creak of doors tin or wood or grass, voices calling out to one another in a thousand languages, the roar of action advancing around the world, awakened like birds by the rising sun.

When night comes now, my friend is able to sleep, and when the dawn comes, she takes up her part of the work that others, exhausted, have laid down. Because my friend is Alaskan singer-songwriter Libby Roderick, her part of the work is to write the songs. Here are some of the words she wrote in "The Cradle of Dawn"—

> Sunset in your country, sunrise in mine
> Lay down your body, hear mine begin to rise
> Sunset in my country, sunrise in yours
> I feel you there in the dawn...
> There are no promises that we will see the day
> The dreams we live for will succeed
> But I can promise you that halfway round the world
> I'll hold the light up while you sleep

Each of us will emerge full-throated from the dark shelter of our private despair. We will find our cause. We will find our chorus. We will find our courage. And then nothing can stop our collective action—not troopers on a North Dakota highway, not uber-bankers, not sniveling oligarchs or complacent professors. Then nothing can distract us—not football, not shopping, not even composting. There might have been a time when our work for the world was in our private lives, focused on exemplary recycling, or some such. That time has passed. Our work now is in the streets, in the statehouses, on the riverbanks, in the college quad, on the path by the flooded field. What we cannot do alone, we can do together.

This is not the end of the small story I offer. This is the beginning.

Courage,
Kathleen

Storm Season

LAURA-GRAY STREET

Dear America, of thee I sing oh please—
not this way. All season spinning up
tangles of words, and look what
comes tearing through, bucking
and snorting. Tell me, my snarled
quarrels, where is this going? Raw
material for millions to make more
millions for a favored few while
more and more are gathering sub
-verse *sotto voce* further evidence
of a storm, an atmospheric system
of domestic—I almost wrote *labor*.
Maybe that's because I was lulled
to the tune of a tornado. It trilled
the way my mother could whistle
arias (*Tosca*, *Madame Butterfly*,
La Traviata), conjuring opera
houses out of housework. But not
that day in a vernacular clapboard
two-over-two, no cellar, no wall
without windows. I'm the newborn bundle pinched in her arms
as the twister hitches toward us
all furrowed, fluted, determined
to shake our sticky hands, kiss our
sour infants, cyclone-wire our
fields with likely scenarios. Such

open-throated testimony. As if
we listen to ourselves anymore.
As if we know how to stop it,
the baby who keeps on crying.

Closing Time

MICHAEL P. BRANCH

Dear America,

I don't hear you laughing much lately. I understand that you're worried and afraid, that everything you've worked so hard for now appears to be in jeopardy, that the system you put your faith in has produced an unnatural outcome, like a lioness unaccountably giving birth to a toad. I realize that the social and environmental justice you've struggled so long to achieve has hit, let's say, a wall. You're feeling angry, sad, vulnerable. Listen, I don't want to talk you out of any of that. But since it is almost closing time, let me buy you a drink, America. Pull up a barstool and we'll pour a bracing chaser for your bitter tears.

Now, I know you're going to say that our present condition is no laughing matter, that things just aren't as funny as they were before the dark night of November 8, 2016. You may even be thinking that humor is an ineffective, even an inappropriate, response to the difficult situation we face—that to welcome laughter at this troubled time is the moral equivalent of fiddling while Rome burns. But hear me out while I sing this short, sweet song of sword and shield. (Take a big swig, America, and then repeat three times fast to get yourself in the right spirit.)

America, never forget the immense power of humor to expose misguided values and destructive practices. Satire is as vital and as useful now as it was when Aristophanes ragged on Socrates in *The Clouds* back in 423 BCE. You remember that gut-buster, don't you? Well, we still have plenty to learn from Swift and Johnson, Bierce and Twain, Orwell and Huxley. Satire is not only funny but also enormously forceful and effective—and, human nature being what it is, the comic exposure of vice and folly has the added benefit of offering great job security. America, I know you feel like you're on the defensive, that even as you try to inspire, persuade, and reform, you secretly fear that you are now a voice crying in the wilderness. The satirist, by contrast, remains ever on the offensive, challenging established power structures, revealing their absurdity or violence, forcing villains to account for themselves. Orwell was right that "Every joke is a tiny revolution," because satirical humor is the enemy of established power—especially power that lacks moral leadership. The satirist's work is the serious business of striking into the troubling gap between what our ideology promises and the often disappointing outcomes our choices actually produce. We don't call them punch lines for nothing.

Consider in this vein the cultural work of innovative comedians like Lenny Bruce, Richard Pryor, George Carlin, and Joan Rivers, who challenged languages of power and used humor to shine a light on the moral failure to promote racial and gender equality, preserve the natural environment, and protect individual freedoms. Or, America, think of the courage of filmmakers who used humor as the vehicle of piercing social critique: Charlie Chaplin, whose *The Great Dictator* (1940) bravely satirized Hitler on the eve of the United States' entry into World War II; or, Stanley Kubrick, whose Cold War classic *Dr. Strangelove or: How I Learned to Stop Worrying and Love the Bomb* (1964) used black humor to expose the terrifying absurdities of the nuclear arms race. Because the logical and moral incongruities these comics and filmmakers attacked were painfully real, every laugh they produced was a small, important blow to a perilous status quo.

It's okay to be pissed, America. I don't blame you a bit. But you can be mad as hell and still preserve your sense of humor. I'm glad you have so much fight left in you, but you can fight without forgetting how to laugh. As my patron saint Edward Abbey advised, "Be loyal to what you love, be true to the Earth, and fight your enemies with passion and laughter." Far from imagining humor as mere entertainment, Cactus Ed is part of a venerable tradition of satirists who have successfully deployed laughter as a tool of battle. This is why Wendell Berry, in recognition of the moral force of Abbey's literary comedy, observed gracefully that "Humor, in Mr. Abbey's work, is a function of his outrage, and is therefore always answering to necessity." And in case you're worried that satire went to the grave with Aristophanes or Abbey, try tuning in to Alec Baldwin's weekly lampooning of the president on *Saturday Night Live*. Why does Baldwin's parody so infuriate the Donald, who watches it each week and then tweets angrily, each week, that it is unwatchable? Not because it is funny (though it is), but because, in its lacerating accuracy, it makes plain the ignorance, hypocrisy, and arrogance that is so richly deserving of comic excoriation.

Look, America, even if you aren't in the mood to brandish humor as a sword, you might at least consider taking it up as a shield—accepting it, humbly, as a small inoculation against the diseases of frustration and fatigue that are epidemic among us these days. Because we love our country and our planet so deeply and yet fear we may be forced to watch them burn—or melt—we find that our love has become a bittersweet affection shot through with grief. But humor, in its power and dynamism, can help us preserve the resilience that enables our creativity and courage—even if, as bluesman Big Bill Broonzy crooned, "When you see me laughing/I'm laughing just to keep from crying." But don't you think Big Bill was right that even when humor is a byproduct of suffering, it is still a healthy response to grief? And I hope I don't need to remind you that in addition to its emotional and psychological benefits, laughing also raises your heart rate and pulmonary ventilation, increases your brain activity and alertness, stimulates the production of endorphins from your ventromedial prefrontal cortex, reduces your perception of pain, and leads you to relaxation. America, please don't feel guilty about laughing. It really is okay to want your ventromedial prefrontal cortex to feel a little better.

Comedy also nurtures empathy, because the appreciation of humor requires flexibility, acceptance, and the capacity to forgive—even to forgive yourself when you've fucked up bigly. Humor has the power to bring us together, helping us reexamine and rebuild our shared values and sense of common purpose. Doesn't that sound pretty good right about now, America? Even that most sober of your sages, Ralph Waldo Emerson, whose Harvard class of 1821 voted him "Least Likely to Ever Get a Laugh," wrote in his essay "The Comic" that "the perception of the Comic is a tie of sympathy with other men, a pledge of sanity, and a protection from those perverse tendencies and gloomy insanities in which fine intellects sometimes lose themselves." And while a sense of humor is impossible to define precisely (after all, "sense" is pretty damned fuzzy), you should be suspicious of folks who lack it, because laughter is essentially a form of self-reflection. Humor, like love and flatulence, is fundamental to our humanity.

Because I'm your Facebook friend I've seen how you're trying to deal with all of this. The disappointment and disillusionment break over you in waves, pushing you back into those old habits of yours, the jeremiad and the elegy—those painful but at least familiar forms of expression for your anger and grief. Listen, America, I get it. Really. But in focusing only on what has been wounded, you risk forfeiting the regenerative potential of laughter. Remember that comedy is a life-giving force because it helps us combat despair. As a writer, I believe that the craft of humor is an essential element of the art of survival.

. Last call, America. Bottoms up. We've both got work in the morning. Important work. I know you've had the wind knocked out of you. But to dig out the old line that desperate stand-up comedians have long used to challenge desperate audiences: "I know you're out there; I can hear you breathing." I can hear you breathing, America. Keep breathing. And then, just as soon as you can, use some of your breath to make the redemptive sound that, even now, is laughter.

Thinking of you,
Mike

Shoes

NICOLE WALKER

Dear America,

I have been writing letters to Arizona governor Doug Ducey for the past year and a half to protest his disembowelment of the higher education budget. I've written more than two hundred of them. I send them to him. I post them on my blog. *Flag Live*, Flagstaff's local weekly, prints them. I have never received a response from the governor. I'm sure he thinks I'm crazy. I don't always write on topic. I write him about fly-fishing and the read-a-thon at my kids' elementary school. I write him about picking up garbage for the Adopt-a-Highway program and the tomatoes I try to grow up here at an elevation of seven thousand feet. I write him about running shoes and how he probably doesn't even own a pair of boots. I offer to lend him my snowshoes if he comes to visit Flagstaff in the winter. If he read my letters, I think he would think I was a snowflake liberal, but he would have to claim that he knows me a little. That, if pressed, he could name my kids and cite their ages and know that my students write hard essays and both my kids and my students are about as empathetic as humans get.

Yesterday five students came to my office hours. Three of them cried. One about the election but another about her sister and the other about his absences. I couldn't fix their problems, but I could sit there and listen and maybe suggest some strategies or plan a collaborative writing project for next summer or invite them into my graduate course in the fall. I could read their thesis proposals real quick and say, yes, I think we'll be able to get that done by spring. I could, in this dark time, be with them and empathize.

My former student, Khara House, was pulling onto the road after a movie last night. Halfway into the street, she was blocked by a woman driving the wrong way. That car needed to move in order for Khara to get out. Instead, the woman in that car called Khara the N-word and told her to go back to Obamaland. Khara wrote, "Please don't pity me. And please don't take your anger out on the woman who yelled. If anywhere, sympathy belongs here. Imagine what HER fears must be to think that her America means striking out so angrily at another person. Imagine her fear, to believe that in the midst of her wrongness, shouted epithets were her only recourse. Imagine her fear, to think THIS was her only option." Not many of us have Khara's capacity to put herself in someone else's shoes. Khara has very strong feet. Would that all of our feet were so tough.

I was in Melbourne eating lunch with my colleagues when the election results came in. My colleagues had to go back to work. I found my way to the bar. They would meet me there when they could. I really could drink only one beer. My throat had closed shut. My stomach flip-flopped like it does when the plane drops ten thousand feet from wind shear. I kept texting my husband for him to tell me there was recourse. Recount. Move to Australia. I placed blame. Russia did this. Electoral College. But Wednesday day in Melbourne continued forth with the news America's Tuesday night had brought. My friends, as soon as they were able, rushed to the bar. They bought me another beer. Talked to me until my throat relaxed. They patted my head. They knew this was bad, but they still tried to make me laugh. They made it as better as they could.

Another of my former students wrote how angry she was at those protesting the election. Didn't they see how some people righteously voted for him? Did they understand that she had lost her job due to immigration and outsourcing? Now she had to pay so much for health care and Trump promised to fix it? I get it. Globalization is hard. And I get that if I had a crappy service job where I once had a well-paying manufacturing job, I would be frustrated too. But there's no real plan to bring back jobs. Technology has replaced as many or more jobs than outsourcing. Robots make cars. Hell, robots are cars. And, more people have jobs now than they did when the last Republican left office. If the 4.5 percent of the population who didn't have jobs voted for Trump, that makes sense. But 24.5 percent of people voted for him. Some of them voted not only for selfish reasons but against the well-being of others. There's a line I draw against empathy. I do not have to get into your shoes to see what it's like to think you deserve more than others because of your race or your religion.

Back when my sister taught students at the alternative high school where pregnant teenagers and teenage moms with newborns go to finish high school, she told them I wrote creative nonfiction. They laughed. Those two words are a ridiculous paradox. But I love it. In the gap between creative and nonfiction is the instruction manual for figuring out empathy. It is between the words where the imagination happens. I tell my own students, like the one who read *Crime and Punishment* over the summer, that creative nonfiction is most interested in the in-between of the genres. It is interdisciplinary, hyphenated, bent. In creative nonfiction, you have to gather things up—hydrogen, carbon, diapers, WIC, governments, *Crime and Punishment*, other people's shoes—and guide the reader to make a connection by offering a unifying image, a repeating phrase, a story about some kids with kids who are trying to bond with their babies while they learn about covalent bonds.

I tell my student, the one who read *Crime and Punishment*, that creative nonfiction is a kind of dialectic too. But no one likes to be preached at. So you engage their senses, like you do in fiction and poetry. You build a whole world for your reader, invite them in, and then tell them that not all governments are created equal. "Mind the gap," you tell your student, who laughs because he's been to London. He rode the Underground. He went outside his comfort zone. He put himself in someone else's shoes.

During the week of the government shutdown, my sister emailed to tell me about her class of chemistry students. As she tried to teach them about hydrogen atoms, she stared out across the classroom into the gaping eyes looking back at her with only one concern: will WIC get shut down? What will my baby and I eat? She looked back with eyes that answered, not hydrogen. She changed her lesson to one about carbon.

I asked my sister how I could help her students. I lived in Flagstaff. She taught in West Valley, Utah. The great gap of the Grand Canyon and five hundred red dirt miles divided us. I thought about sending up formula. I thought I had some frozen breast milk tucked away in the back of my freezer. There wasn't much I could do. The frozen milk had passed its expiration date. My sister said it would be okay. The kids would figure it out.

I don't get too depressed that Governor Ducey doesn't respond to my letters because, once in a while, someone reads my letters. People give me ideas. "Write about teenagers in Tempe." "Write about peach trees." They wait for my letter to appear. They say, "I know you! You're the one who writes those letters!" And they do know me, a little bit, and the way I haven't ever caught a fish with a fly, the way the tomatoes I grow cost about nine dollars each, what with the deer-repellent grow box and fence we had to build, and they know my kids take tae kwon do and I've got two crazy dogs from the shelter at once and that I spend a good deal of my life trying to convince my dogs to empathize with people walking down the street who do not think it is nice to bark. They know that I have one pair of shoes for winter. I wear them every day. Sometimes, they wear them too.

If we're going to be able to change the way people use their vote to vote not only for themselves but for their neighbors or even the betterment of those they have never met but can only imagine, then we're going to have to tell our individual stories to make that imagination fully sensible. Describe the shoes. I'll choose my daughter's. They are red. They have laces. Okay, let's make it easy and admit they are Vans. Red Vans. Now, don't you feel fourteen again? Make the shoes real for the readers and empathy will spread like fire—the good kind of fire. The kind that the seed inside the ponderosa pine cone needs in order to escape its hard shell to germinate.

Truly,
Nicole Walker

The Little Painter

JOY CASTRO

I am just a little painter, a painter of small things.

In the National Palace of Mexico, I saw that artists had painted the walls after the 1910 revolution. They had painted a history of Mexico from the ancient times right up until just before they started to paint.

Tall painted murals showed the green and gold crops of the Toltecs on barges of floating earth. In one, a man climbed to the top of a tree and carved down its trunk in a long spiral so rubber sap would drip down. In another, all the people came for market day, offering tribute to the ruling Aztecs in the complicated city with its pyramids and bridges. There was the god going off to heaven in his dragon boat, the sun with its eyes upside down. Big murals showed the Spanish conquest and Catholic conversions by torture, the chinless soldiers and priests all painted the same sickly pale green. There were huge panels crowded with conflict and hundreds of faces, and an arch full of the decadent thigh-fondling of the pale-skinned robber barons with ticker-tape hearts. In another archway, the good brown worker family sat down to dinner with loaves of bread on the plate and love in their eyes. *Viva. Viva.* And Marx and so on and *la revolución*. Their paintings told a story opposite to the one the imperial palace had told for hundreds of years, after Spaniards had crushed the Templo Mayor and built their own great building on top. With their paintings, the artists made the palace say something new.

I came home to the United States and thought about it all. I thought about my country and I wanted to be historical. So I started painting in my little notebook.

In my notebook I painted the first peoples, their cities and villages and farms and canals and the wild lands where they hunted. I painted pictures of Columbus enslaving the Arawaks. I painted pictures of the Arawaks and Tainos all dead. (I knew the right blue for the water; I knew the right red for the blood.) I painted Puritans putting their own people in stocks, hanging their own people, dunking their own people, burning them, beating their children with sticks, and going to church.

I painted men galloping over yesterday's treaties, their arms out-stretched for free land, and the Iroquois dying, the Apache dying, the Choctaw, Ojibwe, Hopi, Zuni, all dying or crammed onto strange lands. On the shining sea, I painted ships' decks full of blood, I painted grownups and children in chains, the trailing sharks. When I painted the Trail of Tears, I put my great-great-grandmother in, but no one knows what she looked like so I painted her to look like my little sister, beautiful. In the South, I painted lots of rape and whipping and gave the white men sickly green skin and no chins. I made the white women thin and pallid and cowardly, afraid to come down off their porches and fix things, but to be generous I included the sticks their husbands were allowed by law to beat them with and the dicks their husbands were allowed by law to rape them with. I painted white women crying in their canopy beds.

You know what else I painted? Every time I painted a man, I painted a woman. Maybe she was only hoeing the dirt, but she was there. May-be she was only carrying a baby, but she was there. Maybe she was only dying, but she was there. And for every little boy I drew, I drew a little girl. It made my pictures look weird, like there were many more girls than boys, more women than men. But really it was equal. It didn't look like history. *Oh*, I thought. *I'm just not used to seeing that.*

I like to paint, so I kept painting. I don't like wars but I made some: the wars in Texas, the war in the Philippines, the first war in Europe and the second, Korea, Vietnam. I drew My Lai, I drew the fall of Sai-gon with the helicopters, I drew Nixon rising from the lawn. I painted a big video game with boys in suits and army clothes gathered around, excited, and on the screen was the Gulf War. I painted trailer parks, and the last of a family's food stamps, and drive-bys, and school shoot-ings. I drew polluted rivers, and dirty air, and lanes of stalled traffic ringing the cities, and coal miners dead underground. I painted rich families on Long Island whose children go to Paris and Yale.

I forgot the Ku Klux Klan so I went back and drew them in. I thought, *How could I forget that?* But I did forget it. Because I am not black. So I took my book to my black friends and said, "What else did I forget?" and they said, "This and this and this," so I drew those things in. Then I thought I'd better ask my white friends and they said, "This and this and this," so I drew those in, too. I double-checked with my brown friends, too, and then I asked my rich friends and my poor friends, I asked my queer and my straight friends, my cynical skeptical friends and my sweet optimistic ones. I asked my friends whose grand-parents came from China, and my friends from North Dakota whose great-grandparents came from Sweden, and my friends who just got here from Bangladesh last year. I asked all my friends, and I painted everything they said.

Then I realized that those were just my friends, and I began stopping people in the street, and the ones who had time would say, "Oh, yeah, you forgot this and this," and I would paint those things in, too. Until, finally, no one I met could think of anything left out, and my book of pictures was very full.

I didn't know what to do with all my paintings. I couldn't just put them on a shelf, so I took my book and went to the White House. I had a meeting with the president and asked permission to paint my pictures on the walls of the White House, like the Mexicans did in the National Palace, and he said yes, art was very important for society, if I would just be sure to put him in and to please make him look heroic.

"Okay, sure," I said.

So I started painting, and all my friends who could get time off work came and helped, and then people just taking tours of the White House said they wanted to paint, too, so I said, "Okay, sure." With ev-eryone painting, the work went very quickly. Sometimes people want-ed to include someone specific, their grandparents or some historical figure they cared about, and I said, "Okay, sure." Newspeople saw us and stopped to film, so the paintings were on TV, and all over America and all over the world people watched the paintings grow, and all over America psychologists recorded a drop in nightmares. All over Ameri-ca, pharmaceutical companies became alarmed.

More and more people came to Washington just to paint. They came in busloads from churches and neighborhoods and Oberlin, and every-one painted. We sang songs and painted long into the night.

I had to paint four planes crashing out of the sky. I painted tiny bod-ies falling down the sides of buildings and then the buildings falling.

I didn't know how to draw controversy and I didn't know how to draw lies, but I painted little dead children in a cold, rocky place, and a thin-legged man with a black hood on, and ancient cities all bombed up, and the people scared and exhausted or dead.

I remembered I was supposed to paint in the president looking heroic, so I painted him in his Oval Office picking up a big sword and hitting his desk with it, and it became a ploughshare, and people lifted him on their shoulders and looked very happy. Then I called his secretary and said we were finished.

The president came to see the finished murals, which stretched for miles and miles in the wide corridors of the White House. He began before Columbus and looked a long time, walking very slowly and saying, "Hmm," and conferring with his advisers in low voices. Then he got to the end, with him in the Oval Office and the sword that he struck into a ploughshare.

"But that didn't happen," he said.

"Okay, sure," I said. "We can fix that." So we went back to his office together, and I took a big ceremonial sword from history down from the wall. I gave it to him and put my hands around his hands. We swung it high over our heads and down hard onto the desk. Then we were holding a ploughshare.

The president was very surprised.

"What do I do with this?" he said.

"Okay, sure," I said. "I'll show you."

Images from the Front

In Which Twombly and Rader Consider the Letter

DEAN RADER

> The lord of Kulaba patted some clay and wrote the message as if on a tablet. Formerly, the writing of messages on clay was not established.
> ENMERKAR AND THE LORD OF ARATTA, 21ST CENTURY

In the beginning was the word,
                       and the word was with
the letter: the letter / is the beginning &
                            in the beginning
is the letter: first mark, first slash, first line, first sign—
not drawn but notched,
                scored:
the spoor of speech: the trace, the track /
                        of utterance:
the invitation not just to see but to read, to record: to write
and rewrite the self into everything it is
                       and is not:
letter within letter:
line from writer to reader,
                sender / receiver.
What is life but a correspondence,
                a notation,
written / read by & about the self?
                    Dear X, Dear Y . . .
Life, like the sentence,
                ends, but what if the letter is infinite?

lettir, *leitre*, Anglo-Norman and Old French, Middle French: *letre*, *lettre*, Anglo-Norman and MiddleFrench *lectre* (French *lettre*) (in plural) knowledge or learning acquired by the study of written texts, erudition (10th cent. in Old French; in Anglo-Norman also in singular (beginning of the 14th cent. or earlier)), any of the symbols of an alphabet, inscription, text (*c*1160), precise words of an utterance or document, exact or literal meaning of something (*c*1170), written communication addressed to a person or group of people, epistle (*c*1170 in plural *lettres*; in Anglo-Norman, Old French, and Middle French frequently in plural; first half of the 14th cent. or earlier in singular), official or legal document (1234; in Anglo-Norman, Old French, and Middle French frequently in plural), writing, lettering (beginning of the 14th cent. or earlier), individual block of type (1486), (in plural) study of grammar, rhetoric, and poetry (1538) classical Latin, *littera* (also *lītera* (in inscriptions) *leitera*) letter of the alphabet, letter as pronounced,

Dear Twombly,
                    master of the eternal e, unending o—
silent scriptographer of the allusive field,
                                        what letter
would you write to / for our country?
                              What sign, what scrawl
speaks through its own silence into the ear
of our brightest hearing?
                    Calligraphic and metonymic
all at once. Yes, it is true we may not hear,
but we still might read,
                    and yes, it is true that we may
not read, but we still might see.
Darkness blinds but only until it is marked by light.
Blindness darkens
                    but only until it is lit by mark.
What awaits us, Cy, in the mailboxes of the dead?
Here, the glyphs and graphemes
                              of our daily lives
seem at best unreadable,
                    at worst struck through.
It is time to draw the insurgent word /
                              time to write
the letter of our uprising on the envelope that is this land.
To the tyranny of edict,
                    I send the erasing angel:
to the president of autocracy,
                    I post the cancellation.

letter as written, character, style of lettering, script, short piece of writing, (plural *litterae*) elements of education, written form or matter, text of a document, letter of the law (as opposed to the spirit), document, record, inscription, epistle, literary works, writings, literary pursuits, scholarship, erudition, in post-classical Latin also sacred literature, scripture (late 2nd cent. in Tertullian), charter, deed (from 8th cent. in British and continental sources), of unknown origin; the hypothesis that it is connected with *linere* to smear is now generally rejected.

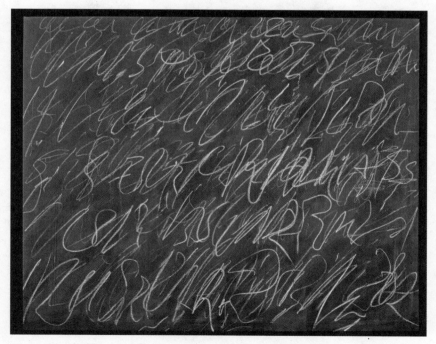

Untitled, by Cy Twombly. [Image courtesy Archives Fandazione Nicola Del Roscio and Cy Twombly Foundation. Photo by Mimmo Capone.]

The Lacunose

ELLEN WELTI

Magma, water, and nutrients, slips and faults, hollowness and opening
fill these holes.

You Are Not the Only America

PATRI HADAD

Dear United States,
    You are not the only America.

My cousins in Argentina would say to me that they didn't understand why *yanquis* would refer to themselves as Americans. As if we were the only country in the Americas. We are in fact one in thirty-six. I would reply, "I'm not a Yankee. I live in Texas."

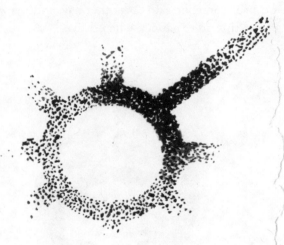

Fifteen years ago I sat in my parents' eleventh floor apartment in Córdoba, Argentina. I could hear car horns, drums, and chants. From high up through a small window, I watched hordes of people, mostly men, pour out of Avenida Hipólito Yrigoyen, a street named after the former president who fought for unions and universal male suffrage in the early twentieth century. These men, presumably taxi drivers, swirled the roundabout Plaza España holding up sagging signs on sticks, painted to their cause. Someone said, "Another day, another *huelga*." I thought, "Things like this don't happen where I live."

My relatives articulate the word machismo with a testicular hand gesture that can easily turn into a fist. In 1995, Mexican poet Susana Chávez wrote a poem with the phrase *Ni una muerta más* to protest the femicides in Ciudad Juárez. This is where the term *femicidio* was adopted. More women are murdered in Latin American countries than anywhere else in the world. On October 19, 2016, I watched on Facebook as women in my family posted links, pictures, and news of women marching in Argentina to protest against femicidio. They adopted the hashtag #NiUnaMenos. Chile, Uruguay, Peru, and Mexico soon followed with their own marches.

After a late night out and an early morning rise, my mother used to say, "Calavera no chilla." A skull, or a dead girl, can't complain. Córdoba is a dry university town, butting against a mountain range. Twenty-three thousand men and women marched there that October day, down Avenida Colón, an avenue of tall sand-colored apartment buildings where all the concrete balconies were empty. The protesters were dressed in black. Some painted red hands across their faces or as *calaveras*. Others outlined bodies in white spray paint on the pavement. The sagging signs they carried were pink, purple, and rainbow. The march hooked a right onto Vélez Sarsfield, gathered at the plaza, and stopped at Avenida Hipólito Yrigoyen.

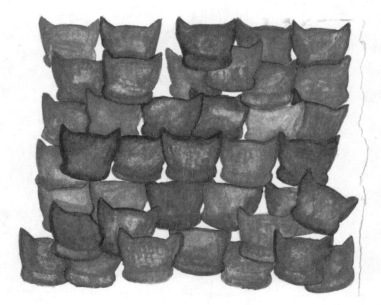

I waited through the Bush years. I waited through the Obama years. I saw nothing like the protest cultures I saw around the globe. And yet...there I was on January 21, among so many in the crowd of fifteen thousand men and women marching in Tucson whose first *real* protest was the Women's March.

While walking up Sixth Avenue, in between chants of *This is what democracy looks like!* and *I don't want no tiny hands anywhere near my underpants!* I marched to stand up to the groping hands that came into power the day before. I marched with millions of others in this country who wanted to say we chose a woman leader. We were joyous, practically giddy in our unity. But I also thought of the sorrow felt by the women who marched in the rest of the Americas—against femicide, mourning their loved ones, fearful for their lives. Even though they marched for something far graver, the women were seen smiling as widely in pictures as we were in the U.S.

Those smiles are democracy. This is what democracy *feels* like.

Afectuosamente,
Patri

Jeffersonian 2016

JOHN GALLAHER

To Tell the Past from the Future

SARAH SKEEN

> ...tell me how
> to turn my head to listen,
> and how, at last,
> to tell the past from the future
> if they both arrive.
> JAKE ADAM YORK, FROM "POSTSCRIPT
> (ALREADY BREAKING IN DISTANT ECHOES)"

Photos from the Granada War Relocation Center, also known as Camp Amache, near Granada, Colorado, March 2016.

Of the Highest Character

PETE SOUZA

(above) President Obama
at Grand Canyon
National Park.

President Obama
thanking a young
letter writer in 2013.

Not of the Highest Character

PÉTE SOUZA

Dear America,

I am concerned about what's happening in our country. More specifically, I am concerned about what's happening at the White House. The man we elected to be our forty-fifth president has shown himself to be a liar, a racist, and a con man.

I say this not just as an American citizen but as someone who has seen firsthand what the presidency requires. I spent eight years visually documenting President Barack Obama's time in office as his chief official White House photographer. I'd also worked as an official White House photographer for President Ronald Reagan.

Both of them took the job seriously and respected the office of the presidency.

Especially for President Obama, my job was unique in that I was the only person who observed him in all compartments of his life.

Because of the trust he instilled in me, he allowed me access to document essentially his every move. I was with him during virtually every meeting he had in the Oval Office and Situation Room. I flew more hours on Air Force One with him than any other person, during our trips to more than sixty countries and all fifty states. I also spent a considerable amount of time with his family. I'd venture to say I spent more time with him than anyone other than his wife. As a result, I can definitively say that he was a president—and a person—of the highest character.

What's become clear in the past three years is that this isn't true of Donald Trump. He does not have high character. Not just as the president but as a human being. What emanates from him is a constant barrage of lies and hateful comments. He doesn't respect democracy or the rule of law. His presidency has become a reality show game show, driven by his primal need to achieve the best ratings and wins—for himself. He doesn't appear to respect women, minorities, or immigrants; he often doesn't appear to respect even his wife. To him, a critical news story is "FAKE NEWS." To him, all our intelligence agencies are corrupt. He shuns preparation for meeting with heads of state. He makes best friends with dictators. He disses our allies. He thinks climate change is a hoax. He tells his supporters how he alone can fix the economy, yet promotes policies that hurt them and instead lines his pockets, as well as those of rich people like him.

Early in 2017, I decided to speak out about what was happening. I did this not as a partisan but as a concerned citizen with a unique voice. Thus began my "shading" of Donald Trump on Instagram. I began to post photographs of President Obama during "normal times" in the Oval Office, juxtaposing them to the latest crazy tweet or news story by or about President Trump. Initially, I tried to be subtle in my comments, and sometimes humorous. But over time, as Trump became more and more brazen in his tweets and actions, so did I.

Like many of us, outrage has continued to bubble up inside of me as I watch him wreck the office of the presidency and wreck the moral fabric of our country. Congress or the courts will eventually decide whether he is a criminal. But even if he isn't, he is not fit to be an American citizen much less the president of the United States. That is why I have raised my voice.

Truly,
Pete Souza

The Power of Satire

Presidential Alert

KIM STAFFORD

THIS IS A TEST
of the National Wireless
Emergency Alert System
No action is needed

This is your President speaking
Please take no action
This is only a test
Please remain calm
and silent

The National Wireless
is invisible and everywhere
Please take no action
No need to be alert
Who says this is an Emergency?

Just because I have your number
No action is needed
This is only a test
of what I can do
if I choose

No action is needed
Please be silent
I am in favor of no action
No need to be alert
THIS IS A TEST

We Need to Talk

JOHN T. PRICE

Dear America,

I've come here to one of my favorite spots of Nebraska prairie to think over our relationship, and I've come to a decision: I love you, but I need some time off. No, this isn't because of the argument we had last night.

Not that you would have noticed, but these last few months have taken a huge toll on me emotionally. I haven't slept well, despite the drinking, and that little tremor in my eyelid has started up again. I've been spending a lot more time in the basement, and less time out here, where I belong—where *we* belong. Yes, I know we've been together for fifty years, and, yes, I know we have had some amazing times together, like last spring on that beach in Malibu when we found the exact spot where, in *Planet of the Apes*, Charlton Heston got down on his knees and screamed, "Damn you all to hell!" Okay, maybe that's not the best example, but still, I think every relationship can benefit from a little time off now and then. Maybe it will give us the space we need to truly reflect on why our relationship, our *love*, matters. Before it's too late.

I realize the problem isn't just you, America. I've taken our relationship for granted. I've been complacent and weak; I've stayed silent when I should have spoken up, which I think you may have mistaken for unconditional support. My country, right or wrong.

But in my defense, there were times when your behavior left me completely speechless. Two summers ago, for instance, when you knew I was grieving a particularly brutal year of grasslands destruction, with 3.7 million acres lost. You may not think that's a big deal, but since you've become obsessed with belittling countries south of the border, let me put it this way: that's more acres than the Brazilian Amazon lost to deforestation.

And how did you respond to my feelings? You bought a gold-plated treadmill and started blabbering about making yourself great again. Can you blame me for thinking that was just a bad joke? And please don't give me that Big Ag crap about being a good provider. I didn't fall in love with the size of your bushels per acre or your checkbook or your ego. I fell in love with your compassionate, democratic, poetic prairie soul!

We used to read actual poetry together, remember? Before you threatened to defund the NEA? Whitman was our favorite, the guy who called the prairies "America's characteristic landscape," the thing that made it truly great—"that vast Something, stretching out on its own unbounded scale, unconfined... combining the real and ideal, and beautiful as dreams." Not to mention all the other passions we once had in common, such as national parks and safe drinking water and feeding poor children and providing medicine for the sick and voting. And facts.

Now I'm just not sure anymore.

I know exactly what you're thinking as you read this: *You don't understand me!* Or worse, you're planning to guilt-trip one of your drinking buddies into leaving me another message on Facebook about how you just "need a little more time." Don't even. I've been there/done that again and again, but every morning it's the same old bullshit. I get out of bed, maybe pick a prairie pasque flower petal (just one, since there aren't that many anymore) to put by your plate, make us breakfast, and then you show up and start in on the immigrants, the Muslims, the Wall, the fake news, the fake science, and it's like I go invisible and you completely forget the pasque flower and the amazing huevos rancheros sitting right in front of your face! It's driving me nuts, America!

And then just last week you proposed "reviewing" national monuments to allow development as well as potentially withdrawing from the Paris Agreement, which you then bragged about at the dinner party we attended yesterday. When I tried to talk with you about it during the drive home, you started yelling at me about how I wouldn't disrespect Sweden like this, or Australia or Russia or China or Canada (I can't recall all the nations you mentioned, but it was a lot). Do you have any concept of how lethal your stupidity can be?

I'm sorry if I sound angry, America, but guess what: you don't have a monopoly on that emotion. Plus, if there's any chance of us staying together, we're going to have to start being honest with each other. And there's no way around it: I *feel* angry. And betrayed. I mean, I've stood by you during some pretty difficult times. Like twenty-five years ago, when I first discovered how you'd spent the entire century before we met destroying prairie ecosystems, leaving them the most endangered in the world, and that you were *still* sneaking off at night to snort "just a few more acres."

I could have left you then, but we talked it out, and even though part of you continued snorting prairie (like during that epic binge in 2014), there is another part of you that joined me in trying to save it. I will never forget the days we spent together seed collecting and pulling up garlic mustard and trying to boost the spirits of those on the front lines of restoring and protecting the native land that I know, deep down, you still love. Not to mention all those hot hours in the tallgrass right here at Glacier Creek Prairie when, despite the ticks, we couldn't keep our hands off each other. Pure sweetness!

We haven't talked about the kids, but then again, you haven't spent much time with them recently. Remember your children? I'm raising three of them right now, and trust me, if it wasn't for them, I might have given up on you years ago. And no, I haven't told them everything you've been up to—I won't put them in the middle—though sooner or later they're going to figure it out. Despite my taking them to this beautiful prairie and telling them about the many good things you've done, are still doing, I can't prevent them from seeing you on TV and on the internet, throwing the ball around with the gun industry and the military drones and the homophobes and the polluters, all of whom are making it less and less safe for their kind to go to school, or even step outside. They're asking a lot of questions I'm finding hard to answer. Still, they love you, and it breaks my heart to think of them losing faith in you. In us.

I guess that's ultimately why I'm writing this letter, why I'm asking for a little honesty and a little space. Not much space—maybe just the distance between our house and an apartment you rent across town, where we can spend the odd night together; just enough for us to gain a little perspective. To remember why we care. And I *really* need you to care right now, truly care, and not just for our children and for our friends and for the prairie, but for every living thing on this planet—because I know you're capable of it. Because I know, despite everything, your soul is big enough.

Did I just say something hopeful? Maybe it's because I'm sitting here in this fragile 320-acre prairie in the middle of Omaha, which, despite the odds, continues to survive. Could it be the same with our romance? Well, you know better than anyone what a bleeding-heart softie I am. Sometimes, between the sheets, you've called me your "sweet little buttercup," even though you know very well that *Ranunculus acris* isn't a native prairie plant. But I guess if we're being honest, that's what I'll always be.

As I said, I still love you, America. Desperately. Let me be clear, though: if you *ever* call me your sweet little buttercup again, I swear to god I'll kick your butt all the way to Mars. From what I hear, you're going there anyway.

With all my love,
John T. Price

#donaldcommanderintweet

RICHARD KENNEY

We mustn't slander our Twitter Commander,
he'll burble our bird and snatch our bander
and fire off a tweet with his hot little hand, or
maybe report us, so stay discreet—

Report us he may, or maybe deport us,
or a whole lot worse than waterboard us
(*all guilty they'll plead, in Superior Court, as
they kiss my ring,* said Commander in Tweet).

Commander in Tweet! Commander in Tweet!
Poke him a little and hear him bleat!
He's a patsy for Putin, is the word on the street—
(*and I think he likes me,* said Commander in Tweet).

Patsy for Putin, Patsy for Putin?—
who bought our election without any shootin'?
Just read the receipt: for whom was he rootin'?
(*I'm* sure *he likes me,* said Commander in Tweet).

Who's his daddy? Why, Uncle Vlad, he
carries his clubs like a nine-hole caddy
(*I think he's sweet—not at all Democratty,
and he really likes me,* said Commander in Tweet).

Commander in Tweet! Commander in Tweet!
Muster the army, commission the fleet!
He's a patsy for Putin, poltroon complete—
(*And that old Constitution? Hit Delete—*)

America: In Theory and Practice

Dear America,

I struggle to keep track and find my way through the pages of your continentally vast volume, a book that could be titled *America: In Theory and Practice*. Its ever-expanding length is stained and scented with all the things that have been "made in the USA" with love and attention as well as recklessness and ill-will.

Dear author of ambition and citizen of uncertainty, I invite you to make any use of this woefully incomplete index, starting scraps for composing a story capacious, and worthy, of its readers.

A

ACT UP
Addams, Jane
affluenza
Agent Orange
air-conditioning
alphabet soup
alternative
    facts
    energy
    press
anthem
app
Apple™
apple pie
Appleseed, Johnny

Arecibo Observatory
Attica

B

bald eagle (*Haliaeetus leucocephalus*)
baloney sandwich
baseball
beef patty
birth control pill
birther
bison (buffalo) (*Bison bison*)
black box
Black Hawk (Sauk chief Ma-ka-tai-me-she-kia-kiak; Sikorsky UH-60 military helicopter)
Black Lives Matter

Fonzie
fortune cookie
fracking

G

gas guzzler
gerrymander
GI Bill
goldenrod (genus *Solidago*)
Gold Rush (1849)
Google
GPA
Grand Canyon
Great
   Acceleration
   Depression
   Gatsby
   God is ____
   Make America ____ Again
greenbacks
greenhouse effect

H

hairspray
hamster wheel
hands-free
Hawai'i
health insurance (lack of)
herbicides
hi
high school
Holiday, Billie
holy moly
hot sauce
hushpuppies
Hutterite

I

ID (voter laws; super-ego)
ICE (Immigration and Customs
   Enforcement)
ice cream
Illini
independent counsel
Indianapolis (Indiana)
Indian Removal Act (1830)
infomercial

J

J, LL Cool
jackalope
Jackson
   Andrew (*see* Indian Removal
   Act)
   Michael
jazz
jeans (blue)
Jell-O shots
jewelweed (*Impatiens capensis*)
juggalo
jumbo jet
jump shot
june bug (beetle, genus
   Phyllophaga)

K

Kaczynski, Ted
Kentucky
   coffee tree (*Gymnocladus
   dioicus*)
   Derby
   Fried Chicken
ketchup

keystone
  cops
  species
Keystone XL pipeline
kickflip
kidfluence
kudzu (genus *Pueraria*)
Ku Klux Klan

L

Lassie
Las Vegas
liability
libel
liberal
Liberty (Statue of)
limitations (statute of)
lobby
  hotel
  political
loblolly pine (*Pinus taeda*)
loot
lottery ticket
Louis, Morris
low-fat

M

marriage equality
Massachusetts
mass shooting
McCarthyism
McClintock, Barbara
melting pot
Merton, Thomas
Miami (*see* sea level rise)
military-industrial complex
milkweed (genus *Asclepias*)

Mississippi River
monarch butterfly (*Danaus plexippus*)
monster truck (*see* capitalism)
moonwalk
moral luck
Mormons
mortality
Mr.
  Peanut
  Rogers
  T
mullet
Muppet Show

N

911
9/11
9/9/11
99% (the)
nachos
national parks
neoprene
new and improved
New Orleans
Nineteenth Amendment (1919)
nuclear
  deterrent
  family

O

OK
OMG
opioid
OPP
Oppenheimer, Robert
opportunity

optics
orange juice
ore
oxbow

P

patent pending
peanut
   allergy
   butter and jelly sandwich
   farmer
penicillin
petro-subjectivity (B. Bloom)
plastics
poetry
popcorn
possibility
poverty
pro-
   gun
   life
   sports
protean
protein
PTSD
public radio
Puerto Rico
pumpkin
purple mountain majesty

Q

Q-tips
quahog
quarter pounder
Quest (Tribe Called)
quilting
quixotic
quiz show

QWERTY

R

raccoons
Radner, Gilda
razzle-dazzle
reality (*see* TV)
redwood tree (*Sequoia
   sempervirens*)
religion (freedom of)
reverse mortgage
Rice, Tamir
riches
Ride, Sally
riot grrl
robber baron
robotics (Three Laws of; Asimov)
rock dove (*Columba livia*)
Rubik's cube

S

Sagan, Carl
saguaro cactus (*Carnegiea
   gigantea*)
Sandy Hook
sea
   change
   level rise
   shore
sí (se puede)
Simone, Nina
Simpsons, The
skyscraper
snapping turtle (*Chelydra
   serpentina*)
soap opera
star-spangled
state

XXX

Y

Yes Men
Yippie
"yo mama" (jokes)
Youth (Sonic)
YouTube
Yo-Yo Ma
Ypsilanti
Yuppie
YWCA

Z

Zamboni
zealotry
zebra mussel
zines
zip code
zip line
zombie economy (*see* Wall Street)
zydeco
ZZZZ

Fourteen Donalds

VINCE GOTERA

To begin, we, sputtering, duck.
With a little bit rock and roll.
Took his Chevy to the levee.
Train with a whole lot of soul.

Scowling with sour pickles.
Presiding evil in a hungry land.
Copping out in neon Miami.
Soaring like a bird in a band.

Read his poems out in the hall.
Read his story to white noise.
Sputtering again like a deputy.
In Miami once more, won twice.

In the rainsong, least of the three.
In the wash, who's despicable me?

ANSWERS: Donald Duck, Donnie
Osmond, Don McLean, Don Cornelius,
Don Rickles, Donald Sutherland, Don
Johnson, Donald Byrd, Donald Hall,
Don DeLillo, Don Knotts, Don Shula,
Donald O'Connor, Donald Trump

Why I Am Not President:
A Campaign Speech

DENNIS HELD

My shallow Americans, in the face of moral decay
And in the absence of justice and humility, let us thank
Ourselves for our brutality and willful blindness
And bury the rotting corpse of human dignity
Now and forever amen and let us also forget
The national debt which we shall never pay
But rather let us hand the burden of our selfishness
To our blessed children whose lives we've ruined
By singeing them with the same list of empty lusts
And heartlessness that hyperdrive our unreflective lives
in the name of the damned Almighty Dollar ah-men.

Give us once more the moolah for bombs smarter
Than ourselves and drones that kill faster than children
Can run and grant us the gall we need to plead
Innocent before the court of history and bribe
Our memories to allow us to believe the cracked
And flaking mask of virtue we besmirch thee with
Oh Lord we beseech thee now and again ah-men.

I Go In

TARFIA FAIZULLAH

I GO IN

TO: All Residents
FROM: The Man

hope

will be

CLOSED.

protocol requires

photo ID's

every time.

remain inside   only.

coals

coals   ashes

The police will be ████████████████████████ getting out of
hand. ████████████████ you are responsible ████████████
██████████
██
████████ question ██████████████████████████████████████
████████████████████ everyone ████████
Happy ████████ dependence Day

Geographies of
Inclusion and Renewal

After His Election,
I Make a Zen Garden

GARY SOTO

A pie tin, five cups of sand,
A thimble with water,
A dry branch, a cotton ball worth of moss,
River pebbles and polished stone,
Maybe a small shell, maybe glass roughed up by the sea...
And by noon I have a garden.
Let me go inside a tree for the next few years.

I offer a spring blossom to my creation.
I hum a three-syllable chant.
I rake the sand and dip my pinkie into the thimble—
So this is the taste of Buddha mind.

This is my garden after the election.
This is my sanctuary on a windowsill,
A monk-like ant trekking the ledge.
A stick of incense is lit, the dead remembered.

I feel a terrible force at work—
A hundred days in office,
Not enough sand to bury his deeds.

The World Is Large and Other Things You Thought You Knew

SEAN HILL

Dear America,

I'd meant to send a postcard from the road last summer, before Charlottesville and tiki torches were in the news. I flew my sixty-nine-year-old father up to Fairbanks to help with my family's move to Georgia, my home state. Dad would make the drive with me and my dog to Seattle, where I'd exchange him at the airport for my young son and his mother, who would continue the drive south. You were with me and Dad the whole way, America, in spirit when not in body—over ten hours a day for four days.

My father summed up that gorgeous drive in a call with a friend once we'd reemerged into coverage after a couple of days of network silence: "I ain't seen nothing but snowcapped mountains and forests for three days!" We still had another day of driving to actually cross the border and get back to you. All that way across first Alaska and then Canada—more than two thousand miles. Dad brought a sense of the world borne out of his relationship with you. His experience of what felt to him like the middle-of-nowhere was shaped by seven decades of living with you—our home.

Between Fairbanks and our first destination—Whitehorse, in Yukon Territory—we saw mountains and braided rivers and possibly a black bear and definitely grizzly bears and small lakes and a vast one and elk and more mountains. The next day while driving through British Columbia, I asked my dad a question I'd been curious about. He and I don't spend that much time together, and this felt like a once-in-our-lifetimes trip. A week of just us round-the-clock. I silenced the podcast about architecture and asked what I hoped would be an open question that would lead to stories and conversation: "What was the great shift in society that happened in your lifetime that you can't help but think about sometimes? You know, what was the thing that changed your world?"

My dad's considered answer was: "Cell phones, the telephone, and radio and television—the things that let people communicate over great distances and keep in touch. We talked to your mother this morning. The internet. People can do business long distance. Those are the things that changed the world."

Communication technology. I was surprised. I'd expected him to say desegregation. I told him as much because that's what I wanted to hear about. America, my father graduated from a legally segregated high school in the mid-1960s. The schools in my hometown of Milledgeville, Georgia, weren't desegregated until the 1970–71 school year, which was about the time that "with all deliberate speed" from the 1955 *Brown II* decision worked to enact desegregation and end the era of legally sanctioned "separate but equal" in many places.

"Your mother would drink out of 'whites only' water fountains out of defiance as much as a political stance; that's your mother," he said.

He went on, "I just thought those were the rules and accepted them. I didn't really think about it."

I found it fascinating that as a young man my dad didn't seriously question being a less-than-equal citizen in a segregated society. You see, America, I've always thought of my father as civic-minded. He's been in leadership roles in civic organizations and the church my entire life—the perfect outlets for his extroverted nature, his need to help others, and his political awareness. But he told me that didn't arise until after high school, when he joined friends marching in our hometown. Only then did he understand how wrong things were and that they could be changed; he could help change society. We continued to talk on down the road.

For our second night, I'd booked us a room at the Tatogga Lake Resort. Tired but with plenty of light left in the high-latitude summer day, we pulled into the gravel parking lot and found the "historic" log restaurant and office closed for the evening. The sign on the door said to find the manager in number 2, but at the row of rustic cabins in clear view number 2 was vacant. I returned to the sign on the restaurant door. A couple of middle-aged white guys dressed in road-trip casual, wearing jeans like us, strolled through the parking lot. They glanced at me and my father but didn't offer any guidance. Dad took their quiet glance for the side-eye of "a couple of good ol' boys."

When eventually we found the manager, Dad thought the flustered big guy in his late twenties or early thirties was a redneck trying to give us trouble at the end of a long day of driving. I thought the burly white Canadian was only trying to stay on his wife's good side—making a show of making sure I understood they'd just recently had a guest with a little dog that messed up the room. He was certain our dog, sixty pounds of what I call "all-American mixed breed," would be fine, but "you know how some people make it hard for everyone else."

When he explained that there were no keys and we should leave our door unlocked until we turned in for the night so as not to lock ourselves out, saying, "It's just us and the bears," I heard fact. Dad heard threat.

The next morning things changed a little. At breakfast, Dad noted that the two men he'd thought were a couple of good ol' boys were German tourists; I had a pleasant chat with them while taking the dog on her morning walk. And the manager shared with me that he'd found out that one of his ancestors a few generations back was Black and from Louisiana, and he wanted to visit one day. Then he warned us to keep watch for black bears the way folks in Georgia will tell you to look out for deer. Indeed, one crossed right in front of us just down the road.

On our last day in Canada, on the phone with a friend who'd called from home, my father expressed how impressed he was with my insouciant driving: "He driving like it ain't nothing. All these mountains. Seem like we been going downhill for over an hour, and we still going down." He said, "Mountain on one side and a river on the other way down below, and if you went off over there they wouldn't know how to get you back." I drove while he carried on his conversation, proud that I'd impressed my father.

After he got off the phone we chatted about road trips. I love them; I've crisscrossed the country more times than a few. Maine's your only state I haven't visited, and I've been to six of Canada's thirteen provinces and territories. This was my second time making this drive from Fairbanks and my third on this stretch of highway. After a while, my father got quiet among those dwarfing mountains, the deep canyon with the rushing river just the other side of the guardrail. I could see his face go still, and then its small gestures didn't fit what was happening outside or inside the car. I asked what was on his mind.

"I'm sitting here thinking about my deck and my little koi pond in my small backyard in my little corner of the world," he said. I heard homesickness and something else—the sound of a rising realization. After a moment he said, "The world is large."

That evening we got across the border and back home to you. Now, I've had problems at borders before. I've had trunk searches on occasion, my residency questioned once, been asked inside the station to answer questions, and a full-on search of my car, its contents, and my laptop. I've thought my color—Suspect Brown, a shade on most law enforcement's color profile chart—was quite possibly the reason for their attention. So with my dog and my dad I was a little nervous but hopeful that things would go smoothly. My dad was cleared, but the border patrol agent raised an eyebrow at me and my story—a professor with his family dog and dad moving from Alaska back to his home state of Georgia. After some questions, he asked if I'd had trouble at border crossings before. It seemed I shared some points of similarity with someone on the wrong side of the law. The agent directed me inside to get our records disentangled. His desire to help me made me hopeful.

Inside I turned over my passport and paperwork. One of the agents asked more questions, including whether I had any tattoos. I don't. He requested that I show him my right arm, so I removed the long-sleeved shirt I was wearing over my T-shirt. He then scanned my passport. Looking at a screen as the data processed he said sternly, "If alarms go off and lights start flashing, you're in trouble." I laughed. He didn't. I nervously asked if that was a joke. No lights or alarms. He looked up, smiled, and said, "Yes." He handed back my passport, and my father and I continued on across the border—returned to you in body.

America, you are the basis of our perspectives; our relationships with you shape and shade the lens through which we look at everything. But perspectives can shift, and I saw my dad's experience and understanding—that the world is big—as hopeful.

That was June. Then came July, and we finally arrived in our new home where we were busy trying to settle in. We'd moved to a small university town below the gnat line—a little farther south than my hometown. It was a slightly different ecosystem, but more familiar than any I'd lived in since leaving Georgia seventeen years ago, when

I was twenty-seven. The flora and fauna sent me into quiet transports of happiness—the smells, sounds, and light of my youth. The human ecosystem seemed a bit different from the South I'd grown up in, as my father's South was different from mine. Interracial couples with biracial children (i.e., my family) don't cause universal and open consternation the way they would have in the 1980s or even the raised eyebrows of the 1990s. But it is still the South, and trying to understand it I noticed little things. For example, one of the options for specialty license plates offered by the state has a Confederate flag framed by the "Sons of Confederate Veterans 1896." I'm still working through how to see these tags and the people who drive cars bearing them.

And then August came, and the weekend before classes began the latest violence that seems to define you more and more took place in Charlottesville. The Unite the Right rally brought together various groups identifying as white nationalists, white supremacists, and neo-Nazis around the cause of saving a statue of Robert E. Lee. Friday evening they held a tiki torch–lit march, chanting, "You will not replace us." On Saturday, one of their numbers drove a car into a crowd of counterprotesters, killing a young woman and injuring nineteen others.

I have a hard time not seeing these men (some of them "very fine people," according to President Trump) as anything but what they proclaim to be—and what their actions show them to be. They've framed their protestations around a fear of obsolescence as they circle around a statue of a man who fought 150 years ago for a confederacy of states in a war that, according to Georgia's declaration of secession, revolved around "the subject of African slavery"—the enslavement of my ancestors. The statue was erected in 1924, almost sixty years after the end of the war. Now, another ninety years later, these men drew demarcating lines of identity. They made their world smaller. They chose to identify with a statue of Robert E. Lee. These men who find their community with the Klan, Citizens' Councils of America, and Council of Conservative Citizens more than they do with me took what most might have thought of as a nostalgic tropical throwback and made it topical. They co-opted the tiki torch. Did they make the bamboo patio torch of summer parties into their great-grandfather's, grandfather's, or even father's torches? How much room is there for doubt that they made it a threat?

The thing is, America, today there's talk of "social media echo chambers" and "confirmation bias," and I get that and am susceptible to those things too. We have all this information and communication technology that has given more people than ever a platform from which to communicate and share ideas widely (my dad was right). And all we seem to do is become more entrenched in our corners. We may think, owing to our experience as a less-than-equal citizen in a segregated society where our neighbors across the color line (if they didn't terrorize us and those who looked like us) rest on the power structure created from our less-than status, that most (not all, but any we're likely to encounter) white men are either rednecks or good ol' boys. Or we may think, owing to our limited experience across the color line or based on what we've learned from the movies and television or word of mouth, that no matter their age, most (not all, but any we're likely to encounter) Black males are threatening thugs or simply less-than-equal people.

As I write this I'm reminded that my father couldn't see the men we encountered on our trip for who they were, not at first. Our trip reminded me that I should always try to see individuals for who they are and be ready to meet them accordingly.

Yours,
Sean

A Still Hopeful Geography

DAVID GESSNER

It has been my lot over the last three years to be working on a book about an American president I admire while living under an American president I despise. Often during this time I have fantasized about an actual confrontation between the two men: 26 vs. 45. Roosevelt vs. Trump.

GESSNER

As it happens, all through his life the president famous for shouting "Bully!" had little tolerance for them. And though Donald Trump is taller and certainly heavier than Theodore Roosevelt, he would have his hands full with a president who boxed and studied jujitsu while in the White House.

Witnessing a physical confrontation would be fun, but a mental and verbal battle would be even better. The great thinker and speaker, the author of more than forty books who read a book a night and whose mind ranged throughout history, debating the nonreader, the non-speaker, the nonthinker. The match would be competitive only in terms of raw belligerence and self-confidence but unequal in all other ways. Particularly since TR was most eloquent when spurred to outrage and since nothing drove him to outrage like the rising tide of commercialism and crassness that was flooding the America he loved. He hated nothing more than "the wealthy criminal class" and "predatory wealth."

While Roosevelt abhorred corruption, perhaps the area where these two men are most diametrically opposed is in their attitude toward the American wilderness. Of that wilderness Mr. Trump has said: "We can leave a little bit, but you can't destroy businesses." Mr. Roosevelt, on the other hand, felt a reverence and wonder toward the land that, despite some bullying flaws of his own, has always redeemed him for me. Perhaps his most famous words about wilderness were "leave it as it is," and I like to imagine him saying those words, sharply, emphatically, and confidently, to our current president whenever he tries to reduce another national monument or park.

I am well aware of recent arguments that undermine the national park ideal, namely that the "pristine" wildernesses that Theodore Roosevelt and others saved had already been inhabited by human beings for ten thousand years. There are flaws in what the writer Wallace Stegner, citing Lord Bryce, called "America's best idea," flaws that recent efforts, like those of the coalition of tribes that helped create Bears Ears National Monument, are trying to correct. But we need to put these flaws in context: the total time of human habitation of this continent is a blink compared to the millions of years that things ran, swam, flew, grew, flourished, and evolved here. There is such thing as being a species bigot too.

It was Roosevelt's genius that he understood this. "For the Benefit and Enjoyment of the People" reads the sign above the arch at Yellowstone. But Roosevelt's secret agenda was to preserve the park not just for the people but for the thousands of animals and plants and lichen and fungi. Seen from a car today while stuck in a mile-long traffic jam, Yellowstone can seem like a disaster. But the caricature of a park is not the park. Only 1 percent of the greater Yellowstone ecosystem is made up of roads; 99 percent is the realm of the elk, bear, wolf, and cougar. Actual wild animals. That's what TR loved about Yellowstone, not the geysers, and that's what he wanted to save. And he did. I remind myself that there are 4,500 bison, 500 wolves, and 10,000 elk who aren't listening when ecomodernist scholars tell us that wilderness does not exist.

Douglas Brinkley writes of Roosevelt, near the end of *The Wilderness Warrior:* "He saw the planet as one single biological organism pulsing with life and championed the interconnectedness of nature as his own Sermon on the Mount. As forces of globalization run amok, Roosevelt's stout resoluteness to protect our environment is a strong reminder of our national wilderness heritage, as well as an increasingly urgent call to arms." Roosevelt found that interconnectedness everywhere, including while birding on the beaches and woods near his Long Island home, but it was in the vast lands of the West, lands that thanks in part to him were to become protected lands, that he found something more.

I mentioned Wallace Stegner. Roosevelt believed in what Stegner called "the geography of hope." That is what the western landscape has always been for me, a born easterner, and that is what it is for so many of us. Not a symbol of hope but hope embodied. This phrase—"the geography of hope"—came at the end of Stegner's "Wilderness Letter" of 1960. He knew the story Roosevelt had spent his life telling, and in his famous letter he retold and articulated it as well as anyone ever has:

> Something will have gone out of us as a people if we ever let the
> remaining wilderness be destroyed; if we permit the last virgin
> forests to be turned into comic books and plastic cigarette cases; if
> we drive the few remaining members of the wild species into zoos or
> to extinction; if we pollute the last clear air and dirty the last clean
> streams and push our paved roads through the last of the silence, so
> that never again will Americans be free in their own country from the
> noise, the exhausts, the stinks of human and automotive waste. And
> so that never again can we have the chance to see ourselves single,
> separate, vertical and individual in the world, part of the environment
> of trees and rocks and soil, brother to the other animals, part of the
> natural world and competent to belong in it.

If the West and its public lands are in fact still a geography of hope, it might be worth it to give some thought to where hope comes from. A country as surely evolves out of its physical features as a human being out of his or her physiology, and the existence of so-called wild places has always been part of this country's DNA. Stegner knew that people were shaped by the place they inhabited. This is common sense, not mysticism. As ideals, hope or freedom grew out of a country with a continent's worth of places laid out in front of it, better places just beyond. The fact that those wild places have shrunken down to islands only argues more strongly that we must protect and expand what is left. "Better a wounded wilderness than none at all," Stegner wrote.

There is still a whiff of the old American exceptionalism in "The Wilderness Letter," but Stegner isn't claiming that we are the only people on earth to have a deep relationship with our place. That would be absurd and jingoistic. Cultures all over the world have grown out of the land and have beautifully expressed people's love for those lands. But while Americans are not unique, it is not absurd to say that we too have developed a certain sort of language, and a kind of spiritualism, in our attitude toward the land. It is reflected in our literature and our art. I recently spoke to a book club in Colorado made up of people whom you would otherwise mostly regard as nonreligious, and I heard their tone shift when I asked them about nature. I don't think it is an exaggeration to say that for more than a small percentage of Americans, nature *is* their religion.

It might seem antiquated and a little quaint to be focusing on saving wilderness in an overheated world full of violence and racism. I don't think it is. I believe that the land we have set aside, land where we have allowed animals, plants, and trees to live and with any luck evolve without too much human interference, is still the greatest thing about our country. For me the land itself is the single best reason for hope in what often seems a hopeless time. Not small and quibbling human plans and contretemps but the land. A physical statement of our belief in the future.

New Names

JOE WILKINS

When I was a boy the fields reached all the way to the dry sagebrush hills, and the hills rose and sloped off to the north, and after school or on summer mornings or with most any given span of minutes on my hands, that's the way I went. I followed the farm road for a time. Then paths of my own devising—up an irrigation dike to the ditch, along the ditch's lip to the barbed-wire fence, through the messy stand of cotton-woods, where I cached my treasures, bones and fossils and slingshot rocks, the kinds of things one finds and needs on journeys such as these.

Eagles cut the sky above me. Antelope shied and shifted and, as was their wont, turned and outran the wind. I was myself and not myself. I was my grandfather, all the many stories he told, but mostly the burning young cowboy he had been so long ago, always at a hard gallop across the flats. I was my grandmother, lolling in the tall grass with a book in her hands, the Crow off near the Big Horn singing their mourning songs. I was my father, jolly and black-haired and strong of back, my father loved and then one hard year dead, and so loved all the harder for his untimely dying. I was my mother, the fiercest of them all, firing the tractor and instructing my brother and me to stand there and there, on the wings of the plow itself, so that as she turned us around the field our small weight might lever the blade that much deeper. Coming through the willows I was Buster Knapp, a man I never met but whom everyone claimed was the best rifle shot the county had ever seen. Crossing the cactus-and-yucca-studded wastes I was lost John Colter. Standing at the threshold of the dead pile, Crazy Horse.

My back against the warm earth, the song of buffalo grass and wind at my ear, I was myself and all these other selves. I was never alone. I was richly accompanied. After some hours I returned from the hills and fields braver, kinder, sadder, wiser, more willing. This is what the land allows, if we let it. A radical, self-shattering, world-building imagining.

. . .

Twenty-three days since the election, twenty-three days of disbelief and grief and donations and letters and phone calls and meetings—and it is time to go to the woods. We pack our pop-up camper and in a mizzling rain drive west into the Coast Range, north up 101, and finally pull in at Cape Lookout, a gnarled finger of volcanic rock poking into the Pacific. In the early dark we set up the camper and heat leftover clam chowder, then despite the rain hike to the angry ocean to say hello. The night falls black and windy. We sleep fitfully, rain threshing the trees.

The next day, though, brings scattered rain breaks, and we hike the woods, my children hiding in the knuckled roots of hemlock and spruce, calling, when I don't find them fast enough, in hoots and hooahs, in the voices of owls. We clamber along the rocks above the frothing ocean. We perch on the highest dune and watch the waves lace and unlace, lift and leap and shatter, the globe itself curving west away from us, beneath the clouds. Later we light a fire, my daughter, five, crunching up handfuls of newspaper, my son, seven, laying kindling sticks just so. I light a match, and flames play across our faces. We gather there, the four of us, a family, and as the embers shift and dim, without a word we click on our headlamps and move once again into the woods, there play shadow and chase, study all that is familiar—fern and salal and Oregon grape—gone in the night so wonderful and strange.

We gather, finally, along a tiny, mossy creek, like a hand holding us the cupped, head-high roots of an ancient Sitka spruce. We crouch down, we touch shoulders, hands. We turn off our headlamps and in the pure dark dub ourselves the No Moon Clan, our names now Shadowclaw, Cloudmist, Moonfire, Starlight.

And when, some moments later, I click my headlamp back on, it's true. My children have transformed. I see it in their rainy eyes, the way they touch and toe the wet earth.

. . .

In the days ahead we will huddle on the banks of creeks and rivers, in the shadows of mountains. We will lay our hands on the hard, good skin of trees. We will be tired, we will be nearly sad to death.

What is coming is not new, true—it is merely, terrifyingly, the worst in us given power—yet it's true, too, that we will need new names to fight it. We will need all of our ancestors, our children, every hero. We need now to be more than what we have been.

Look to the fields and hills and spruce forests, look to the fire, the shadow, the mist running across the moon. How multiple, how yielding and unyielding, how wise in the moment.

Stomach no bullshit.

Be fierce for love, for all the real things.

Dear Milo

LAWRENCE LENHART

Dear Milo,

It is possible to be too much in love with something. For example: the other day, I tossed you in the air (despite Mom's prohibition), hoping to elicit a smile big enough to reveal the pegs of deciduous teeth emerging from your gums. Even though I was bound to catch you (I always will), I forgot the ceiling fan was on and nearly decapitated you. Love can be dangerous like that. I am not sorry, but could have been. Ever since, I've been holding you in the basket of my arms, staring at your neck, imagining it severed. I decide the fan blades are too blunt to amputate even a foam finger. Still, I trace the creases over your trachea, wondering. Sometimes you smile for no reason at all. The tooth eruption has only just begun, and it's likely you'll be gummy for another year. I give you my pinky to gnaw on, and, for the moment, you're mollified.

I add "decapitation" to the long list of concepts I don't yet know how to explain to you. Our "sex talk" will be easy due to an overabundance of resources on the matter. But where's the pamphlet on *How to Talk to Your Kid About*... alternative facts, border walls, travel bans, white-nationalist rallies, national anthems, collusion, Gaza, and seeing other kids in cages? And how to introduce the idea of extinction when you've barely mastered object permanence?

Another thing I love—and you probably know this by now since you hear me speaking its name all hours of the day: the black-footed ferret. It was the first animal (stuffed) to share a crib with you. *Ferret* was the reason I almost missed your birth; at thirty-eight weeks, I volunteered on a remote ranch without a cell signal, drawing blood from small mammals possibly infected with plague. *Ferret* is the thing I try to pick out by itself, only to "find it hitched to everything else in the

Universe," to quote John Muir. The "universe," Milo. I'm not even sure how to explain the "neighborhood" to you yet—let alone "Arizona," "America," the "biome."

The real reason I'm writing: please don't get me one of those ancestry DNA kits for Father's Day. Not this year, not ever. Our extended family has superficially rectified any mystery worth the yarning. They've tattooed national flags on their torsos, struck up correspondences with long-lost relatives, and even bought purebred dogs that hail from the county of their country of origin. There are factions who would have you believe we're so Irish we shouldn't leave the house without a shillelagh. But I refuse to believe that ancestry is some self-fulfilling prophecy you can purchase with a credit card and a loogie. It isn't meant to retroactively inform your consumer behaviors, explain your freckles despite your olive complexion, or stoke tourism to some muddled motherland. I have this sneaking suspicion that the genealogy boom (the local news tells me the kits are the top-trending gift this Father's Day) is a temporary evil that has something to do with the rise of white nationalism and the suppression of cultural globalization. By discovering where we *do* come from, we are able to clarify: we do *not* come from that other place. But I could be wrong. I've always been a miserabilist, son. I apologize now and forever. I know you're my descendant—in fact, you were named after the punk front man of *The Descendents*—and that's enough, genetically speaking, for me. Let's skip the tongue swabs and just spend Father's Day hiking the open spaces in this forest of a city: Flagstaff.

I am no father to a ferret, Milo, but it's important to think I could be. After all, there are thousands of men who abandon their biological children daily; how can we expect them to care for the next generation of wildness when they can't be bothered with their own domestic brood? For example, the other day, we were killing a couple of hours in San Jose. I called six cemeteries in the area, hoping to find a "Nick Leonard." He was "definitely not" in the directory for cemeteries #1, 3, and 5; unlikely to have been buried in the Jewish cemetery (#2); and I just had a hunch, without ever meeting the guy, that #4 was not his style. We went to the sixth cemetery, your mother and I stalking alternate rows, scanning the mausoleums for his name. I carried you for a while, whispering: "We are trying to find your father's father's father's father." You laughed—maybe at the sonic repetition or the way we kept converging upon Mom. Or perhaps you know better than me: he's unfindable.

For most of his life, that was true. When Nick left the family during the Great Depression—goodbye wife, goodbye son, goodbye daughter—he found work in New York, Indiana, and Illinois before choosing a new name, family, and coast. That's how Lenhart spontaneously became Leonard. In the 1980s, Nick's second wife called to tell us how impressive his gravesite was. "It's a one-person mausoleum," she said. "Don't you want to come see it?"

At the time, my dad (your Pap) said, "Not really." But now. Now that I was doing the legwork, he called in a favor. "Piss on his grave for me, will you?" I won't be able to teach you about "desecration" or "grudges" or "intergenerational trauma" until after I teach you how to pee at a specific target. These things take time, Milo.

Most of the names in that Catholic cemetery were Italian, which seemed to mean we were in the right place. Nick's original name was something like Lenbratto, but he changed it to improve his employability in a racist (even then) western Pennsylvania. The more I had to pee, the closer I thought I might have been getting to the grave. Ironically, you were taken from my arms when you wet your diaper, leaving me to continue the charade, now with more velocity. It was the first time I ever craved one of those small drones with the aerial cam. (The drone is the second most popular gift this year; don't get me one of those either!) How quickly I could have whipped through the cemetery, verifying Nick's interment—or not. I think not, after all.

The real reason we were in San Jose, though, was to meet your mother's uncle. Orphaned in rural Vietnam where he was a stable-sleeping cowherd who ate only rice and bananas, Henry (his American name) was discovered by missionaries who transferred him to Manila and then Oakland. Wearing his only outfit, he moved to America and lived just a two-hour drive from his half-sister (your grandmother). Only he didn't know it until his Amerasian friends encouraged him to sign up for Ancestry last year. "Hello, my sister," he wrote to your grandmother who had mostly been using the service to fine-tune the plot of her perfect *Mayflower* story. "Excuse me?" she asked. And just like that, Henry went from being a bastard of the Vietnam War to a Son of the American Revolution.

Before we went into Henry's house, I asked your mother if she was planning on calling him "uncle." She wasn't sure. But Henry was the one to set the tone; speaking in English but with Vietnamese grammar, particularly using kinship pronouns, he began nearly all his sentences with the word "uncle" (rather than "I"). It's like when I say to you, "Daddy is tired, Milo. Daddy is really, really tired." The beauty of the kinship pronoun is that the speaker does all the work for the listener. It seems odd to me that I won't speak to you like this forever. Because it begins to sound patronizing in American English, eventually parents abandon the kinship grammar and begin using the first-person "I."

Your father's father's father's father. Your mother's mother's father's son. Your father's father's father's father's father's father's father's father. Say it enough times, and you'll exceed the DNA kit's capacity to convey an ancestry that can be viably enjoyed. One product promises: "Held within our DNA code is the history of humanity." In reality, our genome reveals much more: the history of all life on Earth.

Come to think of it, Milo. What I *would* like for Father's Day: a frame for my "Certificate of Adoption" for the black-footed ferret. It's the only gift I've ever accepted from a student, and I'm entirely proud of it. I guess you could say this makes you a brother. More symbol than sibling, this "adopted" ferret from the World Wildlife Fund will continue snoozing in a burrow rather than your bunk.

It's been a few months since I've seen a live ferret. Do you remember when I drove to Seligman on Good Friday with some friends? We arrived at that hour the Bible says Jesus died. There's a famous quote in that book in which Jesus interrogates God. "Why have you abandoned me?" he asks. I remember having enough pluck to ask a priest in Catholic school if this meant Jesus was a bastard. His answer, which leaned heavily on the "virgin birth" paradigm, was inconclusive.

After sunset, we got to driving through the ranchlands, flashing lights over the tufted steppe, looking for the eye shine of black-footed ferrets.

When I teach you about "death," Milo... When I teach you about "extinction"... How to explain that sometimes beings are resurrected? This might be my one concession to "faith," so lend me your brand-new ears.

Dead center in white light, we all saw it. And it saw us.

We sprinted jaggedly toward the ferret, just one-tenth of a mile away. Hardwired in those strides and my beating heart: that's where I keep my biophilia, my urge, as Edward O. Wilson puts it, "to affiliate with other forms of life." It was in our recovery hunch, our lungs wheezing like bellows, that we got a good glimpse. The ferret lingered as if it was an act of diplomacy. We had our little tête-à-tête at 35°27′54.1″N 113°01′25.3″W, and then we set the trap.

I wondered if it was born in vitro at the zoo (of virgin birth) or if it was wild-born, a product of conservation well done? It never emerged for us, not even on Easter Sunday, so we all went home with our near-resurrection experience. I slipped into bed at 6 a.m., just as you were stirring. "Good morning," I said to your mom. "Goodnight," she said back. I am often failing to get the best of both worlds.

I toss you in the air, Milo. I toss you again. Don't worry: the fan is off this time. The blades are resting. I say to you: "Father's father's father's father." And you begin to repeat, your bottom lip flinging off your top teeth. It sounds something like "fa-fa-fa-fa."

If you say it enough times, *father* and *father* and *father* and *father*, it begins to sound like *farther* and *farther*, occasionally *forever*, like you're tracing a distant line. "Fa-fa-fa-fa," you say. "Fa-fa-fa-fa." I toss you up just as you've reached the dawning of the Cenozoic. "Fa-fa-fa-fa." You're nearly face-to-face with the ancestor of all placental mammals, humans and ferrets alike. "Fa-fa-fa-fa-fa-fa-fa-fa." There is something urgent in your babbling. There is the semblance of an urge. "Fa-fa-fa-fa." That's how you get your furry sibling after all.

Always your father,
Larry

Geography Lessons

B. J. HOLLARS

Dear America,

We went in search of you but found a storm instead. This was June 8, 2018—a year and a half into a presidential term that would not end, and one day into my son's first day of summer vacation. That final bell of kindergarten in Eau Claire, Wisconsin, had barely rung before I swept six-year-old Henry into the car and began our 2,500-mile drive west.

Our mission: to "rediscover" you, America, by retracing the Oregon Trail. Delusional as I was, I'd convinced myself that vital lessons might spring forth from the earth if we only rolled over enough of it. If we retraced the footsteps of those who came before. If we buckled up, burned rubber, and talked to Americans who were not the Americans we saw on the nightly news. Not the ones bearing tiki torches in Charlottesville but the ones who would fight to snuff those torches out. I needed to find those people, for my son's sake.

But we only made it 575 miles to Doniphan, Nebraska, before our mission became sidetracked by the weather.

At first, it was nothing more than a 2 a.m. breeze rippling against the nylon tent. But soon those ripples become rattles, and those rattles increased in speed.

"Henry, get your butt up!" I hollered. "It's storming!"

"Hmmm?"

"Come on," I said, tugging on his sleeping bag. "Let's move."

Since we were the last tent standing (the rest of the campground had the good sense to clear out), I unthreaded the tent poles from their holders, collapsed the tent, then hustled us into our vehicle.

I took my place in the driver's seat and turned to help Henry assemble his nest in the back. Pushing aside the cooler and the dry bag, I piled both our sleeping bags atop him, swaddling him like the old days. "You okay?" I asked.

He opened his eyes long enough to consider it. "No," he said.

"No?"

"My hat. I lost my hat."

Not just any hat but his favorite—the bright red, big-billed bit of headgear that, for reasons beyond my understanding, we'd determined was surely the talisman for our trip.

I took a breath, preparing myself to brave the storm in search of what had gone missing. But before I opened the car door I spotted a woman's silhouette sprinting toward us: head down, arms pumping, her legs a pair of pistons at full tilt. Backlit by lightning, the woman reached the passenger door. Arm raised, she revealed the red hat in her hand.

"Is this yours?" she shouted over the wind.

I leapt out of the car and ran around to her, gripping the soggy hat in my hands. "Thank you!" I shouted.

"No problem!" she shouted back, and retreated into the darkness.

It was the first kindness.

■ ■ ■

A thousand or so miles later, we ran into a problem of another sort. This was long after leaving Chimney Rock and Scotts Bluff in our rearview mirror. Long after our visits to Fort Kearny, Fort Laramie, Guernsey Ruts, and every other vestige of tangible proof of the overland travelers who'd come before.

We'd just concluded our stop at Idaho's Register Rock—an off-the-beaten-path boulder tagged with immigrant names—when our mission got diverted again. We still had two hundred miles to Boise, though upon starting the engine I noticed an unfamiliar message scrolling along the vehicle's display screen.

"That's weird," I said.

"What's weird?" Henry asked.

"The screen says 'oil change recommended.'"

The brown desert outside sizzled at a sweat-inducing ninety-one degrees, but the temperature inside the car climbed much higher. I'd insisted on making this stop at Register Rock to impress upon Henry the difficult conditions immigrants had to endure. Now, with car trouble looming, I worried that the lesson was becoming a little too real.

B.J. HOLLARS

I put the car in drive, then careened past Rock Creek along Register Road until I spotted the interstate ahead. The miles passed like seasons, and eventually we puttered into a Jiffy Lube near downtown Boise.

"How can we help you?" a young oil-specked technician said.

I explained the situation.

Within minutes, the technician returned with inconclusive news. "The oil's dirty," he said, "but it's sort of right on the line." Since I knew more about covered wagons than cars, this information helped little.

In walked a man named Dave in a Jiffy Lube shirt, pens spilling forth from his breast pocket. Dave and the technician debated the severity of our problem—to change the oil or not—until eventually Dave pulled rank. He turned toward Henry, then me.

"Listen," he said, "I'm not going to have you and your son getting stranded in the desert somewhere." He grabbed the keys and left.

"So, what's happening?" Henry whispered as we took our seats in the waiting area.

"I have no idea."

Dave returned ten minutes later and handed over the keys. "We topped her off," he said. "It'll get you there."

All I understood was the last part. "Thanks, Dave," I said.

"No problem," he said.

"How much do we owe you?"

"Nothing," he said. "Have a great trip with your son."

He vanished into the garage.

It was the second kindness.

■ ■ ■

We arrived in Oregon's Willamette Valley twelve days into our journey. For nineteenth-century pioneers, covering that distance generally took five months. Yet even with the assistance of every modern convenience (GPS, air-conditioning, Wi-Fi), Henry and I were still beat. We'd cooked over enough campfires for a lifetime, slept alongside enough streams too. Which was why, as we neared the end of our journey, we opted for an indoor campout in my friend Ellie's living room in Portland.

We stayed up much too late, Henry mesmerized by the grand return of a TV screen while I prattled on to Ellie about the trip. I shared the many kindnesses we'd been the beneficiaries of, the abundance of goodwill that always somehow steered our way.

America is still good, I assured her. I told her about the hat-snagging woman in the storm, about Dave the mechanic, and a host of other examples of generosity witnessed up close—the woman in the bookstore who'd insisted on buying Henry a gift, the extra scoop of ice cream at dinner, the free sand dollar at the antique store. How quickly every stranger became our friend.

"It's as if people can't wait to help us along," I said, and smiled.

"That's awesome," Ellie said. "But I wonder how your trip might've been different if you weren't a straight white guy with a six-year-old."

My reaffirmation halted faster than a busted wagon.

"I mean, I'm really glad you guys are having a great time and all," she added. "I'm just saying—"

"You're right," I whispered.

In trying to rediscover you, America, I'd missed most of you. I'd been so focused on the geography beyond the window that I'd overlooked my geography within. Become so transfixed by the myths of the pioneers that I'd paid too little attention to the horrors they wrought in their wake.

How easy it is to forget our place in history. And how easy it is to look elsewhere when we can. That we've long exploited our way to our "exceptionalism" isn't merely a historical fact but a current event.

Had Henry channel-surfed his way to the news that night, he would have found plenty of proof of exploitation in the headlines. Including the previous day's acknowledgment by the Department of Homeland Security that some two thousand immigrant children had been separated from their families during border crossings between April and May.

Had he turned on the news a week prior—on the day we'd endured Doniphan's storm—he would have witnessed exploitation of a different sort: coverage of oil now flowing through the Dakota Access pipeline, despite protests from the Lakota and Dakota people whose sacred lands we'd co-opted yet again.

How to explain white privilege to a six-year-old? By telling him that his skin is a shield to hide behind but that he mustn't hide behind it. And by explaining that shields can be weapons, too, and can inflict harm on those who don't possess such protections. I want to tell him that every mile of our lives is a chance to forge a different path. And we must.

But by the time I hit upon these final thoughts, Henry's already fast asleep.

That night we snuggled deep into our sleeping bags alongside one another, enjoying the comforts of a living room floor. But it was the only comfort.

For hours, the moon bathed my sleeping boy's body in light. While I remained awake, unsettled.

Sincerely,
B.J.

Begin Again

SANDRA ALCOSSER

Because of open woodland
With quivering sun patches

A bird's eye might observe a worm
Chiseling under earth's

Skin—because of granite boulders
Full of egg cases holding

Spiderlings—because of purple berries
Come sweet in July—chokecherry

Shadblow Nanking
Hips and haws ripening—

Branch nesters build summer nurseries
On the face of our cabin—the same family

Every year or their progeny
On ridgepole—purlin—crossbeam

Sensitive to each human gesture
Inside the window and when men

Come to paint the fascia or spray
The log base and its foundation

The nester will abandon her clutch
Of eggs—blued by mineral blood—

And begin to weave a new nest
High above squirrels and house cats

For aren't we all pattern-making animals—
Make a beautiful thing and you've done all you can

To battle a friend said to me
And a people-adapted species—

Nuthatch or chickadee or these
Robins—become a kind of mother country—

Like you dear America—offering a body each day
For someone to make a wasteland—

I would like to weave with the surety
Of that robin—only a heartbeat

And a wrist wing to shape her nest—
A shaggy cup of mud and spiderweb

Come greed come windstorm—begin again

Driftless

CHERENE SHERRARD

Blacks have never been, and are not, really considered to be citizens
here. Blacks exist, in the American imagination, and in relationship
to American institutions, in reference to the slave codes: the first
legal recognition of our presence remains the most compelling.

JAMES BALDWIN, *Evidence of Things Not Seen*

But you said there was no defense.
"There ain't."
Then what I do?
"Know it, and go out the yard. Go on."

TONI MORRISON, *Beloved*

My youngest son is already grieving. Today men came to our home to
cut down a very old tree. We will not know how old until we can count
the lines on the stump, and even then, we can only estimate.

"The tree made our house a sanctuary," he says.

His plea startles me. A sanctuary is a holy place, a refuge from one's
enemies. It's true that the tree's long, leaf-laden branches have shield-
ed our 1922 colonial in Madison from harm. And yet fear has led us
to remove it. Seven men, outfitted in orange vests and black helmets,
swing among its branches as they must have done as boys. The work is
laborious, precise, and slow. They navigate a cat's cradle of ropes and
pulleys with chainsaws. Whenever a branch careens into the exact spot
they have identified, they applaud. I explain to my son that in this age
of the superstorm having a tree so large loom over not one but three
houses seems like baiting the gods: Oya, the whirlwind, and Shango,
the lightning. But the casual eloquence with which my preteen drops
sanctuary gives me pause. I'm thrilled that he finds our home a safe

and secure place of comfort, but I'm alarmed: From what outside these walls does he want protection?

The tree is a silver maple, *Acer saccharinum*, also known as the swamp maple, water maple, silverleaf maple, white maple, and soft maple. It's the sugar maple's stepbrother; a less-loved half-sibling with sap too slow to tap, good only for shade; a genus that spews at least four different kinds of "fruits" in the slender window that is Wisconsin's spring. It throws off an abundance of seeds that clog and warp our gutters, funneling rain into our basement. First, heavy clumps of spongy, red cotton, then helicopters—ovoid seedpods that spin and waggle until they rest on every lawn on our block. Its leaves are the last to turn. On Halloween, they backlight our house in saffron.

Once, on a windless day, a branch, so massive it could have been its own tree, fell. It covered the entirety of our shared yard, miraculously missing everything of value from the sungold tomatoes growing against our back fence to our newly installed cedar plank deck to the swing set upon which our neighbor's granddaughter was being pushed by her babysitter. Afterward, as I laid my hand on the prone limb, wide as an oil drum, its earth-shattering thud became an illusory earworm—the answer to the perennial philosophical question. The granddaughter and our youngest son share a middle name: Sage. As in a wise person or mystic, or an herb that proliferates if you plant it in any amount of shade.

Shade is the most apparent loss we will feel. Our air-conditioning bills will skyrocket, our deck become less hospitable between the hours of noon and five. But we won't be afraid anymore. Not of the tree. Which will be gone. Left in its place: unimpeded blue, sharp as any sky above a desert. Like the earth may be one day in our near future. Treeless.

We counted eighty-one rings before the lines on the stump vanished. The tree was older than my mother but younger than my grandfather, who died last year at 101. This tree had barely begun to sprout when he was born to Louisiana sharecroppers in Shreveport. Its thin sapling was stretching up from the weeds when he married my grandmother, just sprouting branches and leaves when they joined the Great Migration of African Americans heading west to California. Whom did the silver maple oversee? How many has it safeguarded?

A sanctuary is a shelter. The evicted squirrels will fight to nest in the black walnut that is now our block's undisputed heavyweight, living on borrowed time. The arborists with their beards and bronzed arms are fearless tree dancers. They sway and swing, limbs interlaced with limbs, unabashed as they fell the ancient giant. Elsewhere in our neighborhood, the culling continues. In the 1960s, ashes replaced the dying elms in the Midwest. Now, the emerald ash borer threatens to wreak the same havoc as Dutch elm disease. We lobby the forestry service for gentler forms of remediation, but treatment is costly.

Madison is technically a sanctuary city, but the designation has proved fungible. As rumors of ICE on the nearby campus where I teach flare, the university administration sends guidelines on how to dissemble and comply. Dissemble and comply is what I have taught my sons to do when confronted with outside authority.

Wisconsin is proud of its abolitionist history, of providing temporary shelter for contraband. In Milton, there's a tunnel beneath an 1844 stagecoach inn that once served as a way station on the Underground Railroad. Visitors can walk 150 feet from the cavernous cellar to a small shed. The same path fugitives traveled by candlelight, which gave off a smoky gleam against limestone. In the anteroom, broken doll parts litter the floor. The key words are *way station*. Freedmen and women were not meant to settle. The state anticipated they would continue on north to Canada. But some did not. One such family laid claim to land that was once a gathering ground for the Ho-Chunk and other First Nations. Notley Henderson purchased forty acres in 1880 and ran a dairy farm on land that now comprises the University of Wisconsin arboretum.

Hiking its many trails with my family, one day we take an unfamiliar path that snakes under the beltline. On the other side, we find a memorial plaque graced with the Henderson family's portrait. Wearing their Sunday best, Martha, Notley, and their children are the very image of restraint and respectability. Their son Allen worked the land until 1927. On March 5 of that year, he and his son Walter were murdered by Charles Nelson, the son of a neighboring farmer: a "shell-shocked" World War I veteran. Many thought Nelson's real diagnosis was racism. Allen's widow struggled to sustain the farm for thirteen years before she was dispossessed. Their square plot, parcel 33 on an aerial map from 1890, now lies under the highway that bisects the arboreal preserve.

What does *sanctuary* mean to a child in Mississippi coming home from her first day of fourth grade in August? She is eager to tell her mother how she won the spelling bee game with the word "asylum." She uses the key tucked under the doormat. The apartment is silent, empty. Her baby brother is next door with the neighbor's teenage daughter. All three sit unattended at the kitchen table, wondering, until someone thinks to turn on the news of the latest raid.

In the backyard of my family home in Los Angeles, lemon and apricot trees created a damp, buzzing glade of clover that I viewed upside down from the seat of a tire swing. Our lemons were the size of Florida grapefruits. Years later, when I first purchased a lemon from a Wegman's supermarket in upstate New York, I was shocked by the diminutive size and exorbitant cost of the wrinkled, yellow fruit that fit in my palm. One of those California lemons from my parents' tree was enough for a pitcher of lemonade. Clusters grew so high and thick that passersby would jump our fences. To discourage trespassing, my mother left paper bags of lemons on the sidewalk. Sometimes we caught men selling our windfall fruit at an intersection adjacent to the freeway off-ramp: one for a dollar.

In Forest Hills, a sprawling cemetery two blocks from our house, my son and I locate the Hendersons' final resting place. Their grave marker is just west of the section in which a sympathetic war widow buried 140 confederate soldiers who had been imprisoned at Camp Randall. After the Charlottesville incident, Mayor Soglin removed the Confederate monument that named the soldiers "unsung heroes." Which parts of ourselves do we preserve and what do we take down? For a moment, we feel that we spiral like the silver maple's helicopters, driftless, ever searching for new ground.

A few of the Hendersons' descendants still live in Madison; others have scattered. We find the stately black-and-pink marble slab with its precisely chiseled names reassuring.

"At least they still have their tree," my son says, pointing directly above the plot. Thick with sun-splashed leaves, a red maple stands sentinel.

Bridge

ARTHUR SZE

Just as the sky brightens over this ridge,
it darkens over that river;

me, my, mine
wants to string barbed wire along this fence,
along that wall;

from a bridge over a river,
lights of two countries
glimmer at dusk;

here, I pull a translucent cactus needle
out of your hand.

The Elwha: A River and a Vision Restored

TIM McNULTY

Dear America,

More than two hundred feet below me, the blue-gray rush of the Elwha River cuts through the narrow walls of Glines Canyon on Washington's Olympic Peninsula like a blade. I am standing on the remnant spillway of a concrete dam that spanned this gorge for nearly a century. The dam and its powerhouse are gone now, making way for the largest salmon recovery project in North America. Upstream the old reservoir basin rustles with autumn-tinged alder and willow saplings, and the newly freed river carves a channel through banks of lake-bottom sediments. It is late in the season. The first pulses of Pacific storms have swept over the Olympic Mountains, and the river is flush with runoff. Returning salmon have entered the river mouth and, keyed to the scent of upstream waters, begun their migrations to spawn. It's an ancient passage for Elwha salmon, honed since the continental ice drew back from this valley some sixteen thousand years ago. But now, with the Elwha's two dams removed, it is altogether celebratory and new.

Fall rains and the epic migrations of wild salmon have always filled me with hope. But this fall, on this river, I'm searching for more. Last November, the electorate took an abrupt turn away from everything I believed in. Overnight our incremental, upstream progress toward peace, fairness, environmental health, and human justice seemed blocked as by a concrete dam. If there is a way through this political blockade, the story of the Elwha River might reveal it.

The Elwha is the largest of Olympic Peninsula's watersheds, and the runs of wild salmon that once plied its waters were legendary. Estimated returns of more than four hundred thousand fish, including all species of Pacific salmon, flooded the river each year. This year-round bounty was the lifeblood of the Lower Elwha Klallam people. Their ancestral village of Tse-whit-zen dates back nearly three thousand years. The tribe's reservation at the mouth of the river is a testament to a people's will to endure.

Early in the last century, when a blind belief in industry and progress held unchallenged dominion over the resource towns of the West, two hydroelectric dams were built on the Elwha. The dams powered a large sawmill and brought jobs, domestic electricity, and a modicum of prosperity to a burgeoning town. But the dams completely blocked migrating salmon, in flagrant disregard of existing law and treaty rights. Their effect on the Elwha Klallam people was devastating.

When I arrived on the peninsula in the early 1970s, the mills were going strong, and timber ruled the local economy. But the once-great salmon runs of the Elwha River were withering to a few thousand fish per year. In the words of my late friend Dick Goin, who moved here as a boy during the Great Depression and grew up subsistence fishing beside his Elwha Klallam neighbors, the Elwha River was dying.

In the intervening years I came to know the river well, working on trail crews for Olympic National Park and on long summer backpacking trips up the valley. The Native American friends I worked with still drew part of their sustenance from the river's depleted fishery. Memories of the predammed river and its abundant fish lived on in their elders' stories. My friend Bruce Brown began researching the history of the river's damming, and in his 1982 book *Mountain in the Clouds*, he brought that story to a wide readership. I and many other conservationists in the Northwest began to envision a different future for the Elwha.

Of course the Elwha people opposed the dams and challenged them for decades. The large mill powered by the dams sprawled over their former village site. In spite of the industrialization of their traditional territory, they never gave up on their river or its salmon. When the Glines Canyon Dam came up for relicensing, a legal avenue opened for addressing a century-old injustice.

The story of freeing the Elwha River has been well told in books, newspaper and magazine stories, and films. The restoration is being rigorously documented by teams of researchers, and visitors from around the world come to witness the recovery. It's no wonder. With the Elwha, hope, perseverance, and a shared vision for the future triumphed. What is also important to me now are the deeply polarized communities who came together to make it happen. As early as 1968 the tribe petitioned the federal government to consider the needs of fish in its relicensing process. Nearly two decades after that, the Elwha Tribe and four conservation groups legally intervened in the process. I remember many meetings, contentious hearings, testimonies, articles, letters to the editor—and more meetings.

Remarkably, the Elwha people remained strong throughout. In the face of dogged opposition by corporate mill owners, local government officials, economic development interests, and more than a few mill-workers, the tribe remained focused. Their persistence, and a conservationist lawsuit brought against the dams' owners, led to the compromise that resulted in legislation allowing the federal government to acquire and remove the dams if necessary to restore the Elwha fishery. That was 1992, and dam-removal advocates celebrated wildly. Little did we know it would be another two decades before the dams came down.

This is the part of the story I returned to on the spillway that chilly autumn afternoon. In no small way, it meant listening to those who disagreed with me over dam removal. Much like today, economic forces were doing away with good paying jobs in the woods and mills of the Northwest. Automation, log exports, shifting markets, and the global economy had unmoored the Northwest resource economy. Millworkers and government officials were justified to oppose what they saw as another attack on their way of life. We who advocated for ecological restoration needed to listen to those concerns and find ways to reach across our philosophical divides to address them.

Again, the Elwha people were exemplary. Compromise measures to supply alternative power to the mill at cost and to protect the community's water quality during the dams' deconstruction and an agreement to stop fishing Elwha stocks during the recovery were worked out. Importantly, a working group of community leaders came together to study the larger scientific, economic, and ethical concerns undergirding the restoration. I have to confess I was skeptical that such opposing perspectives could communicate, share ideas, and come to consensus. But they did. All sides listened. Concerns were assuaged, and with community support, congressional representatives were able to secure needed funds and the removal proceeded. Not on schedule, not by a long shot, but in time. And what is time for a river, for a fishery, for a people?

As the lower reservoir was drawn down, a sacred place for the Elwha people emerged from a century's inundation. "Coiled baskets" rock, the place of the Elwha people's creation, is accessible again. And seventy miles of pristine spawning waters in the heart of Olympic National Park are once more open to salmon. A once wild-eyed vision of a restored river is underway, unfolding by leaps and bounds with each spawning season. The greed and racial prejudice of an unenlightened time has been turned back and a natural order restored. It happened within my fairly recent memory. It can happen again.

Yours,
Tim

Dear Dulce

JEREMY VOIGT

everything hums beneath the surface of the world
STEPHEN DUNN, "GUARDIAN ANGEL"

Let be be the finale of seem
WALLACE STEVENS, "THE EMPEROR OF ICE CREAM"

Did you know in 1890 Eugene Schieffelin, a wealthy German
immigrant, tried to introduce all the birds mentioned
in Shakespeare to North America—released forty pairs of starlings

in Central Park until they established themselves comfortably.
I think they're beautiful, though I know I'm not supposed to.
Also, nine billion passenger pigeons lived in North America

when the *Mayflower* landed. People ate them the way we eat chicken.
Yesterday I saw three juvenile eagles in a tree and half a mile later
in another tree two adults—awaiting roadkill, and silhouetted in winter

trees so their shape on bare branches stood out against the sky.
But enough about birds, Dulce, they're just birds, and I'm a teacher
of words, but in my defense, I read these things in a book

on the history of American English. It turns out most American
locutions are upgrades, thieved, or wholly invented for profit,
like *vitamins* invented to sell supplements, supplementing nutrient

weak food made increasingly nutrient weak to sell supplements.
Also brought to you by America: hangover, commuter, hamburger,
motel, escalator, air brake, and fountain pen. Now: mass shooting,

a term whose definition we don't agree on, much less its prevention.
Dulce, after two years in my classroom can you imagine me
packing heat? As a child, I dreamed my John McClane dreams,

gun in hand, as an adult, now I know my inclinations lean
toward observation, and that I'm just one darkly iridescent
starling among the yard-bespotting masses. Dear Dulce, I'm pleased

you, citizen of the liminal, you brought across as a baby, your
papers lost while your father's back healed, a back broken
working in this hamburger-hangover, escalator ride of a country,

I'm pleased you are in college. May you remain until defining
seem, which is everything, which is Achilles' rage firing
straight up in a column from head to sky, which is the one

moment he does not seem the unbearable whiny teenager
he is, which is when he says *yippee-kay-yay not my friend today.*
May you remain, as I do, a stupid, yellow-eyed songbird,

snatching bits of song wherever you can, you with
your throaty voice releasing pairs of everything you love,
all the stolen words made new as they fly together from your tongue.

January 8, 2017, Antarctica

ELIZABETH BRADFIELD

Dear America,

A wandering albatross just soared by my porthole. I am on a ship in the Southern Ocean, traveling between Antarctica and South America.

Before the bird startled me, I was reading *Antarktische Wildnis: Südgeorgien,* Thies Matzen and Kicki Ericson's beautiful book about their time on South Georgia Island, a hundred-mile-long craggy place at the edge of the Antarctic Convergence, nine hundred miles from the nearest city in the Falkland Islands. They spent two years moving from bay to bay in their small wooden sailboat.

Small wooden sailboat. In bays and fjords that freeze over in winter, in the long dark of howling weather, along a coast with no backup plan. No bluster to their stories. No swagger or machismo. From 2009 to 2011 they were surprised and humbled and charmed and terrified by penguins and glaciers and leopard seals and storms and solitude. For them, the vast, raw place was made of intimate moments. Tenderness, even. America, I want all of us to know wild places in this way.

I've spent the last month working as a naturalist on a ship that spends the austral summer taking tourists to the Antarctic. This trip, we left Ushuaia, at the tip of South America, headed east toward the Falkland Islands and South Georgia, sailed southwest across the infamous Drake Passage to prowl a few bays and shores of the Antarctic Peninsula, and are now heading back.

The boat will do variations of this route all season, carrying visitors from America, Australia, China, India, Europe, and elsewhere, all of whom have found a way to get here—to this longed-for, difficult, leaderless continent set aside in 1959 "for peaceful purposes only" as a space for "scientific investigation...and cooperation toward that end."

In their epilogue, Thies and Kicki write about the phenomenal recovery of South Georgia after industrial whaling sputtered and the island was abandoned by people. Tussac grass returned to trampled hillsides. Skies cleared of blubber-smoke. Fur seals rebounded from near extinction.

Solitude was part of the balm. But so was the hard work of people who began to pull back the harm done: introduced rats and reindeer, asbestos in the ruining buildings. The restoration of that place is both working and not working. Certain things are healing, but other harms encroach. America, recovery is more complicated and simpler than we know.

At home on Cape Cod, I have been tracking the decades-long recovery of the gray seal population since their protection in the 1960s. Some think their return is not restoration but ruination of what we came to know in their absence. Some want to start killing them again. I don't agree, but I'm interested in the different places our understandings come from. Where do we source our information, and how do we scrape down to the truth? How are we going to agree and make a plan to move forward, America, on this one subject in our own crowded, conflicted, contradictory, not-wholly-known land? There are so many matters that require answers to these questions.

In Antarctica, the ocean today feels the same as it did five years ago, the last time I worked in these waters. The same birds soar above the waves, tipping their wings. My wonder is greater upon returning. My knowledge of the threats they face: greater too.

America, some of you have asked, but I can't say that I see the effects of climate change here firsthand. There are differences, but are they moments or trends? I started looking too late. I haven't looked long enough. But that doesn't mean I don't believe the scientific papers about warming oceans, rising seas, acidification, changing weather. It doesn't mean I don't fear the consequences.

Thies and Kicki navigated to South Georgia from the Falklands without a GPS or satellite phone. They brought books and apples. They were cautious and experienced. Time slowed for them. We also need time to plan wisely, to wait out storms, to take a broad view and allow contradictions to have their space.

Now I am headed home. Back to grocery shopping and teaching and bills. Back to neighbors and their conflicting political yard signs. I've been keeping up with the news in small doses, plotting my course. Was it an escape to come to the cold, hard edge of the world? Did I flee? Did Thies and Kicki? Maybe, but I have to believe that we return changed and strengthened. Better able to make new connections and see from new perspectives. Maybe even better at changing.

America, how do we care for what is far from us as well as what is near? How do we acknowledge the legacy of a plastic-wrapped sandwich or throwaway keychain? How do we account for the hidden costs of our technologies?

I embody so many of our modern, American oppositions: my environmentalism and my 120-mile commute, my certainty that wild spaces are necessary and my chugging toward them in a diesel-powered boat, my love of diverse community and my home in a largely white township. It's easy, in the scatter of home, to forget our connections and contradictions.

On a ship, the crew is visible to one another. Here Americans are in the minority. We are Filipino, Indian, South African, Bulgarian, Austrian, Chinese, New Zealander, Latvian, Irish, Columbian, and more. There are fissures between us. Bigotries. But also a clear sense of our interdependence.

But then, one fragile hull holds us all, doesn't it, America?

Yours,
Elizabeth Bradfield

Diversity: A Garden Allegory

CAMILLE T. DUNGY

Dear America,

When we first moved into our house, the yard was tame and orderly. There were three aspen trees in the rear corners of the backyard, but mostly the plant life consisted of severely trimmed juniper bushes and a substantially weed-free lawn. Beds of river rocks, so uniform in size and shape as to seem manufactured, edged these expanses of green. It was a well-manicured yard. This was the first thing about the house I set out to change.

I've been pulling rock for four years now. Every spring before the heat comes on and again in the fall before the cold settles, I rip out a new section of river rock and landscaping fabric. This is a slow process. The rock and plasticized landscaping fabric deplete the soil. Efforts to reduce natural diversity nearly always result in some form of depletion, and this certainly has been true in my yard. What I find beneath those repressed beds would be of little use to a garden. It's hard clay I have to amend with the compost I produce from kitchen scraps and fallen leaves. I also add topsoil hauled in from a landscaping supply store called Hageman Earth Cycle. I love the environmental vision inscribed in the name "Earth Cycle." I also love climbing their small hills of topsoil to shovel some into my wheelbarrow and haul with me back home. It's the full-bodied participation in promoting an ecologically vibrant landscape that excites me.

I try to salvage native earthworms I find under the river rocks, tossing the wrigglers back into my newly enriched beds. The work might go more quickly if I hired a Bobcat to scoop the rock, but I work slowly, extracting and replanting desirable vegetation whose roots have grown into the landscaping fabric. I spare centipedes and pill bugs, do my best to avoid spiders. Once I found an anthill teeming with creatures who were busy tunneling into the difficult dirt. I left them where they were. Proceeding this way, it may take me twelve hours to prepare a satisfactory three-square-foot plot. I'll sow this with wildflower seed, perennial starts, tulip bulbs, and irises' gangly rhizomes. Within months, I will enjoy a riot of color where once there was nothing but a hard, gray expanse.

In the center of my lawn, and also in poorly irrigated corners that had been overtaken by crabgrass and purslane, I've started more flower beds. Making these, too, is a difficult process, but not the kind of process that takes place on my knees as does the reclamation of the rock beds. The object on the lawn is to turn turf into rich soil. I cover the grass with layer on layer of cardboard, kitchen scraps, topsoil, compost, newspaper, and mulch. At the end of the long winter, I'll turn it all with a shovel and pitchfork. Then I will plant my seeds. I begin around Halloween and must wait until nearly June before I can start to see any results. The process of changing my environment from homogeneous to diverse is rewarding but slow.

Because I garden by scattering seed, I never quite know what's going to appear, or where. If, as Michael Pollan writes, "a lawn is nature under totalitarian rule," my yard reveals a very different sort of possibility. My property yields an explosion of color come midsummer. You never know exactly what you'll find on my little patch, or whom.

The August we moved into this house, I found canister upon canister of herbicides and pesticides on the worktable in the garage. That first summer, very few pollinators braved the poisoned turf. They'd flit from one rare dandelion to the next, then buzz away, seemingly forlorn. But this year I've counted numerous species of bee, more than two dozen different kinds of birds, and a slew of moths and butterflies, including monarchs. I've planted milkweed in many places around the yard. I've planted other native plants as well. In some of this year's reclaimed beds, I planted handfuls of sunflower seeds left over from last year's crop. These have grown as high as thirteen feet, delighting many species of neighbors, humans included.

The brilliant goldfinches that hang out near our feeders eat my sunflower petals. I would prefer if they didn't eat my sunflower petals, but the sunflowers are there for them as much as they are there for me, and I'm learning that birds eat flower petals, not just the seeds from the middle of the plants. Next year, to continue to attract these beautiful birds, I'll sow more sunflower seeds. The sunflowers, *and* the birds who eat them, fill me with joy I could not have imagined.

The covenant for our homeowners association specifies that what I've done around my house is technically prohibited. There should be fewer wildflowers in my yard. Banish the milkweed. Banish the tall grass. Banish the front yard onion patch, the sad squash trials. When the sunflowers have finished flowering, rather than leave the dried stalks and seed heads for birds to perch and munch on as they stock up for their winter migrations, I should pull all remnants of the summer plants out of the ground. There should be nothing brown like that around the yard. Nothing that might be construed as aesthetically unsavory.

Did I mention that my family is the only black family on our block? That we're some of the only black people in our neighborhood? That, in fact, we're one of the few black families in our entire town? I say this now because it may help you understand that my resistance to the particular brand of suburban American monoculture my homeowners association promotes is also a resistance to a culture that has been set up to exclude people like me. A culture that—through laws and customs that amount to toxic actions and culturally constructed weeding—has effectively maintained homogeneous spaces around houses like mine.

But I'm lucky. My neighbors claim to be grateful I've moved in and cultivated the most heterogeneous environment on our street. And the bees love the flowers. And the sunflowers shade the low-growing plants at their bases, some of which flower and some of which don't. A whole new ecosystem is thriving in my yard. Hardly anyone used to visit, but now it is alive and full of action. Birds I don't see on any of the neighboring lawns have taken up regular habitation around our place. Several mating pairs chose spots in our various trees and bushes to nest and raise their young. The worms I so carefully preserved provide tasty snacks for robins. I released nine thousand ladybugs to help with an aphid infestation on my rudbeckia plants. Now I've seen an increase in creatures feeding on the healthy black-eyed Susans (and probably on some ladybugs as well). Swallowtails, painted ladies, and the occasional monarch pass through the garden in late summer. When our aspens succumbed to the scale that struck many of the trees in the neighborhood this year and we had to cut them down, there were still plenty of places for bugs and birds and squirrels to congregate, places that did not exist before I began the work of diversifying the landscape I found in my backyard.

Though it fills me with joy to be surrounded by such vibrancy, keeping up with all of this isn't easy. This spring, it was as if every dandelion in the county called its neighbor to join them in our yard. I spent countless hours with my old-fashioned weed remover, pulling weeds at the root. It occurs to me, doing this work, that one of the reasons we prefer homogeneity is that it can seem much easier. There is a man who comes to my house and fixes things. He's handy, smart, and strong. He has an eye for order and structure, and I defer to him when it comes time to decide what type of stain to use on the deck. He recently offered to help me out with the weeds. A couple applications of chemical herbicide, and my yard will surely look as neat as a magazine photo. I will admit I have been tempted. My flower beds are spectacular, but the mounds of clover and bindweed scattered around the unimproved sections detract from the overall grandeur of my lot. It's difficult to strike a balance between acceptance and dominance. I have to come to terms with the fact that maintaining a poison-free yard will mean revising some of my opinions about what plants I want around me and which I do not.

This is one of the key glories of cultivating diversity: when we cultivate diversity, we learn things we never knew we might want to know. Things we may even *need* to know one day. Neither our river rocks nor our turf grass are edible, but the dandelions, purslane, sunflowers, coneflowers, California poppies, and curly dock I either cultivate or tolerate all have some nutritive value. The vibrant variety in my yard can provide sustenance in all kinds of ways!

Our first winter in this house was hard on me. The killing frosts did what they do, and then there were the months without flowers. February came, then March, and then April and, because of all that rock and turf, there was nothing to look at but gray and more gray until May came and, with it, some green. As I've spent the past years planting bulbs and seeds, and as I've put in perennial starts, and as I've swapped plant cuttings with friends, planting plots in their honor, and as I've divided and rearranged tubers, and as I've cultivated the diversity of my garden, I have grown happier earlier and earlier each spring. I didn't know I was that dependent on color, on variety, on watching so many different kinds of life being lived, but evidently I am.

Yours,
Camille

Hell Bent On

PAM HOUSTON

Dear America,

Every day for the last several years my first thought upon waking, and my last thought before going to sleep (and many thoughts in between), have been about our magnificent planet, and how we seem hell-bent on its destruction at every turn. It's a desperation that threatens to double me over, daily...hourly, and I wonder what evolution could have possibly been up to when it gave opposable thumbs and the ability to reason to the only species too stupid to understand that the first rule of survival is to protect one's own habitat.

Since the election of a man who has promised to dismantle the EPA, sell off our public lands to Big Oil, "cancel" (emperor-style) the Paris Agreement, reinvigorate the Keystone Pipeline, and remove all protection from endangered species, that desperation has increased a hundredfold. Simultaneously, every single other thing I value about this country—its diversity, its freedoms, its art and culture, its institutions of higher learning and all other forms of education, its tolerance, its generosity, its many compassions—has already come under direct attack from what promises to be the most toxic administration in American history.

And yet beneath the deep grief that threatens to pull me under, I feel an ember of hope burning in my rib cage. In the five days after the election, the Sierra Club quadrupled its monthly donation record, and in the same amount of time the ACLU received roughly 120,000 donations totaling $7.2 million. I have been heartened to read San Francisco's manifesto of resistance and resolve, and the letter all Vermonters just received signed jointly by the outgoing Democratic governor and the incoming Republican governor promising to disavow intolerance and hate. I am encouraged by artists and actors and scientists and the 365 corporations who have banded together to speak out against one unconstitutional campaign promise after another, and principled political leaders from both parties standing up for what America has always tried to be. What I feel in the collective atmosphere makes me believe that this time we will not go to sleep, we will not wind up in divisive squabbles between people who hold the same essential beliefs, because if we do so many will suffer and the suffering will be unmitigated and like nothing we have ever seen in this country before.

I live in the high Rockies, in a valley that has so far been not much touched by corporate greed. It snowed overnight, and this morning my elderly horses wear a ridge of bright white along their dark spines and snowflakes in their eyelashes. Earlier, when I went out to feed, the pair of bald eagles who return to my property every other year were using the new snow to spot small moving creatures in my pasture. I heard the elk bugling last night before sunset, and at first light this morning coyotes were singing with such full voice outside my bedroom window that my two Irish wolfhounds threw back their heads and sang along.

I had a father whose tactics resembled those of our president-elect so precisely that in the aftermath of this election season, I can scarcely remember my father at all. My mother, now that I think of it, was not unlike our new first lady (in absentia), in the way she always kept her jaw so tight, turned her attention to looking good, and never kissed anything but the air. For parenting, I turned to the patch of remnant woods that ran behind our subdivision, to the railroad tracks that lead into the dappled light of relatively undisturbed deciduous forest. When we went as a family to the beach for a week, I spent the last hour of every trip standing at the edge of the ocean saying an individual goodbye to each wave.

The natural world did not just heal me from the abuses I suffered at the hands of my father. It raised me up to be the person I am. I am ready to give my money, my time, and, if it comes to it, my life for the right to save the earth, and if it is too late for that I will give all those things to at least have the freedom to sit at her bedside and grieve.

I have no time or energy anymore for cynicism, anger, vanity, or even despair. We must work together to cultivate hope and courage. A lot of us have had the good fortune of living in this beautiful country, in this improbable democracy, without being asked to participate fully in its care. Now we have been given the opportunity to fight for our freedoms. Now we have been given a mandate to lead more radically meaningful lives.

Sincerely, and with love,
Pam Houston

Togethering

November 2016, a View from the National Zoo

DEBORAH FRIES

I am lost at the National Zoo
this leafy warm Thanksgiving weekend,
somewhere near the bipedal red pandas,
whose wedding-hat tails drape like wisteria
from branches just 2.6 miles from the
White House kitchen garden where puckered
kale will soon freeze and curl, but closer
I think to the source of sweet whiffs of straw
and dung from another large species, which,
even armed with prehistoric hide and horn,
may also feel sad in this afternoon light, despite
swarms of polyglot children squealing *Bei Bei*,
soft wave of kids licking the glass, short slice
of the 2.5 million visitors who've come
to your zoo this year, even on Election Day
when I was in a Philadelphia suburb,
twitchy from the swing-state full-court press
but not lost like now—skirting Small Mammals,
searching for The Think Tank, wanting
to see Batang kiss her new son, Redd,
glimpse daddy Kyle brachiating overhead,
orange as acid mine drainage, hoping
that from his place in the sky he might
be able to see through bamboo stands
and light-wrapped trees, throngs of stroller
pushers, zebra-stalking cheetahs, first-date

nuzzlers, and point me to a place beyond
the screechy flamboyance of flamingos,
higher, where I can see all 2016 zoo-goers
at once, crowded against cages, spilling
into the moats that separate us from beasts,
and recount their sweet upturned faces,
earnest otter eyes, extant and assembled,
to picture them in sum—plus 365,000 more—
scared, sandwiched together on Lion-Tiger Hill,
rounded up with goats in the Kids' Farm corral,
waving from the roof of the Great Cats Gift Shop
—who together are your Lost Citizens,
the 2.8 million who each believed a vote
was a voice that would be heard, each
a peacock's scream or lioness's roar—
soundstorm of animal certainty, derecho
of deep human desire, so very sure our
collective shout would have your impartial
ear, rightly grab your untamed heart.

High-Dollar Papayas

JOHN LANE

Dear America,

I guess your in-box is blowing up, so I will be brief. Since I am writing a letter I should address my grievances and fears about our shared political future point by point, but most of what I am feeling is still hard to explain. My mood is still more storm than cold front. These past few weeks since the election have been surreal, America. No, these weeks have verged on Dada, or even early 1980s punk or bad game-show TV. Reality at times has felt like a Johnny Rotten solo, and at other times like a faulty Vanna White spin of the Wheel of Fortune, and at other times like a low-budget movie so bad Ronald Reagan wouldn't even star in it. I am telling you how I feel because I want your heart's voice to shout down my head, America. I want riots in my aortas. I want to stun this mealy month in its tracks and not let it be normalized by passing time. That is what's most important. I am telling you we are living in strange dangerous times and should not abstract them.

I want to bore you with the details, so here goes. I've heard them all because I have been awake through this Dark Night—the plywood cabinet he's hammering together full of billionaires used as nails, the Twitter wars, the vigil at the Tower on Fifth Avenue, the speculation about the family move, the Facebook live broadcasts from the barricades, the endless calls not to normalize, the case for recount, the appeal for the overthrow, the lawsuits bouncing like radio signals off the dome of justice, hate pooling like greasy runoff in the nation's outer swales, the vanquished candidate shopping in an indie bookstore for solace, the parading dark suits animated by coal plants, the syntactical terror of the full transcript, whole zip codes in Portland lining up at the metaphoric cliff edge like the Zealots at Masada.

But I digress. I'm told I am better at anecdote than polemic, so here goes. I was shopping for Thanksgiving yesterday, America, and I decided to try to be full of reconciliation and not judge the 63 percent of my neighbors who voted for him for the decisions of their own hearts or minds, but just to smile and be kind. After all, didn't Leonard Cohen tell us there is a crack in everything and that's how the light gets in? I'm religious too, America. I believe in synchronicity, so it's no coincidence Leonard Cohen died on election eve. ("No whining," that's what Cohen told an interviewer he'd learned after decades of religious practice.)

So, America, back to the checkout line where I am standing behind a colleague we'll call Thomas. "Hello, Thomas!" I say, generating enthusiasm for my newfound nonpartisanship. I smile warmly and shake his hand as if he is another companion in the huge surging mess of human existence just demonstrated by our election process. "Happy Thanksgiving." He shakes my hand and seems surprised I'm so bubbly after such a defeat, probably thinking, "What's up with one of the most notorious liberals on campus being nice to me when he's usually coming at me like a buzz saw about climate change?" and once he sees my guard is down he launches into a friendly lecture, as he always does, explaining how he is headed up to spend the holiday with his highly successful corporate daughter and that she has requested he bring these "high-dollar papayas." ("Can you believe it! These two papayas cost me six dollars!") I smile more, trying to listen, as David Brooks has prompted us liberals to do, and say, "That's great, Thomas, have a happy Thanksgiving!" I shake his hand as he exits, and he strides out, the victor that he is.

The checkout clerk says, "Oops, your friend didn't pay for his papayas."

I paid for his papayas, America. I know this isn't as clear as one of those Jesus parables I learned in Sunday school, but I'm afraid this is all I've got. Looks like we've all been left holding the bag.

For our shared future,
John Lane

Unfold Your Love

AISHA SABATINI SLOAN

Dear America,

Once, after a bad breakup, I made myself do yoga every day for two weeks. I dedicated myself to some limitations for this daily routine: I ad-libbed from a sequence in the practice manual we used when I completed yoga teacher training and listened to an hour-long episode of the radio show *On Being*. I tried to let Krista Tippett determine the duration of my practice, but usually after a half hour of stretching and some super-abbreviated sun salutations I was up and googling the Beatles song about the weepy guitar and writing the lyric on Facebook and crooning, "I don't know why nobody told you how to unfold your love" into the computer screen while snot ran down my face.

Settling into Savasana, I marveled about what Joanna Macy said in her interview with Krista about how pain, when faced, turns. I brought my knees into my chest as I sobbed while she read her translation of Rilke: "Let everything happen to you. Beauty and terror. Just keep going. No feeling is final. Don't let yourself lose me." I don't know that this practice hastened or lightened the mourning process, but it felt important to harness my grief and shove it into something potentially transformative.

Last week, my girlfriend and I flew to New York for a visit. Even though I had lived in Brooklyn for a couple of years once upon a time, I felt nervous to go back, ride the train, and be in a big city after being so used to a small one. Almost immediately we traded in our big-world anxieties for the excitement of the everyday. Late one night we were led into a room where Ocean Vuong and Juan Felipe Herrera and Natalie Diaz and Saeed Jones and Rigoberto González were eating dinner. It didn't feel so delusional to believe, for a spell, in magic. We decided that everything was going to be okay, president-wise, in order to get through the trip. Toward the end we noticed that we were starting to float away into a kind of delusional paradise, using the term "dissociation" a lot when someone brought up politics. When we got home we found the fear waiting for us in the living room. I realized we seemed to be moving beautifully through the real-live stages of grief—depression, denial.

I entered into "bargaining" the other day when somebody on Facebook mentioned writing letters to the electors. I decided to throw myself into it the way I tried to get *really effective* when called upon to write letters to the staff of a prison that held my nephew in solitary confinement for over a year. I am mostly an ethos-pathos kind of girl, so these letters had the tone of Oliver Twist cowering with a bowl in his hands.

With the electors I tried to think of the fastest trick to their heartguts. I peered at their names and chose from a list of heroes on a Wikipedia page for action-adventure movie heroes/villains and wrote in big, bold letters: *This moment in time is like the end of an action adventure film. You are Matt Damon. You are the hero. Be the hero. Please.* I also tried Will Smith, the Girl with the Dragon Tattoo, Julia Roberts, Russell Crowe, and Liam Neeson. I never did Catherine Zeta-Jones for some reason. Quick question: Is it just me or are most of those electors white?

A day after I sent that batch of letters, I decided to reach out to another set of electors with a different approach: watercolors. I put on Issa Rae's show, *Insecure,* and tore watercolor paper that I'd meant to use for Christmas cards the year before into postcard-sized sheets. I addressed them and then painted on them using a very dried-out watercolor set running low on blue and yellow. I brought out my acrylics. I got abstract for a few hours. There were some, how do you call it, pink *washes.* Some dots. I like to do a red line across the page sometimes. A Diebenkornish gesture. There were a couple of good ones. I'd had half a bottle of wine by the time I wrote, "I emplore you. No, I implore you," to somebody in Texas or Arkansas, followed by a message that conveyed my very specific hopes for their electoral vote decision.

I woke up feeling dehydrated and exhausted from hours of the nonsleep you get when you drank too much bad red wine and kept the salt lamp on while *Frasier* played for several hours and you didn't bother to brush your teeth until 2 a.m. after eating Karamel Sutra ice cream and you never asked your dog to move over so your back is sore. And then you're faced with this fiasco: your girlfriend is out of town with the car. You have a bike, an empty stomach, lots of caffeine in your system, and no stamps. How do you buy stamps without going all the way to the post office?

After I put a bunch of abstract art in the mail for twenty-nine strangers, I got back on my bike and felt so empowered that I entered swiftly into the "I need to jog and clean the house" phase that I usually require if I'm going to stop spinning out into a destructive mess. So I had my dog drag me half a mile up the road and back and I mopped to *Pop Culture Happy Hour*, and eventually I realized that it was time to start doing yoga again. And that it might be necessary to do yoga and meditate every day now, and not drink so much, and feel my fear more. And clean up the dog shit from the backyard. And listen to music that might let my soul maneuver itself around all those feelings. Feelings like: an orphanage of children in Aleppo asking to live.

In a recent article in the *Guardian*, Rebecca Solnit asked us to take responsibility for coming up with the big idea that could keep Trump out of office: "It's up to us, which means it's up to you. Think big. And act." Inspired, I quoted her to some friends over dinner. We sat under a lamp made from deer antlers. We were talking about what we could do. Every time we had an idea that made my heart beat faster, the light dimmed or surged. We looked at each other like kids in a movie hovering hands over a Ouija board, baffled by the possibility of our own power.

Every few days, I realize that I have the responsibility to clear a path for better ideas, as Solnit has pleaded. Less wine, more meditation. As this year comes to a close, I hope we can all use the tools we have cultivated, whatever they are, in order to make space for the idea that could save us.

Love,
Aisha Sabatini Sloan

Thoughts from an Empty Courtroom Following the Hung Jury of a Man Tried for Harboring Migrants

AMY P. KNIGHT

Dear America,

When people want to talk to God, they go to church. Of course, you can talk to God anywhere, but a church is where you can feel pretty sure he's listening.

Where, then, do we go to talk to our country? I have come to this courtroom because what is it, really, but a kind of church? It was built on the faith that we will agree to resolve disputes by the rules of a peaceful system. It has practical features, the jury box and witness stand and bench for the judge; it has symbols, the flag, the seal. When judge or jury enters, we all rise.

Now everyone has left and I have come back, pleading a left-behind object. I have something to say to you, America.

Over the last year and a half, I have defended a man who spends his time in the desert, searching for the bodies of migrants who died crossing the border. He leaves water to prevent more people from dying there. When two men making the journey turned up tired, thirsty, and in pain on the doorstep where he does his work, he gave them water, food, and a place to rest and recover. He treated their blisters and other injuries. On the fourth day, he sent them on their way. For this, America, lawyers acting in your name charged him with three felonies—for which the law allows a prison sentence of up to twenty years.

Did those attorneys really believe, as they have claimed, that contrary to all evidence, he was actually part of an organized scheme to smuggle people from Mexico into the United States, helping them avoid the Border Patrol until they were safely deep inside our country? Is it because the Border Patrol's enforcement strategy depends on putting people, in their words, in "mortal peril," such that making the journey a little less deadly undermines the effort to keep people out? Is it because they could not grasp that a person—a fellow American— could be so deeply unselfish that he would offer strangers what he had to share, for no other reason than because they needed it? Can they not see the difference between simply aiding a human being in need, and condoning his every choice and action?

We tried everything, America. We explained to the judge that my client was acting on his spiritual beliefs about helping others in their time of need. We exposed the motives and the improper actions of the agents who arrested him. We brought in all our treaties and agreements expressing our collective obligation to save lives whenever we can. We filed hundreds of pages of legal documents and argued for hours at the podium. And no matter how right we were, those lawyers—acting in your name—didn't budge, and because they wore your colors, they had the power to keep him under tight control. They took his passport. He was forbidden to leave the state without explicit permission. Their power is startling.

But here in this empty courtroom I want to remind you: however grieved, even terrified you may feel in seeing the damage a handful of misguided people can do when they're acting in your name, you have always had a limit. Government agents can accuse and arrest and seize and detain, but before they can actually punish, you have always insisted that they convince twelve of your citizens, your own precious children, that punishment is warranted. And *that*, these lawyers could not do. Twelve men and women listened while the lawyers made their case. Four said yes; eight said no. The good man went free.

These lawyers wear your colors, America. They have your flag pinned in miniature on their lapels. When they speak in court, they say it is "on behalf of the United States of America." But ultimately, they are not you; the jurors are. In the jury room they—you—argued for three days, and when it was all over, they didn't agree. They—you—spoke with many voices. They said that the predicament at our southern border is far too complicated for the black and white of a federal crime.

So much is changing. Limits that have always felt solid and real have begun to erode, and many of us are losing our faith. But please, let's hold fast together to this: America is not defined by the people whose paychecks bear her signature, but instead by the people who are called upon to decide. Never surrender that.

Our system is far from perfect—jurors are often chosen unfairly, the instructions we give them are impenetrable, and the versions of the truth we are allowed to tell them can get badly distorted—but it stands as a necessary barrier. Without boundaries, there are no countries. And the ones we can see on a map are not the ones that matter. It is the limits of power, not the limits of land, that make us America. They are meant to restrain *us*, not to be wielded as weapons against anyone who approaches from beyond. Without them, America, you cease to exist.

I can't stay long in this empty courtroom; the marshals need to secure it. Other lawyers are waiting, other defendants, other juries. On my way out the front doors of the courthouse, I will pass two framed portraits, the president and vice president of the United States. The same portraits hang in the entrance of every federal courthouse in the country. The portraits change every four or eight years, but the courtrooms do not. There is always a place, guarded and sacred, where the jury will sit, and no matter who is in those frames in the lobby, nobody leaves this courthouse in chains without their say-so. Remember that, America. Hold on to that.

Yours,
Amy

Letter to the Future President

STEVEN AND SOPHIE CHURCH

Dear America,

On the morning of Tuesday, November 8, 2016, in Fresno, California, we took our eight-year-old daughter, Sophie, to the polls to vote with us. This was her third presidential election, but I'm not sure there's ever been more at stake for her. My hands began to shake from some unexpected panic, as if my body were registering the tremors of the coming divide. My daughter stood with me in the recreation room of the church, watching as a diverse roomful of people cast their votes and expressed their vision of the future of our country. A couple of hours later, her third-grade teacher asked the students to pen letters to the future president, whomever they thought that might be. They were asked to contribute at least two ideas or suggestions. What follows, then, is my daughter's "letter to America":

Nov. 8, 2016
Election Day!

Dear Future President,

Congrats on being elected president! This is probably going to be a great experience (hopefully). I'm writing this to tell you my opinions of how we could change the USA.

Here are the things I believe are important to change in the next *4 years*!

My Platforms:

1. End global warming
2. Equality for every race, sex, and religion
3. Education

4. Gun control
5. Better cafeteria food
6. Less abusing animals
7. Save water
8. Free college for all
9. Love everyone (all races, all genders, and all religions)
10. Less misogyny
11. Homeless shelters
12. Less (no) student debt
13. Free health care
14. A fair world
15. Better housing
16. Help children get food
17. Fight world hunger
18. Help us have a safe world
19. No WARS!
20. Nobody should be discriminated against
21. Lower taxes for the middle class
22. Treat other countries with respect

Kids need healthier things in cafeterias. Because they can't afford to pay for home lunches, they should be able to have healthier food at school. And we should stop war now and have peace on earth, and keep everyone alive!

Thank you, President!

These are the things I feel very strongly about in our country.

Sincerely,
Sophie Church
Age 8, Fresno, California

I guess if I could say anything to America right now, perhaps I would just tell you to listen to our children. They have things to say. I saw a statistic somewhere, backed up by anecdotal evidence from my daughter, that if children were allowed to vote in the 2016 election, Hillary Clinton would have won in a landslide. What does that say about us as a country? When I asked Sophie why her classmates didn't like Donald

Trump, the general consensus was "he's a bully." But it's more than that, of course. She knows, on some level, that you, America, voted that day to affirm centuries of sexism, racism, xenophobia, homophobia, and oppression. You elected to continue marginalizing her. And she won't forget that. What I see in my daughter—this fierce, smart, and driven young woman—and in her classmates is a kind of imaginative optimism and uncorrupted hope for a better world, an idealism I think we have to find a way to recapture and hold on to. We have to make art, put words on pages, and fight. But we have to remember to love one another too and to keep the vision of a better world alive. We need to listen to the wisdom we have apparently lost, the wisdom of our youngers.

Sincerely,
Steven Church
Age 44, Fresno, California

Defying Hatred

SCOTT RUSSELL SANDERS

The first television images I can recall seeing, as a boy in the 1950s, were of white southerners attacking peaceful black demonstrators with police dogs, fire hoses, tear gas, clubs, and curses. Even black children, neatly dressed and carrying books, were turned away from schools by white sheriffs and politicians and mobs. My parents could not explain those bewildering images to me. They could not explain why people with dark skin were prevented from going to school or sitting at a lunch counter or voting. According to my own skin color, I should have identified with the angry whites, but instead I felt the fear and bruises of those who were attacked.

That sympathy was instinctive, as in any child who has not been taught to despise some group of people defined as Other. The Other may be distinguished not only by skin color but also by gender, religion, age, class, national origin, disability, and any number of other markers. Our evolutionary inheritance predisposes us to divide the world between Us and Them—between an in-group toward which we are loyal and protective, and one or more out-groups, whom we treat as enemies. Members of a tribe that exploits, enslaves, or slaughters neighboring tribes—thereby acquiring more territory and resources—are likelier to pass on their genes to future generations. At least they are likelier to do so in an era of low population density and primitive weaponry. Today, on a planet crowded with over seven billion human beings and armed with murderous technology, from malware to missiles, tribalism may prove lethal for the aggressors as well as for their intended victims.

The risks of tapping into tribalism in the twenty-first century do not make it any less appealing to demagogues, as we saw in the 2016 presidential campaign. One candidate addressed his audiences as the in-crowd, while demeaning and demonizing various Others, and he stoked a penchant for violence against anyone he defined as an outsider, including rival candidates. It was a dangerous as well as a shameful strategy. After the election, rather than speaking to the press about his plans or seriously preparing himself for the presidency, he continued holding rallies laced with ridicule and contempt. Even if he wished to temper the hatreds he had roused, he wouldn't be able to do so without alienating his core followers. Fear of the Other is easy to evoke, difficult to allay.

Fortunately, our evolutionary legacy includes not only a predisposition for aggressive tribalism but also a countervailing capacity: in its everyday form we call it empathy, and in its more refined, often deliberately nurtured form, we call it compassion. Without empathy, we could not have survived and flourished as social animals; language, culture, and cooperative behavior all rely on our ability to intuit the inner states of the people around us. Empathy alone, however, does not assure that we will treat one another fairly. Con artists are expert at reading the emotions of those whom they exploit or manipulate—again, as illustrated in the 2016 presidential campaign by the demagogue who was declared the winner. What con artists lack is compassion, which involves not merely sensing what others feel but sympathizing with them, caring for them, wishing to address their needs and relieve their suffering.

Figures famous for their compassion range from the Buddha and Jesus to Mahatma Gandhi, Martin Luther King Jr., and Mother Teresa. In each case, their caring for others reached across the supposed boundaries that separate humans into tribes. But this potential resides not only in saints and cultural heroes. We can see it demonstrated by countless followers of Islam, Buddhism, Judaism, Christianity, and other religions that uphold compassion as the highest human virtue. Quite apart from religion, we have all encountered unsung, dedicated, kind people whose actions defy divisions between black and white, male and female, native and foreign, straight and gay, Jew and Gentile, rich and poor, and every other variation on Us and Them. This capacity for all-inclusive caring is as much a part of our inheritance as tribalism.

On the national stage right now, tribalism appears to be ascendant. A tyrant occupies the White House. He has surrounded himself with people who share his prejudices and flatter his vanity. Most of his nominees for cabinet posts are hostile to the public purposes that their agencies are designed to serve—such as defending civil rights, protecting the environment, assuring access to health care, and advocating for the poor. The dominant news media, having profited for years from publicizing his slightest and nastiest blurts, have been slow to challenge this betrayal of the public trust. The members of his own party in Congress either align themselves with the tyrant or lack the courage to stand against him.

The menace may seem overwhelming. But we should remember that the forty-fifth president does not represent the majority of Americans. His tribalism has drawn into the spotlight a throng of white supremacists, misogynists, xenophobes, anti-Semites, and others animated by envy and hatred, but such people constitute only a small, if dangerous, fraction of his supporters, and his supporters, in turn, constitute only a small fraction of our fellow citizens. He won the Republican nomination with votes from fewer than 10 percent of eligible adults. His Electoral College victory was decided by fewer than sixty thousand votes in three swing states, and he lost the popular tally by more than three million votes. Forty percent of eligible adults—over ninety million people—did not vote at all. He garnered 46 percent of the votes cast, which works out to just over a quarter of eligible adults. He did not come close to securing a popular mandate. So we should not allow his election, his divisive views, or his callous policies to define our nation.

With or without a mandate, the forty-fifth president has proceeded to shred the social safety net, reignite the nuclear arms race, replace diplomacy with military threats, set off trade wars, shun refugees, free global corporations from all constraints, abolish environmental regulations, and stymie efforts at reducing climate disruption. Compassion may seem too weak a force to counter so much malice. But compassion is not our only source of healing and courage. We should not underestimate the strength of neighborliness, generosity, and hospitality. We should not forget the power of reason, especially as manifested in science and medicine. Nor should we forget the power of imagination, as shown in the arts and humanities, and in the creativity that wells up in each one of us.

Vicious policies have inspired strong resistance. Churches and other places of worship are offering sanctuary to immigrants threatened with deportation. Cities, towns, and households are welcoming refugees.

States and municipalities are renewing commitments to reduce carbon emissions. Citizens are organizing to defend public schools, public lands, the oceans and fresh waters, biodiversity, and other portions of the commonwealth. Scientists are collaborating with filmmakers to dramatize the reality of climate disruption and other threats to Earth's living web, and to lay out paths for recovery. Writers and musicians are opposing tyranny by giving voice to our sympathies and affections. Nonprofits, buoyed by an unprecedented inflow of donations, are redoubling their efforts to meet human needs, advocate for justice, protect wildlife, and foster peace. These and many other efforts of resistance and healing are unfolding all across our land. Aided by reason and imagination, powered by love, they arise from our capacity to see beyond all seeming divisions, to recognize our common humanity and our membership in the web of life.

Everything we loved and cared about before the 2016 election, we still love and care about, only now we realize more vividly how endangered those precious people, places, creatures, and causes are. Now we realize we must defend them with all our heart and might. When my hope falters, I recall those TV images from my childhood of white mobs abusing peaceful black schoolchildren and demonstrators. Some of those whites are still with us, clinging to their prejudices; some have taught the same tribal hatred to their children and grandchildren. But they no longer rule our country, not even the South. Enough Americans of all shades and ethnicities have sufficiently freed themselves from racism to elect and then reelect an African American man to the presidency—a man who far surpasses his white successor in character, intelligence, and concern for human well-being. That successor, an accidental president, is a holdover from a cruder and crueler time in our history. We must not let him dictate our future.

Dear Soon-to-Be-Sprout

ELIZABETH RUSH

Dear Soon-to-be Sprout,

It's possible that as I write you are rooting yourself deep in my uterine walls. It's also possible that your will-be dad's sperm missed the rendezvous we arranged with my eggs and that we will have to try for you in another three weeks' time. I love that phrasing: to try for someone. I suppose that is what motherhood will hold, a whole lot of attempting on behalf of another being.

As I write, I'm not thinking about what color to paint your room or what name you might carry, tender spark, I'm thinking of a letter Alexis Pauline Grumbs wrote to her past self from a changed future where society is no longer steeped in cheap fossil fuels. Imagine that. One line of her missive reads: *Now life, not exactly easier, is life all the time.* I first encountered those words back in the spring after I returned from a reporting trip to Antarctica, where I'd watched a chunk of one of the world's key glacial systems collapse right in front of me. It augmented my already extraordinary ability to conjure up endings. Though my skill, mind you, is not born of delusion. Last year the Spix's macaw, a wily blue bird with a long tail that I'm certain you would have loved, went extinct in the wild. Also gone: a songbird called the cryptic tree-hunter (how fabulous a name is that?) and the Hawaiian land snail. In the year before we began to try for you, human beings—and in particular human beings from the country where you will be born—forced a few species from the earth forever.

Were I a weatherman I would call my mind a tidal wave; a temperature gauge, broken and blistering. Which is why, I guess, I needed those words *life all the time,* fiercely. Sure, they gave me solace, but they also lent me something even more crucial: an alternative to work toward. Sometimes, I think, reason mixed with laziness and fatigue fills the future I often imagine with drought and famine and death. It's more difficult to know that something will persist and that it's our job to shape that something into something good.

I'll admit, I fear your absence and also my presumptuousness in writing you so soon. I wake up in the middle of the night, anxious that whatever could become your consciousness might not grow in my belly. And I try to tell myself that, if that does happen, it isn't my body's betrayal but rather some basic biology and that I will find another way to make a family.

Which is to say when I think of you I think of all the things that don't have to exist—your feet and clavicles and little soon-to-be eyelashes—but that might just become part of the world. I think of the nothingness in which beginnings begin. I think of the hard country where we live now and what it can, with work, become: a place where all of our energy comes in renewable forms, where high-speed, zero-carbon trains connect here and there, a home where for the first time in a long time living doesn't also mean systematically dismantling the weave of life we depend upon.

Often we talk about what we'll have to give up to turn the future livable, the sacrifices we will have to make—the flights, the single-family homes, the pleasure derived from regular purchases of things we do not need and that will not last. Some say sacrifice is something a mother makes, in particular, of her body when it becomes a place where someone else might reside. But thinking of my flesh and bone as your shelter does not diminish my own being; instead of one body I begin to see two.

Recently, Elizabeth Swain, a mother and climate organizer, recommended that we shift our focus away from what we alone cannot accomplish and toward thinking that helps us to glimpse what is possible when people come together to demand change. Instead of focusing on "your own carbon footprint (which you can never drive low enough in a society awash in cheap fossil fuels)," she writes, we must work collectively "to apply pressure so that the incentives and infrastructure investments help to lower everyone's footprint." Because the keyboard I type on is made with petroleum, the plane I fly home powered by jet fuel, sometimes I feel impotent at best, ashamed at worst. As it turns out, none of my personal choices about what and how to consume can, on their own, actually build for you the world I want you to inhabit. They cannot guarantee you a home beyond my body, one that you nourish and nourishes you in turn.

Something about Swain's words got me thinking about Staten Island again and how in the wake of Hurricane Sandy six hundred people there sold their houses to the state so that they might be bulldozed and the land returned to nature to act as a buffer against the storms to come. If one person moved away, nothing would have changed. Yet, counterintuitively, Sandy brought the community closer together. They fought as a group for a fair recovery. When I visited five years after the hurricane I found that the overwhelming majority of people relocated nearby, just up the hill, out of harm's way. They still ate fried fish sandwiches at Toto's and danced at the VFW. What had changed was their immediate vulnerability to flooding.

Rosebud, it has taken me a long time to connect what I have seen playing out along this country's transforming shore to my own life, but with the hope of you inside of me here I finally am: the only personal action that can slow the tide of the climate crisis is to create a coalition that is bigger and more powerful than the individuals of which it is comprised.

You are an idea that I pray will become a zygote, unfurling as tendril from a seed. To prepare for your soon-to-be presence, your residence on planet earth, I've decided to try something new. As the sun set last Tuesday, as I sent my prayers up into the glowing sky that you were there inside of me glowing a little too, I walked toward the George Wiley Center in Pawtucket. There I joined a dozen other people who were advocating for the establishment of a public utility in our home state. Together we drafted letters, made outreach plans, and vowed to meet again in two weeks' time. All these actions might seem small, but when you connect them to those taking place across America, the reach of this groundwork is wide.

I want to say to you, little seed, change is the only thing that is true, and it starts when we join one and one to make more than two.

Yours,
Elizabeth

The Augury

KIMIKO HAHN

August 3, 2019

Dear America,

I will meet him in November
In upstate New York
Knowing that with grand ardor
He will begin to cry.

In upstate New York
He will love me and take a breath
As we both begin to cry.
No one needs a seer to see

He'll love me and take a breath
Of the rank air
That no one needs a seer to see.
He'll not love the ripe water

Complementing the rank air
Thanks to the factory owners.
He'll not love the stench
Concocted by our president.

To protect him from factory owners,
I'll meet him in November.
To protect him from this president
I'll attend his birth. I am his grandmother,

Kimiko

July Fourth

CATHERINE VENABLE MOORE

Dear America,

I spent much of today reading about union activists in the coalfields of West Virginia a century ago, who found political salvation in the stick-together notion of solidarity at a time and in a place where nearly every instrument of democracy had failed them through and through. The old Wobbly poet Ralph Chaplin wrote the union anthem "Solidarity Forever" in response to a coal strike he witnessed here in Fayette County in 1912, when mining families lived outdoors in tent camps for over a year, facing down the barrels of machine guns wielded by private police. *We can bring to birth a new world from the ashes of the old, for the union makes us strong.*

"Charming," I can almost hear you thinking. "Another leftist's essay about solidarity!" But indulge me, America, while I try on this belief that my well-being and your well-being are mutually dependent. Indulge for a moment my romantic notion of wholeness through the many. The grace of belonging to a "we," entirely integrated by common concern. Today I actually *ache in my body* to feel close to you, my country. I have to admit, I've never felt more without a society. This morning, I read about tanks arrayed on the apron of the Lincoln Memorial and saw pictures of the detention camps at the southern border, and sat stewing in our national shame.

My alienation from you is a loneliness I try to fill with other things. I fantasize about getting pregnant, or I imagine a man who's going to come along and fix me. I eat delicious food from a container advertising itself as a "Deep Fried Box of Love."

Antsy this afternoon, I headed outside, to the place I always seek relief when I'm feeling moody—a rock outcropping along the rim of the

New River Gorge, its vastness usually a cure for my tiny woes. There's a comfort, too, in the simple act of returning to the same rock ledge, over and over across a life. In the soft drift of the rhododendron blossoms that fall across the path, in the light that ripples along the finger ridges.

But here in West Virginia, the pastoral is never more than a field or two apart from a scene of human disturbance, as the blasts from the surface mine near my house remind me every afternoon at 4 p.m. In this way, West Virginia most resembles the nation. None of it—the vastness, the blossoms—brought me any closer to the kind of union I longed for. I walked back toward the road just as dusk began to fall.

■ ■ ■

Oh, amnesiac country, let's just agree that your freedom has always been suspect. Pretending otherwise is getting too exhausting. Across your brief 244-year life (155 if we count 1865 as your rebirth), that word has taken on various shapes and shades, some more benevolent than others.

Certain factions have translated freedom as independence, as in self-rule, as in the degree to which one can author one's own life. In this sense, the fewer hindrances to our individual autonomy, the freer we are as a people. *Yet what force on Earth is weaker than the feeble force of one?* Ralph Chaplin sang, to the tune of "John Brown's Body."

Another conception of freedom locates interdependence at its core. Rather than self-interest, this school of thought organizes its decisions around a "common good." In such a territory, liberty is measured by participation in public life and access to democratic practices. This is the one we're starving for, America.

■ ■ ■

As darkness fell, I headed toward town for the fireworks, still hoping for some last-minute catharsis, cheap and commodified though it might be. An indigo storm cloud hovered over the park where the town's display was scheduled to appear. People sent up their own little streams of light into the cloud from their backyards, as though egging on the thunder. Everywhere, police cars flashed their red, white, and blue lights, reflecting in the smoke of the fireworks. I heard someone say on a podcast the other day, "bullets are men's tears," and, under the exploding rockets, that felt true.

■ ■ ■

The union I hunger for is the same one that the labor agitator Mother Jones described to an assembly of United Mine Workers in 1901: "the school...where you learn to know and to love each other and learn to work with each other and bear each other's burdens, each other's sorrows and each other's joys." America, can we build more schools like that?

In my foster-parenting class the other day, we learned that there are certain needs beyond food and shelter that drive us as humans; needs more emotional than physical. One of those is the need to belong. Without a sense of belonging, we quickly lose all motivation. And starved of love and human touch, a baby will quite literally die. I read in a neuropsychology book that the female brain is "a machine... built for connection," hardwired to seek "social harmony," unlike the competition-seeking male brain. In this way, America, women are the more dialectical sex, and perhaps the better suited to forging this new union, if it's to be.

We also talked about building positive attachments to meet that human need for belonging. About pathways through the grieving process. When we got to the lesson on discipline, the trainer asked how many of us had been hit when we were children. Almost everyone in the overflowing room raised their hand. Most are grandparents raising the addicted children of their addicted children in a situation called "kinship care." The trainer calls it "coming into care," a phrase my tongue turns over to soothe itself.

■ ■ ■

Back at home now, I write three words on a slip of paper—
Solidarity
Solace
Solitude
—and stare at them as the night deepens around me.

The part of my soul that tries to make sense of life through language notes their common beginning, "*s-o-l,*" and hopes it might reveal some shared linguistic ancestry. Language, at its best, provides wiring for connection, unlike a bullet, the ultimate anticonversation.

I look up their Latin sources but find that they descend from three entirely different words: solidarity from *solidus,* meaning "whole" or "solid." (*Solidus* also described a coin of the Roman Empire made of nearly pure gold.) Solace, from *solacium,* for "comfort." Solitude, from *solus,* which is most commonly translated as "alone," though it had other senses as well. Forsaken, for one. Extraordinary, for another.

So I dig even deeper, trace the words to that theoretical *ur*-language, Proto-Indo-European, searching for a common root.

This dream of a unifying tongue is a strange, racist myth at worst and a set of imperfect conjectures at best. Proto-Indo-European is an imagined language—like you and me and us, America—which we nevertheless use to parse our own very alive one.

It's murky, but there appears to be some connection, deep in the past, between the idea of being whole and the idea of comforting another. We can't say for sure, but some have theorized that *solidarity* and *solace* both go back to a single root, *sol,* meaning something akin to "whole and well-kept." I hold tight to this tiny piece of sense.

■ ■ ■

I fold up the piece of paper with the three words and set it beside my bed, like a charm to usher in good dreams.

■ ■ ■

There's a glint of mirage to the idea of union; that *we* can be singular, uniform. That *we* can in fact be a *you,* America, seems in a lot of ways like a blind myth. That *you* were born on any particular day, independent or otherwise, seems increasingly impossible. There's no you at all, I realize, no recipient of this letter—there's just us, a bunch of I's living inside a collective identity, which, like all identities, is a thing constructed over time, malleable like the flickering of consciousness within an infant, seeking love and connection to grow into itself.

■ ■ ■

Anyway, if you're out there, America, write back soon.

Yours (Ours?),
Catherine

Dear Katrina

KATRINA GOLDSAITO

Dear America,
   I don't know what to say. Every draft ends up in the trash.

Katrina

■ ■ ■

Dear Katrina,
   I hope it's okay, I pulled your letters out of the recycling bin. I read how heartbroken you are, how you swing between despair and hope, activity and exhaustion. Of course you are confused, unsettled, and very, very scared. And in every line you cannot, nor should you, hide your disappointment in me.
   It is a strange thing to be a mother. You watch your land swollen and ravaged by your children, watch them take with impunity, as children do, sure always of your never-ending generosity.
   It's strange the way they see you only in parts: broken or godlike, joyful or haunted, grasping or noble. It is difficult sometimes to feel whole, when your children reflect back all of the ways you've done them wrong, not been the mother they need, not handed them the life they deserve. You hesitate to let them know: they are creating this image of you.
   There are moments, of course, when you delight in the way they notice you: they wade into your deep waters and lean their heads back and float; they fall back into your cool grass: still and listening and breathing. They walk through your paths and brambles, climb with determination to your highest point, and in that moment where they look out on your canyons and forests and rivers and oceans, in that moment

where they sigh with contentment, you feel seen, though all you can do is echo back the words that they call out.

One of your sisters, Alice Walker, said that having a child is like having your heart walk around outside of your body. The ache of watching every one of your children confront heartache and violence and sorrow and hatred until they are so full with it that they turn on each other is a pain that I hope you will never fully comprehend. Or maybe I am being too protective; maybe if you could comprehend the pain of that division it would be the medicine you need to come together. I want to remind you how the palettes of your emotions are identical. I want to awaken your basic empathy, but I am only a mother, I can only nag so much.

As a mother, I refuse to distribute love according to goodness, will not dole it out like an allowance for chores finished: to be a mother is to love everyone, even the children riddled with hatred. Because hatred is just old festering pain, and you remember when that pain was fresh, can see how it paints a fluorescent streak to the present. Even when you think, that's it, I've had it, even when they get on your last nerve—you realize suddenly that there are always new nerves you can grow.

Did you know that nerves are "cordlike bundles of fibers" and that they have an astounding ability to regenerate? That the two ends of a peripheral cut nerve can and will knit themselves back together in time? That is what you hope for your children, though for now they continue yanking each other back and forth in a giant tug-of-war. Did you know that to be a mother is to always be teaching whether you realize it or not? Did you know that sometimes those lessons are not the ones you intended but ones that are learned nonetheless?

I know you wrote to me wanting some guidance. I know you wrote to me because you see me as wise, as responsible, as the one in charge, but I don't know what to say. I don't know how to comfort you. This, perhaps, is the most difficult part of being a mother. To admit that I am not all-knowing, I am not all-seeing, I do not know how to knit the disparate parts of our country together.

But I think you do. Because I can see the whole of you. I've been there all this time. I held you when you were colicky and sick, I kissed scraped knees and rushed you to the hospital when you fell from my branches, I've been here for every iteration of your human life. I see your resilience, your generosity, your human creativity. I see your capacity for radical empathy, and how you too have this ever-widening capacity for love.

I ask, simply, that you try. That you try to be both understanding and firm, that you speak out and act out against injustice, that you remind your brothers and sisters of their duty to one another. Be both patient and tenacious. Big-hearted and steadfast.

Love,
America

Dinner with America

RICK BASS

When I was a child growing up in Texas, in the 1950s and 1960s, time capsules were a big thing. There was a quaint, almost querulous child-like quality to the capsules. Preserving things the way they used to be. We did it every year, in grade school.

But folks had been burying things in Texas for a long time. There was a famous horned toad named Rip who was buried in the concrete poured in the foundation of the Eastland County Courthouse in 1898, and, when the courthouse was torn down thirty-one years later, the foundation was broken open and Rip was still alive.

This idea that things, even the past, can stay the same is not uniquely Texan: but there was certainly fertile ground for it, back then.

What I want to say tonight, I know, already has a time-capsule quality to it—a few months from now, all manner of dramatic things will have happened, and no small amount of them will be heinous. And since this is to be a letter to my country—a nation founded on genocide, which rose to economic power on slavery—we've already read *that* letter. We could recite it with every hangdog step as we are carried into our future.

Tonight I could chat with America about the long-standing fetish with guns. Again, not a peculiarly Texas affliction, the idea that might makes right, and that whenever a conversation lags, just whip out a gun and fix whatever's inconveniencing you.

It could be mild fun to call Donald Trump a grotesque idiot, a bloated manifestation that has nothing to do with our country's soul—an unwitting Trojan horse foisted upon us by Russian oligarchs—

—It would feel okay, to say something like that—

But the truth is, things could get worse; this railing could in a year be as antiquated as a time capsule.

If America were a person—and it occurs to me, in this fast-evolving speciation where we are willingly transferring ourselves from individual voices into corporate-proxy voices, that personhood seems ever more remote—well, I really don't think I'd write a screed about what's wrong. It feels too much like telling a sick person you're afraid they're dying.

I think if she were here at the table with me, on this porch, at the end of summer and beginning of fall, with the rich green scent of marsh grass flowing up toward me, and no birdsong, no frogs, just stillness (later tonight, there will be wolves), I'd fix her a meal. It would be elegant and heartfelt—potatoes and meat—elk backstrap cooked in an iron skillet with a dash of cream and sautéed morel mushrooms picked from last season's fire and then dried, stringing them on this same porch with thread and needle to twist and dry in the summer sun and breezes, before rehydrating.

I wouldn't feel the need to preach or complain. Being sentimental I might even tell her I'm grateful to her for much. Later in the evening, as we got near the bottom of the wine I'd opened—a Côtes du Rhône or Bordeaux—I might read some poetry to her. American poetry; American art, created in hard times, leaning hard on those old crutches of beauty, creativity, imagination.

We'd save room for dessert, because even though I think there's going to be a tomorrow, one never knows. Huckleberry rhubarb.

We might talk about what makes a great American. Great ones we've known. Teachers would be thick among them, and older people of integrity we've been lucky to know. My grandfather. My parents.

Artists are my heroes, too. I'd talk about Berger, and Merwin's poem "Thanks." We'd stay up late. I'd plug in the porch lights.

The pie would be pretty great. She'd want to know the recipe for the crust, but I wouldn't give it to her, not yet. I'd want to keep her coming back.

And after we caught up on her last ten thousand years—*Say what you want about global warming*, she'd laugh, *but I was pretty excited at first, when that last ice sheet started to go away*—she might ask what I've been up to.

I'd tell her. While all the other shit's going on, I've been living like a hermit here in this little bowl of a valley on the Montana–British Columbia border—this island, separated from all other mountain ranges—fighting to protect the last twenty-five grizzly bears that are hanging on here. It's the most endangered population in North America. You see one family unit of four, you're seeing 15 percent of the entire population.

But you don't see them. They live deep in the woods, in this low-elevation swampy rainforest garden. They're ghosts.

Why do they matter? she might say. *With all that's going on, do they really even matter?*

I've thought about that, I'd tell her. I'd shake my head. They're beautiful, I'd say. Just because there's so much going on doesn't allow us to extinguish them. Doesn't allow our government to extinguish them. Remember, I'd say, haven't we seen this story before?

I love them for what they are: ice-bound astronauts, sleeping five months of the year beneath the ice, their hearts beating two to three times a minute, dreaming in slow motion. I love that they're largely vegetarian, eating hundreds of pounds of grass and berries. I love how the adults slide down the ice with their cubs and splash each other in the lake. I love how they will protect their young with a ferocity not seen elsewhere on this continent. I love that they possess the greatest growth disparity between newborn (less than a pound) and mature adult (six hundred pounds or more). I love that they came over the land bridge and lived on top of the ice—that they were the first thing here, when the ice left. Waiting.

I love that Native people call them Teacher or Grandfather. I love that theirs is a maternal culture, that the female takes her cubs all over their territory, showing them where to catch fish when the berries are dry, where to go when they hear rifle shots, where—

You don't like being around people much, do you?

Do I have to?

No. There is plenty to love about America other than people. Just curious.

I like people, but I don't like being around them.

How can I help, she'd say, leaning forward. *You're right: a country that can't protect its last twenty-five grizzlies. . .*

. . . doesn't deserve them, I'd think, but neither of us would say that.

Write Senator Tester, I'd say: tester.senate.gov/contact. Write Senator Daines, and Representative Gianforte. Read about it at yaakvalley.org.

All right. Good night, she'd say, getting up. *I have to be up early. Thank you for the pie. Thank you for the elk.*

Thank you, I'd say. Thank you.

But we wouldn't be finished talking.

Acknowledgments and Credits

The editors would like to thank the contributors for joining us in donating all royalties from this anthology to the Union of Concerned Scientists, the Natural Resources Defense Council, and the American Civil Liberties Union. We thank these organizations and so many others for their essential work.

Special thanks to Alison Hawthorne Deming for her initial letter to America and her ongoing support, energy, and wisdom. She is our hero.

Thanks also to Kurt Caswell and David Gessner for their publishing support of this project, not to mention their friendship. Many thanks to the *Terrain.org* editorial board and editors for their insight and support for the Letter to America series as well as to the many contributors to the series, both online and in this book. Kind thanks to Tom Payton and Steffanie Mortis Stevens at Trinity University Press for their belief in and careful stewardship of *Dear America*. And thanks to our editorial intern, Vilune Sestokaite—we weren't always easy to work with, we know.

Simmons would like to thank Billie, Ann-Elise, Juliet, Nangia, and Lacey for their love, hope, support, and good old-fashioned American progressiveness.

Elizabeth would like to thank her family and friends for their love and support for—and during—this project, most especially Dave Rintoul.

Derek would like to thank his friends and family for their love and support, especially Dennis, Andy, Kevin, Allen, Joe, Jack, Gabrielle, Zoey, Kelsea, Georgia, Lonny, Diana, Jodi, Mindi, Jerry, and Loyd.

Thank you, dear readers, for believing in what America can still become.

Poetry, essays, and artwork by the following authors and artists originally appeared in *Terrain.org*, usually in an earlier form: Seth Abramson, Sandra Alcosser, José Angel Araguz, Todd Boss, Elizabeth Bradfield, Michael P. Branch, Taylor Brorby, Rob Carney, Jennifer Case, Joy Castro, Kurt Caswell, Victoria Chang, Steven and Sophie Church, Miriam Marty Clark, Todd Davis, Alison Hawthorne Deming, Elizabeth Dodd, Chris Dombrowski, Camille T. Dungy, Blas Falconer, Bob Ferguson, Deborah Fries, Suzanne Frischkorn, Allen Gee, Katrina Goldsaito, Vince Gotera, Patri Hadad, Amanda Hawkins, Dennis Held, Lee Herrick, Sean Hill, Jane Hirshfield, Jen Hirt, Erin Coughlin Hollowell, Pam Houston, Barbara Hurd, Sarah Inskeep, Fenton Johnson, Ever Jones, Richard Kenney, John Lane, Karen An-hwei Lee, Lawrence Lenhart, Erin Malone, Debra Marquart, Tod Marshall, Anne Haven McDonnell, Colleen McElroy, Rose McLarney, Gregory McNamee, Tim McNulty, Sandra Meek, Christopher Merrill, Kathryn Miles, Scott Minar, Kathleen Dean Moore, Naomi Shihab Nye, Georgia Pearle, John T. Price, Heather Ryan, Scott Russell Sanders, Lauret Savoy, Martha Silano, Sarah Skeen, Aisha Sabatini Sloan, R. T. Smith, Ana Maria Spagna, Kim Stafford, Catherine Staples, Laura-Gray Street, Alexandra Teague, Nicole Walker, Debbie Weingarten, Lesley Wheeler, Joe Wilkins, Christian Wiman, Sholeh Wolpé, Robert Wrigley, and Andrew S. Yang.

Parts of Francisco Cantú's essay "Assembly-Line Justice" originally appeared with the title "Tucson, Arizona," in the October 2017 issue of *Harper's Magazine*.

Contributors

Simmons Buntin is the founder and editor-in-chief of *Terrain.org*. He is the recipient of an Academy of American Poets Prize, the Colorado Artist's Fellowship for Poetry, and grants from the U.S. Forest Service, the Arizona Commission on the Arts, and the Tucson-Pima Arts Council. He is the author of a collection of community case studies, *Unsprawl: Remixing Spaces as Places*, and the poetry collections *Riverfall* and *Bloom*. He lives in Tucson, Arizona.

Elizabeth Dodd is the nonfiction editor of *Terrain.org*. She is the author of the nonfiction collections *Horizon's Lens: My Time on the Turning World*, *In the Mind's Eye: Essays across the Animate World*, and *Prospect: Journeys & Landscapes* and the poetry collections *Archetypal Light* and *Like Memory, Caverns*. Her honors include the Association for the Study of Literature and Environment's Best Book Award, the Elmer Holmes Bobst Award for poetry, and fellowships from the Kansas Arts Commission. She lives in the Flint Hills of east-central Kansas.

Derek Sheffield is the poetry editor of *Terrain.org*. His poems have appeared in the *Southern Review*, *Poetry*, the *Georgia Review*, and several anthologies. He is the recipient of the James Hearst Poetry Prize and fellowships from Artist Trust and the Sustainable Arts Foundation. He is the author of the poetry collections *A Mouthpiece of Thumbs*, *A Revised Account of the West*, and *Through the Second Skin*. He lives in central Washington.

■ ■ ■

Seth Abramson is an attorney, professor, columnist, editor, and author whose most recent book is the *New York Times* best-seller *Proof of Collusion: How Trump Betrayed America*.

Sandra Alcosser is the author of *A Fish to Feed All Hunger* and *Except by Nature*. The founder of San Diego State University's MFA program and editor of *Poetry International*, she was Montana's first poet laureate.

José Angel Araguz is the author of several chapbooks and poetry collections, including the 2019 Oregon Book Award finalist *Until We Are Level Again*.

Diana Babineau is managing editor for *In These Times* and a consulting editor for the *Kenyon Review*. Her poetry has been published in *North American Review* and elsewhere.

Ellen Bass is a chancellor of the Academy of American Poets. Among her poetry books are *Indigo* and *Like a Beggar*. Her nonfiction includes *The Courage to Heal: A Guide for Women Survivors of Child Sexual Abuse*.

Rick Bass is an award-winning short story writer, essayist, and novelist. He lives in the Yaak Valley of Montana and is board chair of the Yaak Valley Forest Council.

Anne P. Beatty is a high school English teacher whose nonfiction has been published in the *American Scholar*, the *Atlantic*, *Creative Nonfiction*, and elsewhere.

Sherwin Bitsui is an award-winning Diné poet and the author of *Shapeshift*, *Flood Song*, and most recently *Dissolve*. He teaches creative writing at Northern Arizona University.

Todd Boss is a poet (*Tough Luck*, *Pitch*, and *Yellowrocket*), film producer, public artist, librettist, and inventor who sold everything he owned in 2018 and has been house-sitting his way around the world.

Elizabeth Bradfield divides her time between working as a naturalist on boats and teaching creative writing at Brandeis University. Her most recent book is *Toward Antarctica*.

Michael P. Branch is the University Foundation Professor of English at the University of Nevada, Reno, and the author of nine books. He is working on a book about jackalopes.

Traci Brimhall's most recent book is *Come the Slumberless to the Land of Nod*.

Taylor Brorby is a contributing editor to the *North American Review*.

Jericho Brown is a poet, author of the award-winning books *Please*, *New Testament*, and *The Tradition*, and director of the creative writing program at Emory University.

Francisco Cantú, a former U.S. Border Patrol agent, is a writer, translator, and author of *The Line Becomes a River: Dispatches from the Border,* winner of the 2018 Los Angeles Times Book Prize.

Rob Carney is the author of six books of poems, most recently *Facts and Figures* and *The Book of Sharks.* He lives in Salt Lake City.

Jacob Carter is an ecologist and science policy advocate who lives in Washington, D.C., with his boyfriend, Justin, and cat, Ruth Bader Catsburg.

Jennifer Case is an assistant nonfiction editor of *Terrain.org* and the author of *Sawbill: A Search for Place.*

Joy Castro is the Willa Cather Professor of English and Ethnic Studies at the University of Nebraska–Lincoln and the author of two novels, an essay collection, a memoir, and a short fiction collection.

Kurt Caswell teaches writing and literature in the Honors College at Texas Tech University. His most recent nonfiction work is *Laika's Window: The Legacy of a Soviet Space Dog.*

Victoria Chang is the author of *OBIT, Barbie Chang, The Boss, Salvinia Molesta, Circle,* and the children's books *Is Mommy?* and *Love, Love.* She is the chair of Antioch University's low-residency MFA program.

Sophie Church lives in Fresno, California, where she fights for human rights and maintains a blog at sopheminist.weebly.com.

Steven Church is Sophie's dad and has written some stuff.

Miriam Marty Clark is an associate professor of English at Auburn University, where she teaches and writes about contemporary American poetry and fiction.

Andrea Cohen's most recent poetry collection is *Nightshade.* She directs the Writers House at Merrimack College and the Blacksmith House Poetry Series in Cambridge, Massachusetts.

Todd Davis is the author of six books of poetry, most recently *Native Species* and *Winterkill.*

Alison Hawthorne Deming is a Regents Professor at the University of Arizona. Her most recent books are *Stairway to Heaven* and *Zoologies: On Animals and the Human Spirit.*

Anita Desikan is a research analyst at the Union of Concerned Scientists whose work examines the impacts of science policy on public health and the environment.

Chris Dombrowski is the author of four books, most recently *Body of Water*, a Bloomberg News Book of the Year. He writes, teaches, and plies the rivers of western Montana.

Camille T. Dungy is a poet, essayist, and editor whose most recent collections are *Trophic Cascade* and *Guidebook to Relative Strangers*. She lives in northern Colorado.

Rhina P. Espaillat, a former high school English teacher, is the author of numerous books and chapbooks, including a book comprising poetry, essays, short stories, and translations into and out of English and Spanish.

Tarfia Faizullah wrote *Registers of Illuminated Villages* and *Seam*. She lives in Texas.

Blas Falconer is an award-winning poet and author of *Forgive the Body This Failure*, *The Founding Wheel*, *A Question of Gravity and Light*, and *The Perfect Hour*.

Bob Ferguson is a fourth-generation Washingtonian and the attorney general of Washington State.

Deborah Fries is a Philadelphia-based writer, teacher, and printmaker and the author of the poetry collections *Various Modes of Departure* and *The Bright Field of Everything*.

Suzanne Frischkorn is the author of several poetry collections and the recipient of a Connecticut Individual Artist Fellowship, a Writer's Center Emerging Writers Fellowship, and the Aldrich Poetry Award.

Amanda Gailey is an associate professor of English at the University of Nebraska–Lincoln and an advocate for gun control and antifascism.

John Gallaher is a poet and artist who lives in rural Missouri and coedits the *Laurel Review*.

Allen Gee is the author of the essay collection *My Chinese-America* and editor of the multicultural imprint 2040 Books.

David Gessner is the editor-in-chief of *Ecotone* and the author of eleven books, including *All the Wild That Remains: Edward Abbey, Wallace Stegner, and the American West* and the forthcoming *Leave It as It Is: A Journey through Theodore Roosevelt's American Wilderness*.

Katrina Goldsaito is the author of *The Sound of Silence*. She would love to hear from readers about peaceful places, living in outer space, and modern nomadism @katrinagoldsaito.

Vince Gotera is the editor of the Science Fiction and Fantasy Poetry Association's journal *Star*Line* and author of the poetry collections *Dragonfly, Ghost Wars, Fighting Kite,* and *The Coolest Month.*

Patri Hadad is a writer, editor, illustrator, and painter and the former managing editor of the *New Ohio Review.* She works for the University of Arizona Poetry Center.

Kimiko Hahn's most recent poetry collection, *Foreign Bodies,* revisits the personal as political. She teaches in the MFA program at Queens College, City University of New York.

Amanda Hawkins is the recipient of the *Florida Review* Editors' Prize for Poetry, and her work can be found in *Orion,* the *Boston Review,* the *Orison Anthology,* and *Tin House.*

Allison Hedge Coke's books include *The Year of the Rat, Dog Road Woman, Off-Season City Pipe, Blood Run, Burn, Streaming,* and the memoir *Rock Ghost, Willow, Deer.*

Dennis Held is the author of the poetry collections *Betting on the Night* and *Ourself.*

David Hernandez's most recent book of poems is *Dear, Sincerely.*

Lee Herrick was born in South Korea and adopted to the United States. He is a former Fresno poet laureate and the author of three books of poems.

Sean Hill is the author of *Dangerous Goods and Blood Ties* and *Brown Liquor* and the recipient of fellowships from the Cave Canem Foundation and National Endowment for the Arts. He directs the Minnesota Northwoods Writers Conference.

Brenda Hillman is an award-winning poet and translator and the author of ten books of poems, most recently *Extra Hidden Life, among the Days; Seasonal Works with Letters on Fire;* and *Practical Water.*

Jane Hirshfield is a former chancellor of the Academy of American Poets and the author of nine poetry books, two essay collections, and four books presenting the work of world poets from the past.

Jen Hirt is an associate professor at Penn State Harrisburg.

Linda Hogan is a poet, storyteller, playwright, novelist, environmentalist, and Chickasaw Nation writer-in-residence.

B. J. Hollars is a writer, professor, and arts advocate living in Eau Claire, Wisconsin.

Erin Coughlin Hollowell is an Alaskan poet, the executive director of Storyknife Writers Retreat, and a teacher for the Kachemak Bay Writers' Conference and the University of Alaska Anchorage low-residency MFA program.

Pam Houston is the author of *Deep Creek: Finding Hope in the High Country* and *Cowboys Are My Weakness*, among other books. She directs Writing by Writers and teaches at the Institute of American Indian Arts and the University of California at Davis.

Barbara Hurd is the author of *Listening to the Savage: River Notes and Half-Heard Melodies*, *Tidal Rhythms: Change and Resilience at the Edge of the Sea*, and several other books and teaches at the Vermont College of Fine Arts.

Sarah Inskeep is an undergraduate student who is passionate about bridging the gap between scientific progress and the policies that influence social and environmental justice.

Fenton Johnson is the author of seven books of fiction and literary nonfiction, including *At the Center of All Beauty: Solitude and the Creative Life*.

Ever Jones (they, them) is a queer/trans artist and writer and the author of the forthcoming poetry collection *nightsong*.

Richard Kenney's most recent book is *Terminator: Poems, 2008–2018*.

Robin Wall Kimmerer (Potawatomi) is a mother, scientist, teacher, writer, and citizen of Maple Nation.

Amy P. Knight is the author of the novel *Lost, Almost* and practices law in Arizona.

Brian Laidlaw is a poet and songwriter whose books include *The Stuntman*, *The Mirrormaker*, and the forthcoming *Summer Err: A John Muir Erasure*.

John Lane is a writer and poet living in South Carolina.

J. Drew Lanham is a cultural ornithologist at Clemson University and the author of *The Home Place: Memoirs of a Colored Man's Love Affair with Nature* and *Sparrow Envy*. He is the poet laureate of Edgefield, South Carolina.

Karen An-hwei Lee divides her time between Seattle, where she teaches in Seattle Pacific University's low-residency MFA program, and San Diego, where she serves in the administration at Point Loma Nazarene University.

Lawrence Lenhart is a founding editor of *Carbon Copy* and the author of *The Well-Stocked and Gilded Cage*, *Of No Ground: Small Island / Big Ocean Contingencies*, and a book-length essay about the reintroduction of the black-footed ferret on the Colorado Plateau.

Diana Liverman is a professor of geography and development at the University of Arizona and a lead author for the Intergovernmental Panel on Climate Change.

Erin Malone is the author of *Hover* and serves as editor of *Poetry Northwest.*

Debra Marquart is the author of six books, the senior editor of *Flyway: Journal of Writing and Environment,* and a professor in the MFA programs at Iowa State University and the University of Southern Maine.

Tod Marshall lives in Spokane, Washington.

Anne Haven McDonnell lives in Santa Fe, New Mexico, where she writes poetry, explores mountains by foot and ski, and teaches at the Institute of American Indian Arts.

Colleen J. McElroy, winner of the American Book Award for *Queen of the Ebony Isles* and finalist for the Walt Whitman Award for *Here I Throw Down My Heart,* has published ten collections of poetry, most recently *Blood Memory.*

Rose McLarney is the author of the poetry collections *Forage, Its Day Being Gone,* and *The Always Broken Plates of Mountains* and the editor of *A Literary Field Guide to Southern Appalachia* and the *Southern Humanities Review.*

Gregory McNamee is an editor and the author of more than forty books. He lives in Tucson, Arizona.

Tim McNulty is a poet, conservation activist, and natural history writer living on Washington's Olympic Peninsula.

Sandra Meek is the author of six books of poems, including *Still, An Ecology of Elsewhere, Road Scatter,* and the Dorset Prize–winning *Biogeography.*

Christopher Merrill is the author of many books of poetry and nonfiction, most recently *Self-Portrait with Dogwood.*

Kathryn Miles is a staff writer at *Outside* and the author of four books, most recently *Quakeland: On the Road to America's Next Devastating Earthquake.*

Scott Minar is the consulting editor of poetry translations for *Crazyhorse,* and the author or editor of eight books, two of which are in Arabic translated by Saleh Razzouk.

Catherine Venable Moore is a writer and cofounder of the West Virginia Mine Wars Museum in Matewan.

Kathleen Dean Moore is an environmental ethicist and essayist whose work bears witness to the glories of this world and the sins against it, most recently in *Piano Tide* and *Great Tide Rising: Towards Clarity and Moral Courage in a Time of Planetary Change.*

Juan J. Morales is the son of an Ecuadorian mother and Puerto Rican father, chair of the Department of English and World Languages at Colorado State University–Pueblo, and the author of three poetry collections, including *The Handyman's Guide to End Times*.

Aimee Nezhukumatathil is a poet and essayist whose most recent book is *World of Wonders: In Praise of Fireflies, Whale Sharks, and other Astonishments*. She teaches in the University of Mississippi's MFA program.

Naomi Shihab Nye is the Young People's Poet Laureate of the United States for 2019–2021.

Elena Passarello is the author of the essay collections *Let Me Clear My Throat* and *Animals Strike Curious Poses*.

Georgia Pearle was born and raised in the Gulf South and is at work on a collection of poems and a memoir.

John T. Price is the award-winning author of three nature memoirs and the editor of *The Tallgrass Prairie Reader*. He teaches in the University of Nebraska at Omaha English department.

Dean Rader, a professor at the University of San Francisco, has written, edited, or coedited eleven books and is a 2019 Guggenheim Fellow in poetry.

Yelizaveta P. Renfro is the author of the essay collection *Xylotheque* and the short-story collection *A Catalogue of Everything in the World*.

Lee Ann Roripaugh is the author of five volumes of poetry, most recently *Tsunami vs. the Fukushima 50*.

Elizabeth Rush is the author of *Rising: Dispatches from the New American Shore*, a finalist for the Pulitzer Prize.

Heather Ryan teaches English at a rural community college and is working on a collection of short stories entitled *Documentation*.

Scott Russell Sanders is the author of *Earth Works* and twenty other books and lives in the hardwood hill country of southern Indiana.

Lauret Savoy is the David B. Truman Professor of Environmental Studies at Mount Holyoke College. Her book *Trace: Memory, History, Race, and the American Landscape* won the American Book Award and the ASLE Creative Writing Award.

Cherene Sherrard is the Sally Mead Hands-Bascom Professor of English at the University of Wisconsin–Madison and the author of several books, most recently the poetry collection *Vixen*.

Peggy Shumaker's most recent book is *Cairn*, new and selected poems and prose.

Martha Silano is the author of five poetry books, most recently *Gravity Assist*.

Sarah Skeen lives in Denver, where she uses her photography skills in support of her nonprofit clients.

Aisha Sabatini Sloan is the Helen Zell Visiting Professor of Creative Nonfiction in the University of Michigan MFA program and the author of *Fluency of Light: Coming of Age in a Theater of Black and White* and *Dreaming of Ramadi in Detroit*.

Jasmine Elizabeth Smith is an African American poet at work on her first poetry collection, *South Flight*.

R. T. Smith edited *Shenandoah* for more than two decades and is the author of numerous books, most recently *Summoning Shades: Poems*.

Dana Sonnenschein, whose most recent book is *Bear Country*, has watched wolves in Yellowstone and howled with them at the Wolf Conservation Center in upstate New York.

Gary Soto is working on a feature-length film based on the work in his book of poems *Oranges*.

Pete Souza is a photojournalist, the former chief official White House photographer for U.S. presidents Ronald Reagan and Barack Obama, and the former director of the White House Photography Office.

Ana Maria Spagna is the author of several books, most recently *Uplake: Restless Essays of Coming and Going*.

Kim Stafford is a writer of poetry, fiction, memoir, and biography whose most recent book is *Wild Honey, Tough Salt*.

Catherine Staples teaches at Villanova University and is the author of *The Rattling Window* and *Never a Note Forfeit*.

Sandra Steingraber is a biologist and Distinguished Scholar in Residence at Ithaca College. Her charges were dismissed.

Laura-Gray Street is the author of *Pigment* and *Fume and Shiftwork* and editor of *The Ecopoetry Anthology* and *A Literary Field Guide to Southern Appalachia*. She teaches at Randolph College in Lynchburg, Virginia.

Arthur Sze's tenth book of poetry is *Sight Lines*, winner of the 2019 National Book Award for Poetry.

Alexandra Teague is the author of a novel and several books of poems, including *Or What We'll Call Desire,* and the coeditor of *Bullets into Bells: Poets and Citizens Respond to Gun Violence.*

Deborah Thompson teaches creative nonfiction and literary theory in the English department at Colorado State University.

Jeremy Voigt is a schoolteacher, poet, and father of three living by a large lake in western Washington.

Nicole Walker is the author of the nonfiction collections *The After-Normal: Brief, Alphabetical Essays on a Changing Planet, Sustainability: A Love Story, Where the Tiny Things Are, Egg, Micrograms,* and *Quench Your Thirst with Salt.*

Scott Warren is a cultural geographer and humanitarian aid volunteer who lives in Ajo, Arizona.

Debbie Weingarten is a writer and community organizer based in Tucson, Arizona.

Ellen Welti works on food webs and insect community ecology as a postdoctoral researcher.

Lesley Wheeler is the author of several books, most recently the poetry collection *The State She's In* and the novel *Unbecoming.*

Joe Wilkins is the author of a novel, a memoir, and several poetry collections, including *When We Were Birds,* winner of the 2017 Oregon Book Award.

Christian Wiman's most recent book is *He Held Radical Light: The Art of Faith, the Faith of Art.*

Sholeh Wolpé is an Iranian American poet and playwright whose work includes more than a dozen books of poetry, anthologies, and translations.

Robert Wrigley is the author of twelve books of poetry and lives in the woods in northern Idaho.

Andrew S. Yang is a transdisciplinary artist working across sculpture, writing, and natural-cultural history. He teaches at the School of the Art Institute of Chicago.

Founded in 1997, *Terrain.org* is the world's first and longest-publishing online literary magazine of place. In addition to poetry, fiction, and creative nonfiction, *Terrain.org* publishes articles, editorials, interviews, reviews, the ARTerrain gallery, Unsprawl community and regional case studies, and the *Soundscape* podcast. Named after A. R. Ammons's poem "Terrain," the award-winning, nonprofit journal publishes three or more contributions a week from an array of writers and artists, all without advertisements and at no cost to access.

■ ■ ■

Visit terrain.org/dear-america for multimedia and other resources to support the reading, discussion, and teaching of *Dear America*, including audio readings of letters by authors; author interviews in print, audio, and video; online-only letters to America; writing prompts; lesson plans and curriculum ideas; talking points for book clubs and other gatherings; links to activist organizations; and *Dear America* events.